P9-API-985

Writing | Techniques for Survival

Second Edition

Mary Ellen Grasso, Ed.D.
James Ledford

Broward Community College

KENDALL/HUNT PUBLISHING COMPANY
4050 Westmark Drive   Dubuque, Iowa 52002

Copyright © 1988, 1996 by Kendall/Hunt Publishing Company

ISBN 0-7872-2708-0

All rights reserved. No part of this publication may be reproduced, stored in a retrieval system, or transmitted, in any form or by any means, electronic, mechanical, photocopying, recording, or otherwise, without the prior written permission of the copyright owner.

Printed in the United States of America
10 9 8 7 6 5 4 3 2

Contents

STAGE 12 Cause and Effect   263

PART II | Finding and Using Information: The Basics of the Resesarch Paper   283

STAGE 1 Beginning the Research Paper   285

PART
III | **A Brief Guide to Mechanics and Style   421**

Acknowledgments

It is rare that a textbook is the product of one single person. It is instead a collaboration of many who in one way or another contribute to the final product. This book is unique because, first, the methods have been piloted for a number of years in our classes and those of our colleagues so that we have had the benefit of many constructive suggestions. Second, the book presents many student models, indicating that it is possible for average composition students and even those with minimal composition skills to learn writing "survival techniques" in order to pass successfully their freshman composition courses. The text first allows the students to review the skills necessary for writing a paragraph before asking them to write multi-paragraph essays.

Because of the composition examples, our special thanks go to our students who proved to be gifted writers and who served as models for those students who followed them: Janet Beline, Newton Berwig, Amy Brown, Lorraine Commerford, Steve DiMattia, Debra Dolphin, Suzanne Driscoll, Marcia Franz, Karen Foglio, Joseph Gannon, Stephen Grasso, Joseph Hone, Robin Ann Kessler, Rebekah Malloy, Terry McCullough, Susan Owen, Terry Petrenchik, Natalie Phalgoo, Aundrea Plummer, Rebecca Rasanen, Joanne Salters, Richard Smith, Joseph Swails, and Susan Swails. Third, we feel that the purpose of the book is to show that average students can learn to write well by first following a structured pattern. Once students feel comfortable writing, they realize that many other composition students in similar situations have been able to achieve competency.

In addition, teaching assistants, first-term faculty, and adjuncts, we are told, are much more comfortable teaching from a textbook that has a definite organizational pattern. However, even more important are those tenured faculty who feel that a structured textbook is most appropriate for today's college student, especially those in freshman composition courses.

We also wish to thank our colleagues, especially Bonnie Hilton, Phyllis Luck, and Patricia Menhart, who have provided us with either student models or suggestions; as well as the photographer, Stephen Grasso, who not only shot most of the photographs, but who also assisted us in selecting those that were most appropriate for the text. Of course, no textbook could have been completed without the help of the college librarian, our secretaries—Toula Bouchoc, Flora Cohen, Susan Heslekrants—and Susan Swails, who assisted in the editing.

Finally, our thanks go to the members of our families who have supported us during the two-year writing period.

Part

I

The Writing Process: Saying What You Mean

Getting Started

How many times have you said, "I know what I want to say, but I just can't seem to get it down on paper"? How often have you heard yourself say, when trying to explain something to another person, " Well, you know what I mean" ? These short circuits in communication happen to anyone and are always frustrating. For example, consider the process of writing to a friend, preparing a committee report for an organization to which you belong, working up a campaign speech for a political candidate, or preparing a resume of your background to apply for a job. As a person who has had little experience in writing or as one who has had to do some writing and has had difficulty expressing ideas, you may have found that a gap exists between the ideas you want to communicate and their final presentation. Recognizing this gap is discouraging, but it is also the beginning of learning to write well.

You need to realize that writing is a skill, and like any other skill, it can be learned in stages and steps. Suppose that you want to play a musical instrument, learn a new sport, or use a word processing program. Before you can play chord progressions on a guitar, you must learn to position your fingers on the frets. When you first go out on the tennis court, you learn to grip the racket properly before you can execute an effective serve. Similarly, when you first use a word processing program in your computer, you need to learn basic terms such as screen formatting, and editing commands before beginning to work with the program itself. In the same way, you can learn to say what you mean when you write and to say it well. If you follow the stages and steps necessary to produce effective writing, just as you would work through the stages and steps of mastering an instrument or a sport, you CAN write.

Mastering Words

1. Recognizing Different Language Situations
2. Distinguishing Denotative and Connotative Meaning
3. Recognizing How Bias Words Work
4. Recognizing Special Problems in Word Choice

STEP I   Recognizing Different Language Situations

The first step in writing is to recognize the right word for the situation. Think for a moment about how you might talk during a job interview. Would you conclude the interview by saying, "O.K., this job looks like a good deal to me, and I'm sure that I can handle all these types I'll run into"? Would you be likely to say, "I think I have enough experience to handle the various kinds of people I will be meeting on this job"? Or would you say, "I'm an individual with background that would enable me to facilitate the interpersonal relationships necessary for this position"?

If you are to be considered for the job, you should use the second comment. The first might be used in everyday conversation with your friends, but the extreme informality of this response might indicate to a potential employer that you would be unable to adapt your language to a more formal situation. The third comment sounds false; the employer could infer from it that you are making a misguided attempt to appear educated and competent.

What different styles of language do you need to recognize to be an effective speaker and writer? First, you will need to distinguish standard from nonstandard English. Standard English refers to patterns of grammar and syntax widely accepted as preferred usage. Nonstandard English is any usage that doesn't follow these patterns. Standard English may be either formal or informal. depending upon the situation.

Standard English

Informal English

You use informal English at home, in conversation with your friends, in the classroom, in informal business situations, and in writing personal letters. When you use informal

English, you are fairly relaxed about word order and rules of grammar; you use contractions, and you use many colloquial expressions.

Formal English

You use formal English in professional situations. in business transactions, in business letters and in expository writing. When you use formal standard English, you pay careful attention to word order and rules of grammar, and you avoid contractions and colloquial expressions. Just as you shift your other behavior according to the situation, you must become adept at shifting language gears in moving from informal to formal standard English. Some differences between informal and formal English are shown in the following paired expressions:

	Informal	Formal
Contractions	We'll go to the concert.	We will go to the concert.
	The press isn't sure about the facts.	The press is not sure about the facts.
Word Order	Who are you going with?	With whom are you going?
	What are you going to panel the room with?	What type of paneling will you use for the room?
Agreement	Everyone has their complaints	Everyone has his or her complaints.
Case	It's me.	It is I.
Split Infinitive	The men want to quickly finish the job.	The men want to finish the job quickly.
Clipped words	phone	telephone
	TV	television
	ad	advertisement
	exam	examination
Colloquialisms	How come the concert was cancelled?	Why was the concert cancelled?
	You're mad at me.	You are angry with me.
	A lot of us are going.	Many of us are going.
	This bike is O.K.	This bicycle is satisfactory.

[handwritten: no in writing]

Because colloquialisms occur so often in informal English speech, you will find that it is hard to leave them out of your writing. The ones listed above will be obvious to you, but you will want to become aware of others which are frequently used but which are not suitable to formal standard English.

Colloquial	Formal
That's a funny thing to do.	That is a peculiar thing to do.
This model is different than the first one.	This model is different from the first one.
The plan is identical to the other.	The plan is identical with the other.
Herman can't help but be a joker.	Herman cannot help being a joker.

The vacation package is a good deal.	The vacation package is a good arrangement.
Stand in back of me.	Stand behind me.
The key must be someplace in the house.	The key must be somewhere in the house.
The kids were here today	The children were here today.
I was mighty happy about my promotion	I was very happy about my promotion.
How about going to dinner?	Would you like to go to dinner?
Try and go tonight.	Try to go tonight.
He blamed it on Herman.	He blamed Herman.
We'll leave inside of an hour.	We'll leave within an hour.
The salesman didn't say if he would return	The salesman didn't say whether he would return.
That girl is just beautiful.	That girl is very beautiful.

Nonstandard English

Nonstandard English is usage which does not conform to the patterns considered correct or standard by most well-educated people. The following expressions are examples of nonstandard English.

It don't matter to me.
I can't hardly wait to see that movie.
I seen that show on television before.
Herman done that on purpose.
Hand me that there magazine.
My sister could of done the dishes for me.
Leave me be.
We was afraid we wouldn't get there on time.
I got the book off of Tom.
Herman ain't there.
We could of gone to the game.
The teacher done everything she could to pass me.
He give me the wrong answer.
I should have stood in bed.
You could have went with me.
The shot won't hurt none.

Slang

Slang is language which relies heavily on newly coined words or on existing words used in some special sense. It is unconventional language that may be vivid, grotesque, comic, or vulgar. Carl Sandburg characterized slang as "language that takes off its coat, spits on its hands, and goes to work. "

One of the chief characteristics of slang is that it is short-lived In the 1920s. for instance, the greatest thing was the *cat's pajamas* or the *cat's meow*, but in the 1980s it was *awesome* . The

1920s expression *"go cook a radish"* translates to *blast off* in the '50s and *get lost* in the '70s. Slang often changes not just from decade to decade but from month to month, so if a person uses slang that is even slightly out-of-date, he may be a *nimrod* one month and a *boob* another. He might even be considered a *jerk* today. The word *jerk* itself illustrates the changing nature of slang. In the thirties and forties when students went to a soda shop to jitterbug to the sounds of the big bands, they often ordered sodas from the boy who worked behind the counter, the *soda jerk*.

While most slang is short-lived, some slang words are so useful that they become a permanent part of our language. *Lousy*, for example, has been around for 250 years. *Booze, blab, cram, lily-livered, laughing stock, dame, clod, bloody*, and *wench* have been around over 400 years. Some other slang expressions which are now accepted as standard English are *okay* as a sign of approval, *hoax*, which in George Washington's day was slang for falsehood, and *blind date*, slang in the '20s, but now a standard expression.

Argot is slang, or code language, specific to a particular social group. *Gat, hit, contract heist, moll*, and *fence* are all 1920s underworld argot. Jazz music is a particularly rich source of slang: *hop, dig, beat, groovy, hip, pad, gig*, and *dude* are just a few of the terms it has produced. In recent years, the drug culture has expanded an already colorful argot that includes *shooting gallery, layout, crack, manicure, nickel bag*, and *mainline*.

Occupations, sports, and special interest groups all have their own slang, known as *jargon*. The term originally meant meaningless chatter, but jargon now refers to terms for objects, processes or operations, prices, and transactions understood by a particular group. A person associated with the theater, for instance, will refer to a stage hand as a *grip*, to the various curtains as *teasers, tormentors*, and *travelers*, and to two people talking at the same time as *overlap*. Much of the jargon of special groups eventually becomes a permanent part of the language. For instance, the general population understands what an aviator means by being *socked in, flying blind*, and *bailing out*; and what the short order cook means by a *BLT* and *one over easy*; what Armed Forces personnel mean by *gold brick, blockbuster, black market* and *running afoul*; and what students mean by a *bull session, brainstorming, cribbing, cramming*, and *acing an exam*..

While slang enlivens the language and is widely accepted in everyday conversation, you should not rely too heavily on it. Using slang will make the transition from speaking to writing expository prose difficult, since slang is seldom acceptable in formal expository writing.

STEP 2   Distinguishing Denotative and Connotative Meaning

Just as you need to distinguish formal from informal uses of language, you will need to recognize that words can carry two kinds of meanings, denotative and connotative. The denotative meaning of the word is the factual or dictionary meaning. The connotative meaning is the emotional or imaginative response to the word The denotation of *mother* for instance, is simply "female parent." The connotations of *mother* might be warmth, protection, consolation, good food, and cheerful surroundings for one person, and nagging, misunderstanding, and restriction for another. The denotative meaning of the word *red* is "the light primary of the long wave end of the spectrum." But *red* has many connotations: blood, war, anger (to see red), or joy (a red-letter day). Politically, it is associated with the red banner of revolution (red scare) and with communism, as in Red China.

Think about names of commercial establishments and the names of products. They are often made up of words which taken individually have specific denotations. When used in association with the firm or the product, however, these same words carry connotations. Consider, for example, Singer's *Touch and Sew*. Each word has a generally agreed on denotative meaning. Yet the image connoted by the combination is that of a machine which almost sews by itself. Or consider an air conditioning shop for automobiles called *Arctic Air*. Once more each word has a particular denotative meaning, but the name of the firm takes advantage of their combined connotations. The customer, seeing them together, gets the impression that the air conditioning unit for his vehicle will have maximum cooling. Even automobile manufacturers have taken advantage of the space-age, giving cars names such as Omni, Spectra, Pulsar, Polaris.

Now read the following two descriptions of a hospitalized patient to see how denotation and connotation work in longer passages of writing. The source for these descriptions is unknown.

A Sick Patient

Denotative Description

A man of forty-five, unclothed above the waist, lay on a bed in the hospital. His skin was deeply jaundiced except over his palms and soles, where a red color predominated over the yellow. His extremities were thin generally although the feet and ankles were swollen. The abdomen was distended with fluid, and its superficial veins were abnormally conspicuous. The hair was sparse in the axillae and absent on the chest. The breasts were unusually prominent for those of a man. The patient's breath smelled of alcohol. If an examiner pressed upon the right side of the abdomen at the margin of the ribs, he could feel a resistance revealing an enlarged, hard, but smooth liver. The aggregate of the patient's physical abnormalities, combined with his medical history of heavy drinking for twenty years, were diagnostic of advanced Laennec's cirrhosis of the liver.

Connotative Description

On the white sheets of a hospital bed, a human ruin was sprawled; his spidery extremities extended like vines from his misshapen yellow body. He lay naked except for pajama bottoms that could not close across his bulging abdomen. The huge belly was striped longitudinally by distended dark veins, and in its middle a navel protruded like a stubby thumb. The pathetic abdominal mountain sloped to meet a hairless, sunken, jaundiced chest. At the apex of this disaster was a small head, fitted on a skinny neck and topped with a tangle of hair that was unevenly brown and gray.

The face, of indeterminate age but vaguely suggesting a man past fifty, was freshly shaven, and the body was clean, thanks to the recent scrubbing applied ceremoniously by the orderlies against feeble protest. Only the stench of the man's breath, resembling rotten fruit, still lingered to remind one of the human derelict lurching from the barroom. The face that presented itself from the white pillow appeared one of defeat and resignation except for the yellow eyes. These revealed a piteous hope that some magic medicine could return him again to the delicious aroma of spilled beer, ragged cigars, and Woolworth perfume. The eyes seemed to long for the nostalgic sight of scarred mahogany bars littered with ash trays and steins, draped with elbows, and canopied by the grim, intent faces of debauchers; and the magic medicine would restore to his ears the amalgamated din of jukeboxes pinball machines, shrill laughter, and loud, empty conversation.

Exercise 1-1 Identifying Denotative and Connotative Meaning

A. What was the writer's intention in the denotative description? In the connotative description?
B. Which words evoke a strong emotional response?
   Underline them
C. What pictures are conveyed by each of the underlined words or phrases'?

STEP 3   Recognizing How Bias Words Work

Some words which have a denotative meaning may each carry very different connotations. Consider the word *smell,* the denotation of which is a sensation perceived by the olfactory sense. Synonyms of smell which have unfavorable connotations are *stink* and *stench;* synonyms with favorable connotations are *aroma, scent, perfume, fragrance,* and *bouquet.* Some of these words even connote masculinity of femininity: advertisements refer to the aroma of a cigar but to the fragrance or scent of perfume.

When certain connotations of words are emphasized over others, the word is being used as a bias word in that context. By selecting an emotionally charged word over a neutral one, an author can slant his writing by using bias words. Depending on his intention, a writer uses favorable or unfavorable bias words. He does this by choosing one of a group of words with similar denotations but different connotations: e.g., *overweight, fat, plump; common, ordinary, universal,* or he may choose from a group of words which refer to a category of objects which have different denotations and different connotations: *lawyer, shyster, counselor at law; freedom, license, independence.*

Bias Words and the Commercial World

Bias words are frequently used in the world around you; they can lead you to patronize an establishment, purchase a product, or make a judgment. Consider the implications of the following words, or phrases used in advertising: Soft and Pretty, Smoke Scan Smoke Alarm, Young and Tender Chicken, Rubbermaid, Superbrand, Sunkist, Wonder Bread, Lestoil, Less (bread), Flaming Pit restaurant. Then consider the importance of word choice in the following newspaper headlines: "State: A Hot Bed of Mail Order Fraud," "Growing Up: One of Life's Grim Tasks," " Nature's Year of Ferocity," "New Fangled Equipment and Old-Fashioned Cars."

Exercise 1-2 Supplying Bias Words

For each of the neutral terms below, supply one or more synonyms with unfavorable and favorable connotations. Compare your lists with those of other students to determine whether you all agree on the connotations of the words substituted for each neutral term.

Unfavorable	Neutral	Favorable
Chic	female	lady
bloke	male	Gentleman
mutt	dog	Puppy
lemon	automobile	hot rod
Quack	doctor	specialist
	reporter	
	actress	
Mule headed	stubborn	Strong willed
kid, punk	child	
haughty	pride	self confident

Exercise 1-3 Finding Bias Words

Find four brand names, four names of establishments, and four captions of newspaper or magazine articles which contain words that are biased or words which in context are biased.

Brand names

1.

2.

3.

4.

Names of establishments

1.

2.

3.

4.

Headlines or news captions

1.

2.

3.

4.

Exercise 1-4 Determining Impressions from Bias Words

What impression comes to mind when a customer sees the following brand names:

1. Wonder Bread _____

   _____

2. Pledge (Furniture Polish) _____

   _____

3. Craftsman Tools _____

   _____

4. Wrangler Jeans _____

   _____

5. Equal Sweetener _____

   _____

Exercise 1-5 Recognizing Bias Words in Journalism

Read the editorial page of your local newspaper. Find an editorial, letter to the editor, or new commentary that you think contains more bias words than it does factual information. Clip the passage, underline the bias words, and bring it to class for discussion.

Don't use

STEP 4 Recognizing Special Problems in Word Choice

Now that you recognize the levels of language, the distinction between denotative and connotative language, and the use of bias words, you will need to consider several special problems that can interfere with communicating specific ideas and information.

Euphemisms

In the interest of a socially accepted word, people sometimes substitute an indirect or vague expression for one thought to be offensive or too blunt. They may say *benign neglect* rather than deliberate disregard for the well-being of a person, *furlough* for fired, *underemployed* for overeducated. Alcoholics are people with a *drinking problem,* undertakers are now *funeral directors,* and the former funeral home has now become a *memorial chapel.*

Jargon

In addition to the specialized language peculiar to an occupation or interest, there is a kind of general jargon characterized by wordiness or verbal fuzziness. Sports seem to be the language of politics and business Corporate administrators speak of *game plans* and *teamwork,* and politicians speak of the political *arena.* The sports world itself speaks of *a world series* when the American and National Leagues do not really represent the world. The word *destiny* has now become a catchall word for many writers and newscasters. Superstars now wrestle with their destiny and superbowl football teams talk about the *destiny factor.* At registration we *scramble* for classes; and if they are closed, we seek *options which sometimes aren't viable.* Too often jargon is substituted thoughtlessly for words with more specific meanings. For example many Madison Avenue writers use the word *concept* instead of *organization, technique, idea, definitions, principles, trend, plan,* or *arrangement* Four jargon word families are to be avoided at all costs; these are families of *-wise, -type, -use,* and *-oriented.* A writer who can't leave these jargon families alone could conceivably write a horror like this: "Computerized mechanisms for executive-type employees are both good moneywise and for time-oriented purchases. "

Pompous Words

Pompous words are first cousins to euphemisms and jargons. Immature and careless writers sometimes use them to give the impression that they are well-bred or well-read. As a result they might write *cogitate* for think, *elucidate* for explain, *masticate* for chew, *fabulist* for a liar, *tonsorial parlor* for a barber shop.

Unnecessary Words

Writers are often unaware that they are fogging their meaning by being redundant, that is, they are repeating an idea in another word, phrase, or sentence. Thus you see such expressions as *large in size, descended down, empty out, red in color each individual person, modern world of today's twentieth century, endorse on the back,* and *tall in size.*

Trite Expressions

If a phrase is repeated often enough, it may lose its original freshness and become meaningless. These overused expressions, or clichés, are usually used by people under pressure, but they should be avoided at all costs. Phrases such as *tried and true, bury the hatchet, at loose ends, at death's door, add insult to injury, hit below the belt, beyond a shadow of a doubt, few and far between, it stands to reason that, a raging inferno, in a word, in my opinion, all in all, last but not least, calm before the storm, in this day and age, high hopes, all walks of life* were once appropriate, but today because of overuse they are stale and commonplace.

Gobbledygook

Gobbledygook is involved, unclear, sometimes completely unintelligible language that combines a number of language problems. Government workers, sociologists, psychologists, educators, lawyers, and armed forces personnel are particularly guilty of producing such language. A sociologist or a government worker may inquire "What is truth?" in gobbledygook as follows:

> It behooves us at this time and period to seek for that which will conform to fact or reality in such a way that we are cognizant of the veracity and the faithfulness or fidelity of a thing, or idea, because the fundamental reality is conceived as being partly or wholly transcendent of perceived actuality and experience since it conforms between judgment and externally existent things in their actual status and relation in such a manner as to be an actual elaboration of concepts, meanings, or implications.

On the other hand, a corporate employer might report that

> Bill Barnes's inability to accurately negotiate the distance between his corporeal bulk and the projection protruding from the adit caused pain and suffering as the result of an ecchymosis.

Evidently, Bill Barnes suffered a bruise after bumping into a hallway door, according to a supervisor's report.

Objective and Subjective Writing

Why all this attention to the use of words? You have seen that there are several kinds of writing and that the types of writing depend upon the writer's intention. The author of the denotative paragraph about the sick patient was probably an internist or a pathologist. His purpose was to report, as factually and as accurately as possible, the condition of a patient with acute cirrhosis of the liver. His intent, obviously, was to reach the understanding rather than the emotions of his reader. His tone was, therefore, objective; and he achieved this objective tone by the use of denotative language. His method was the logical presentation of medical data which could be objectively verified. From this logical presentation of facts, the writer then drew his conclusion. This denotative passage, then, is an example of expository writing.

On the other hand, the second passage about the sick patient, full of connotative words and phrases was probably written by a novelist. His purpose was to produce in the reader a feeling of horrified fascination at the physical deterioration of a human being. His intent was to reach his reader's emotions first. Some readers would no doubt respond with pity at the portrait of a life so wasted; others would react with scorn or revulsion at this picture of a skid row alcoholic. The writer's method was primarily pictorial rather than logical; his tone was subjective, and he achieved this subjective tone by his use of connotative language. Because of its subjective tone and the different emotional responses possible on the part of the reader, this passage is an example not of expository writing but of fiction writing.

The two types of writing differ in intent and, therefore, in word choice. The writer of fiction interprets human life or some aspect of it from his or her particular viewpoint—that is, subjectively. The expository writer tries to report more objectively. To do so, the expository writer considers four questions:

Think about before beginning

1. What is my particular point about this subject?

2. Who is my audience? *— use background & description*

3. What do they need or want to know about this subject?

4. How can I best convey my point to my audience?

The expository writer then sets about listing facts, examples, and incidents; analyzing the subject by classifying information; defining terms; comparing and contrasting the subject with similar topics; and demonstrating causes and effects of the subject. In the following Stages you will learn how to use these methods to demonstrate your points, and then how to combine these methods in an interesting and well-written paper.

Generalizations and Facts

1. Recognizing Generalizations
2. Recognizing Facts
3. Distinguishing Between Generalizations and Facts from a Source
4. Finding Suitable Sources for Expository Writing

STEP 1   Recognizing Generalizations

Your first concern as an expository writer is to communicate specific information, rather than vague or general ideas. However, a special difficulty for you as a beginning writer is that most people speak in generalities. As an illustration, listen to a conversation among your friends at the cafeteria. You might hear remarks something like this:

"The food prices are *reasonable* and the portions are *large.*" "But the atmosphere in here is *pretty depressing.*" Or: "That instructor is *demanding,* but he does have a *knack for* making the class *really interesting.*" Or. "You ought to vote for Tony for president of student government, he's a *great guy.*"

Ask yourself what all of these remarks really mean. What specific information has been transmitted? For instance, what does your friend mean when he says that the atmosphere of the cafeteria is *depressing*? Ask him. He may answer that "It's *dreary.* " Do you know yet specifically what he means? Not exactly; ask him to explain further. Now he may tell you, "The walls are painted gray, the room is lit with bare sixty watt light bulbs. The only decorations are bulletin boards, and the windows are blocked out by the new wing under construction." Now you know what your friend meant by *dreary and depressing.*

Go back and examine all the other statements in the conversation. You will notice that every italicized word or phrase is also known as an inference An inference is an *opinion, a conclusion, a generalization, a preference, a prediction,* or a *vague statement.* An inference raises one or more of the following questions: *what? when? why? where? how? to what degree? under what conditions?*

STEP 2   Recognizing Facts

When these questions are answered. they are answered with facts. Facts make up the evidence which explains, supports, or clarifies the generalization. You can verify a fact with evidence obtained by sight, sound, smell. touch, measurement, and mathematical computation. A generalization, then, is an inference, an abstraction; a fact is a concrete statement.

You will need practice in leaning to recognize inference words and their location in a sentence. As an alert reader, you will soon recognize that the inference term can be one of several parts of speech (noun. verb, adjective. or adverb) and that it can appear in any part of a sentence (subject, subject complement, object complement, or modifier). Furthermore, you will see that there can be more than one inference in a sentence. In addition, you will begin to notice the many unsupported generalizations you find in textbooks, newspaper and magazine articles, television commentaries, and advertisements. The following sentences and explanations illustrate the various roles played by the inference terms, which are in italics.

> *Femininity* is an asset to any woman.
>> *Femininity* is a noun, and it is the subject of the sentence.
>> *Asset* is a noun, but it is the subject complement in the sentence.
> Peggy Parks *really hates* eight o'clock classes
>> *Really* is an adverb modifying the verb hates.
>> *Hates* is a verb.
> *Old* people are often *lonely* and *neglected*
>> *Old* is an adjective modifying people.
>> *Often* is an adverb modifying are.
>> *Lonely* and *neglected* are adjectives used as subject complements.
> *Neo-Nazi* racists are found *guilty* of *racketeering* by *all-white biased* jury,
>> *Neo-Nazi* is an adjective modifying racists.
>> *Racists* is a noun and is the subject.
>> *Guilty* is an adverb modifying the verb *are found.*
>> *Racketeering* is a noun used as the object of the preposition *of.*
>> *All-white* is an adjective modifying *jury.*
>> *Biased* is an adjective modifying *jury.*

It is possible for an entire sentence to be a generalization even though none of the words in it can be identified as inference terms. Slogans, sayings, and propositions are in this category. Consider the following: a rolling stone gathers no moss; legalize pot; if guns were outlawed, only outlaws would have guns.

Exercise 2-1 Recognizing Inference Terms in a Generalization

In each of the following sentences, underline the inference, name the part of speech, and tell how the word functions.

Example:

There are many adverse psychological effects of anorexia.

Many is an adjective modifying *effects*.
Adverse is an adjective modifying *effects*.
Psychological is an adjective modifying *effects*.

1. Bulimia is an abnormal appetite that has a detrimental effect to the human body.

2. The health fitness instructor motivates a mature audience with body dynamics.

3. A lethal amount of cocaine found in the superstar's body caused his untimely death.

4. The employment agency lists employee fidelity and reliability as two desired traits.

5. Most facilities and activities are easily accessible for the handicapped.

Exercise 2-2 Supporting Generalizations with Facts

Following are examples of several kinds of generalizations. Underline the inference term or terms and supply at least two facts to support the generalization.

1. Opinion
   Sara Jayne is an excellent hostess.

   A. (Fact)

   B. (Fact)

2. Conclusion
   Smokeless tobacco is dangerous.
   adjective noun

   A. (Fact)

   B. (Fact)

3. Generalization
   Students work too many hours while attending college.
   noun verb   noun

   A. (Fact)

   B. (Fact)

4. Preference
   I prefer to rent an apartment rather than live in the college dormitory.

   A. (Fact)

   B. (Fact)

5. Decision
   Jason plans to become a television broadcaster.
   is future

   A. (Fact)

   B. (Fact)

6. Prediction
   I will probably pass algebra.

   A. (Fact)

   B. (Fact)

7. Vague Statement
   Longevity is causing Americans many problems.

   A. (Fact)

   B. (Fact)

Exercise 2-3 Distinguishing Generalizations from Facts

In the blank to the left of each sentence put an G if the sentence is an generalization and an F if the sentence is a fact.

_G_ 1. The Marjorie Kinnan Rawlings State Historic Site is located not too far from Gainesville, Florida.

_G_ 2. Human beings tend to make uncritical remarks about one another's behavior.

_F_ 3. On January 27, 1966, a U.S. B52 bomber carrying four hydrogen bombs crashed southwest of Cartagena, Spain.

_F_ 4. One in every four American households was touched by crime in 1985.

_F_ 5. Nearly 22.2 million households reported a crime in 1985 compared to 22.8 million in 1984.

G _F_ 6. Peter will inherit his uncle's farm in Illinois.   future

_G_ 7. Some students fail to work up to their ability.

_G_ 8. Since I mailed the catalog this morning, you should receive it by Wednesday.

_F_ 9. The college alumni scheduled the dance for June 20 and sent invitations to all of the four hundred graduates.

G _F_ 10. He made a fortune by discovering a new type of automatic can opener.

_F_ 11. Gettysburg, a town in southern Pennsylvania, is the site of a Union victory in the Civil War in 1863.

_F_ 12. The singular of data is datum.

_G_ 13. The difference between democracy and totalitarianism is evident by the differences between the United States and Iraq.

_G_ 14. There are many educational programs on public television.

_G_ 15. Delegates to the NAACP Convention will discuss issues vital to U.S. Blacks. including poverty among minorities.

future

_____F_ 16. There were 214 crates used to ship the Statue of Liberty to the United States.

_____G_ 17. Ken Alworth, my tutor, speaks distinctly although not always with sufficient volume.

_____G_ 18. Westinghouse Electric Corporation will develop a machine editing system for the military that balks at overlong sentences or cumbersome expressions.

_____F_ 19. The Navy and Bell Laboratories have a 4,000 word controlled vocabulary for a computer.

_____G_ 20. The Westinghouse automatic readability system has 1,800 words in a floppy disk that can be substituted for 900 objectionable words.

_____G_ 21. All training manuals must be written in highly readable English because many servicemen do not understand directions that are printed in factory-written training manuals.

STEP 3 Distinguishing Between Generalizations and Facts from a Source *— somebody else said it.*

Often a statement indicates that the information came from a source other than the writer. If a fact comes from another source, the statement is a fact from a source. The information may come from books, periodicals, interviews, lectures, or others. If the generalization comes from another source, the statement is a generalization from a source. The following sentences are examples of these types of statements.

Facts from a Source

The emergency room doctor told me that Amy had seventeen stitches on her arm.

According to a 1986 demographic study "Marriage Patterns in the United States," white college-educated women born in the mid-'50s who are still single at 30 have only a 20 percent chance of marrying.

Researchers David A. Waldman, Ph.D., and Bruce Avolio, Ph.D., of the State University of New York, Binghamton, reported that persons 65 or older had a median income of $18,236 in 1984, compared to the median income of $29,292 for those under 65.

Muncie, Indiana, has a population of 71,034, reports the 1995 *World Almanac*.

The paper copier, according to the manufacturer's representative, will reproduce fifty copies a minute.

Generalizations from a Source

The emergency room doctor told me that Amy had quite a few stitches on her arm.

According to a 1986 demographic study "Marriage Patterns in the United States," white college-educated women born in the mid-'50s who are still single at 30 will have only a slight chance of marrying.

Researchers David A. Waldman, Ph.D., and Bruce Avolio, Ph.D., of the State University of New York, Binghamton, reported that persons 65 or older received substantially less household income than those under 65.

Muncie, Indiana, is a middle-size town, reports the 1995 *World Almanac*.

The paper copier, according to the manufacturer's representative, will reproduce a large number of copies per minute.

Exercise 2-4 Recognizing Generalizations, Facts, Generalizations from a Source, and Facts from a Source

Identify the following statements according to the key:

G   Generalization
F   Fact
GS   Generalization from a Source
FS   Fact from a Source

___F_1. The Silver Reed typewriter has a great frame.

___FS_2. According to essayist Otto Friedrich, "One nation's freedom fighter is another nation's terrorist."

___G_3. Valspeak was California's answer to the lexicon of the New England Preppie.

___FS_4. Associates of Boston's Massachusetts General Hospital reported that as of 1986, 33 patients had kidney stones removed with the laser.

___F_5. Clearcutting is the practice of cutting all trees on a given stand of forest regardless of the age or size of the trees.

___FS_6. "Valspeak is a state of mind, not a state of mouth," said Moon Unit Zappa.

___GS_7. Dr. Lillian Glass, a Beverly Hills speech pathologist, insists that Valspeak is a national speech disorder of monumental proportions.

___F_8. Slang is a highly informal language in which words and phrases either disappear or continue into formal usage.

___FS_9. G. K. Chesterton said, "Good slang is the one stream of poetry which is constantly flowing.

___F_10. "Bones" is a 14th century word for dice.

___F_11. The 1986 Nissan 300 ZX is advertised as the "Car for the performance generation."

___GS_12. There is more comfort than class, according to the manufacturer of the new recliner chairs.

___FS_13. A study in 1996 reported that college-educated women who are still single at the age of 35 have only a 5 percent chance of getting married.

_____14. The world's largest metal statue, the Statue of Liberty, is a pledge of American-French friendship as well as a beacon to immigrants.

_____15. The 850-mile long Fraser River in British Columbia has never been dammed although it is considered to be a good candidate for hydro development.

_____16. According to National Geographic, the Statue of Liberty arrived in New York on June 17. 1885, but it was presented to the U.S. minister on July 4.

_____17. Looters entered the palace of the Philippines ex-President Marcos just two hours after his departure.

_____18. Manila's Center for Research and Communications reported that in 1985 three-fourths of the Filipinos lived below the poverty level of $1,000 per year.

_____19. Gobbledygook is often called "Bureaucratese."

_____20. "Slang," says Theodore M Bernstein authority on words for *The New York Times* often develops out of an individual's need to identify with a group."

_____21. Argentina won the 1986 World Cup in soccer by defeating Germany 3-2.

_____22. Laboratory tests confirmed that the athlete died of a lethal overdose of cocaine.

_____23. The first seat belt patent was issued in 1885.

_____24. In today's culture, young people as well as adults, "are most likely to pick up their history from the mini-series' docudrama than the schools," believes television critic Steve Sonsky.

_____25. Cigarette smoking is harmful to your health.

Exercise 2-5 Supporting Generalizations with Facts

Supply at least four facts for the following generalizations. Include a few facts from sources. Indicate in the blank to the left of the number whether you have written a Fact (F) or Fact from a Source (FS).

A. *Generalization:* After one glance at my sister's apartment, I could see that she was not a housekeeper.

1. _____

2. _____

3. _____

4. _____

B. *Generalization:* The University of New Technology has stringent entrance requirements.

1. _____

2. _____

3. _____

4. _____

C. *Generalization:* Upon visiting Washington. D.C., the students found that there was more to see than the Congressional Building and the White House.

1. _____

2. _____

3. _____

4. _____

Exercise 2-6 Supplying a Generalization for a Series of Facts

Following are three groups of facts or facts from a source which support separate generalizations. Write a generalization for each group.

A. Generalization: _____

_____

_____.

1. The Christmas display tree at Lantana, Florida, grew for 53 years in an Oregon forest and stood 126 feet high.
2. The Douglas fir was taller than a twelve-story building; it weighed more than 8,000 pounds.
3. The silver star that topped the tree was six feet high.
4. Its trunk circumference at the base was 99 inches, and the spread at the bottom was 45 inches.
5. It was decorated with 15,200 lights, over half mile of garland, 1,050 colored balls, 225 red bows and 225 candy canes.

B. Generalization: _____

_____

_____.

1. The primary needs of the beginning scuba diver are mask, snorkel, and fins; this combination costs between $80 and $120.
2. As the novice advances, he will need a buoyancy compensator, which costs $190.
3. Since renting air tanks is expensive, $150 deposit and a $5.00 rental fee, divers may consider purchasing an aluminum air tank which costs $129.
4. A regulator rig, separate but necessary items for underwater diving, range in price from $220 to $650.

C. Generalization: _____

_____

_____.

1. On the basketball courts to the west of the shore, the boys are running back and forth, making points as they drop the ball in the hoop.

2. Further to the north, children are building sand castles on the water's edge.

3. Just beyond the children on the sand, a mother and a child are wading in the salt water ocean.

4. Three teenage boys are body surfing on the waves that keep bringing them back to the shore.

Exercise 2-7 Supplying Generalizations for a Series of Facts

So much for generalizations drawn from personal experience. Now you can deal with the kinds of statements that you are likely to come across in your reading. Following are three groups of facts or reports of facts. Write an inference for each group.

A. Generalization: _____

_____

_____.

1. According to Hugh Downs, narrator of "Growing Old in America," the life expectancy at the turn of the century was 47. In 1985 it was 74.

2. One out of every five persons over the age of 65 in 1985 will live to the year 2000.

3. In 1945 the average worker could expect to work only 13 more years. Today, it is 17.

4. Retirees in 1985 can expect to have twenty to thirty years remaining after they leave work.

5. One third of all people 65 or older live near the poverty level; sixty-five percent of the elderly live only on their social security income.

6. Early retirees take jobs that pay minimum to supplement their social security.

B. Generalization: _____

_____

_____.

1. Environmentalists trying to clean up one of the country's polluted waterways, the Miami River, discovered that the water turned orange because of rotting material from derelict boats and decaying automobiles.

2. The Pollution Board reported that forty industrial drainage pipes added to the 100,000 gallons of raw sewerage dumped into the river each day.

3. Volunteer observers reported that tourists and natives alike discard piles of rubbish and beer cans into the river.

4. The Geological Survey explained that industrial pollution of the river is caused by dumping of such items as carbonless carbon paper, paint, brake fluid, electric transformers, ink dyes, and plasticizers.

C. Generalization: _____

_____

_____.

1. An electrical engineer in Long Beach, California, invented a robotic arm that is used for brain surgery.
2. This arm aids physicians to insert radiation inside the brain for treatment.
3. It can locate points in the brain within .002 of an inch.
4. Furthermore, with its use, doctors can perform surgery without a general anesthesia.

STEP 4 Finding Suitable Sources for Expository Writing

You have met one of the crucial challenges of expository writing—distinguishing generalizations from facts. You have supplied statistics, incidents, and specific examples to support generalizations. You have also drawn generalizations from the enumeration of statistics, incidents, and specific examples on a particular topic.

Now you will be meeting the second challenge of expository writing-recognizing and using suitable sources for the content of your papers. Once you recognize the wealth of source material available to you, you will never have to say, "But I have nothing to write about."

Personal Experience

For your first papers in this course, you may use personal experience as a source. Personal experience gives a wide range of subject matter: hobbies, jobs, sports, school, travel, family, friends, cultural activities, organizations, and social life. Drawing on your personal experience involves participation, observation by looking and listening, conversation, and interviewing.

During World War II, newspaper reporters wrote detailed accounts of the battles since television was not available. One such reporter was Ernie Pyle, who traveled with the infantry and was part of the Normandy Beach invasion. His account of the first few hours is filled with specific descriptive details.

DESCRIPTION

I walked for a mile and a half along the water's edge of our many-miled invasion beach. I walked slowly, for the detail on the beach was infinite.

The wreckage was vast and startling. The awful waste and destruction of war, even aside from the loss of human life, has always been one of its out-standing features to those who are in it. Anything and everything is expendable. And we did expend on our beachhead in Normandy during those first few hours.

For a mile out from the beach there were scores of tanks and trucks and boats that were not visible, for they were at the bottom of the water—swamped by overloading, or hit by shells, or sunk by mines. Most of their crews were lost.

There were trucks tipped half over and swamped, partly sunken barges, and angled-up corners of jeeps, and small landing craft half submerged. And at low tide you could still see those vicious six-pronged snares that helped snag and wreck them.

On the beach itself, high and dry, were all kinds of wrecked vehicles. There were tanks that had only just made the beach before being knocked out. There were jeeps that had burned to a dull gray. There were big derricks on caterpillar treads that didn't quite make it. There were half-tracks carrying office equipment that had been made into a shambles by a single shell hit, their interiors still holding the useless equipage of smashed typewriters, telephones, and office files.

There were LCTs turned completely upside down, and lying on their backs, and how they got that way I don't know. There were boats stacked on top of each other, their sides caved in, their suspension doors knocked off.

In this shoreline museum of carnage there were abandoned rolls of barbed wire and smashed bulldozers and big stacks of thrown-away life belts and piles of shells still waiting to be moved. In the water floated empty life rafts and soldiers' packs and ration boxes, and mysterious oranges. On the beach lay snarled rolls of telephone wire and big rolls of steel matting and stacks of broken, rusting rifles.

On the beach lay, expended, sufficient men and mechanism for a small war. They were gone forever now. And yet we could afford it.

We could afford it because we were on, we had our toe hold, and behind us there were such enormous replacements for this wreckage on the beach that you could hardly conceive of the sum total. Men and equipment were flowing from England in such a gigantic stream that it made the waste on the beachhead seem like nothing at all, really nothing at all.

But there was another and more human litter. It extended in a thin little line, just like a high-water mark for miles along the beach. This was the strewn personal gear, gear that would never be needed again by those who fought and died to give us our entrance into Europe.

There in a jumbled row for mile on mile were soldier's packs. There were socks and shoe polish, sewing kits, diaries, Bibles, hand grenades. There were the latest letters from home, with the address on each one neatly razored out- one of the security precautions enforced before the boys embarked.

There were toothbrushes and razors, and snapshots of families back home staring up at you from the sand. There were pocketbooks, metal mirrors, extra trousers, and bloody, abandoned shoes. There were broken-handled shovels, and portable radios smashed almost beyond recognition, and mine detectors twisted and ruined.

There were torn pistol belts and canvas water buckets, first-aid kits, and jumbled heaps of life belts. I picked up a pocket Bible with a soldier's name on it, and put it in my jacket. I carried it half a mile or so and then put it back down on the beach. I don't know why I picked it up, or why I put it down again.

Soldiers carry strange things ashore with them. In every invasion there is at least one soldier hitting the beach at H-hour with a banjo slung over his shoulder. The most ironic piece of equipment marking our beach-this beach first of despair, then victory-was a tennis racket that some soldier had brought along. It lay lonesomely on the sand, clamped in its press, not a string broken.

From Ernie Pyle, *Brave Men*, Henry Holt & Co., 1944.

Media

The sources from which you will draw for your other papers—especially research papers come from the media. Here again you have many possibilities: newspapers, magazines, journals, books, and advertisements; television, radio, and movies.

In Exercise 2-6 you noticed that generalizations were drawn from such personal experiences as visiting the Christmas display, scuba diving, or watching the activities on the beach. For example, you might read these statistics: The average Puerto Rican in the United States

Excerpted from *Brave Men* by Ernie Pyle. Reprinted by permission of Scripps Howard Foundation.

lives in New York, is 22.3 years old, and earns $14,200. The average Cuban in the United States lives in Miami, is 37.5 years old, and earns $24,400. The average Mexican lives in Texas or California, is 21.8 years old, and earns $20,000. You might make this generalization: "Among immigrants of Hispanic origin, Cubans have the highest medium income." Another generalization, equally correct might be: "The Mexican immigrant is among the youngest of those from Spanish-speaking countries. "

As generalizations vary somewhat, facts drawn from personal observation vary according to individual experience. For example, ask five people to give what they consider to be an accurate fact for each of the following inferences. Record and observe the variation in responses.

Inference 1: A *moderately priced,* unfurnished two-bedroom apartment.
Inference 2: A *satisfactory income* for a recent college graduate.
Inference 3: A *reasonable number* of hours a college freshman should work.

Why do the responses vary? In these instances, they vary because of relative circumstances. For example, the inference term *moderately priced* when applied to a two-bedroom unfurnished apartment depends on a number of circumstances: the number of people sharing the rent, the amount of income available, the area of the country, the size of city or town, the particular location of the apartment in the city, the facilities and services available, and the size of the rooms in the apartment.

If the writer or speaker took into account all these points and explained them, you would understand what he means by *moderately priced* for that particular circumstance. Consider the variables that would enter into the response for the generalized terms *satisfactory income* and *reasonable number of hours.*

You are now aware of legitimate variables in the wording of generalizations and in the reporting of facts. However, you may have noticed in the discussion of the generalizations supplied for Exercises 2-6 and 2-7 that one or more people wrote generalizations with which the rest of the class did not agree. These students made inaccurate generalizations either because they did not take all the facts into consideration or because they misinterpreted one or more of the given facts.

As you learn to distinguish between generalizations and facts, you become more skillful at observing the world around you. You will also find that you will read more analytically.

At first, you may think that the objective facts that you need to support your generalizations in expository writing are cold and impersonal. You may also think that accumulating these facts is not a very exciting activity. However, as you gather these facts, store them in your mental sourcebook, and reflect upon them, you begin to make relationships. These relationships will lead you to form accurate and, therefore, effective inferences. It is your evaluation, then, that gives an original view to the subject matter of objective writing and persuades your reader that what you have to say is worth reading or acting upon.

You have seen how to assemble facts one by one from the various sources available to you and how you make generalizations from these facts. Working in a sequential manner, you transmit the experience or the information to your reader.

The photographer transmits experience too. However, he is able to capture a number of facts at one time. Different but equally correct generalizations can be drawn from a particular photograph. A writer using photograph titles (captions) it according to his purpose, using either a generalization or a fact. However, the photographer is able to capture a number of facts at one time. Different but equally correct generalizations can be drawn from a particular photograph. A writer using a photograph titles (captions) it according to his purpose, using either a generalization or a fact. Therefore, it is possible to use a photograph as the basis for writing a paper. One student chose to write about her grandmother.

PHOTOGRAPH OF MY GRANDMOTHER

Being only two years old when my paternal grandmother died, I was never able to know her. But the photograph I have of her serves as a link to the woman that she was. From her picture, it is apparent that she was a strong woman; her heavy frame indicates that she was a typical farmer's wife of the 1940's. The lines on her face are a result of raising ten children in the poor country of Guyana during times when frogs swam in the drinking water, women picked rocks out of huge bowls of rice before cooking, and indoor plumbing was a fairy tale. Her long hair is pulled back into a bun, a functional if not fashionable hairstyle. Her dress is plain with no collar or belt and the beaded necklace she wears is one of the few luxuries she is afforded. She is not smiling; maybe this is because cameras were not common in her world. Perhaps cameras made an old-fashioned farm dweller uncomfortable. This moment, frozen in time, is the only one I remember sharing with my grandmother. As a result, it is with this countenance that I always think of her: serious and stern, but loving.

Natalie Phalgoo

Photograph 2.1 (Photo by Stephen Grasso)

Inference Caption: A cute toddler presses his nose against the glass showcase of shiny racing cars, hoping that he will be able to persuade his mother to buy one for him.

Fact Caption: A small child, kneeling on the floor, presses his nose against the glass of a showcase in order to look at the toy cars displayed.

Discuss the circumstances under which a writer might use each type of caption.

Exercise 2-8 Captioning Photographs

The following are three photographs. First write a caption which is a generalization; then write a fact caption. Be prepared to discuss the circumstances under which you as a writer would use this photo and the two types of captions.

Photograph 2.2

Generalization Caption: A sweet little boy hugs the cute puppy he ~~just~~ received for his third birthday sits on his favourite ball a ste

Fact Caption: The little boy and his dog pose for a picture

Photograph 2.3

Generalization Caption:

Fact Caption:

Photograph 2.4

Generalization Caption:

Fact Caption:

Now you are ready to see how generalizations and facts work together in expository writing. Because the paragraph is the basic unit of expository writing, you will want to try out your generalization/fact distinction skills first on a paragraph. Following are two paragraphs written by college freshmen. In the first paragraph, the student focused on a photograph of a rusting refrigerator. The first sentence of the paragraph was to contain an opinion (generalization) of the subject, and the writers opinion was to be supported with a minimum of five facts and/or reports of facts.

THE PORCELAIN TOMB

(1) Our barn has become a mausoleum for all our discarded farm equipment and household items. (2) As I look around, I see a broken-down tractor, an ancient plow, buckets with holes in them, a refrigerator with its door removed, and a child's bedroom set with a broken mirror. (3) The one thing in particular that catches my eye is an ancient refrigerator which has become a final resting place for unwanted and unusable articles. (4) On closer inspection, the largest of these outdated goods is a pitchfork with its handle broken and prongs bent. (5) A scrap can keeps the tool pointing upward, awaiting an unsuspecting victim to fall prey to its lethal points. (6) On the same shelf, two napkin holders, from the restaurant we once owned, are found transformed from a shiny luster to a tarnished rust. (7) Towering over these two dispensers is a generator that came off an old tractor. (8) The power unit, frozen where it should move, is unable to produce electricity if it were attached to an engine. (9) On the lower shelf, three U-shaped iron bars lean against the back wall of the refrigerator. (10) These rods had six different uses just three years ago, from mending fences to making hold-downs for cattle; the small rails now have no use at all. (11) In front of the bars, hidden beneath the pile of wet leaves, which have accumulated on the bottom shelf, is a rusted hand sickle, dull and lifeless; it was once used everyday for harvesting the wheat, but now is decaying away, almost unnoticed. (12) As I turned to walk away, I am saddened by what I see: once the storer of all our perishable foods, the aged refrigerator is now the grave for idle, undesirable materials.

—Richard Smith

In the second paragraph, the student decided to discuss an assignment that he had written the previous week.

MY WRITING: A WORK OF ART

(1) Last week I wrote this really great paragraph for English class. (2) When I handed it in, I knew that it had to be ten times better than Mary's paragraph or John's paragraph. (3) In the topic sentence I used some neat wording to catch the reader's attention. (4) Then I really got my pen rolling as I wrote the body of the paragraph. (5) I let the reader know exactly how I felt about my subject because it was a topic that was near and dear to my heart. (6) Believe me, I really laid down the facts, not caring whose toes I stepped on. (7) Then to help my reader to remember the opening idea, I repeated words similar to the ones that I used in the beginning of my paragraph. (8) But when

my paper was returned, it had a lousy low grade. (9) I can see my instructor doesn't know a really great paragraph after reading one.

Exercise 2-9 Criticizing Inferences and Facts

The paragraph about the refrigerator contains twelve sentences. Label each of the sentences as Inference (I), Fact (F), Report of Fact (RF), or Report of Inference (RI). After you have labelled each sentence, be prepared to discuss the extent to which this paragraph fulfilled the assignment. Your instructor may also ask you to comment on the sentence structure in the paragraph.

1. _____

2. _____

3. _____

4. _____

5. _____

6. _____

7. _____

8. _____

9. _____

10. _____

11. _____

12. _____

Exercise 2-10

Identify the sentences in the paragraph about the assignment exactly as you did for the one on the refrigerator. Discuss the inferences and/or reports of inferences that occurred in the body of this paragraph. Did you think they were justified? If so, why do you think so? How do they relate to the inference in the first sentence? How do they relate to facts in the paragraph?

1. _____

2. _____

3. _____

4. _____

5. _____

6. _____

7. _____

8. _____

9. _____

Discussion: Which of the paragraphs is written in formal English? Which has concrete information? Can either paragraph be improved? If so, how?

The Paragraph

STEP 1 Writing the Controlling Inference in the Topic Sentence

The paragraph is the basic unit of expository writing. In the paragraph the writer develops a single unit of thought. He introduces this single unit in the controlling inference sentence, commonly known as the topic sentence. The topic sentence consists of two parts-the limited subject and the controlling inference. The controlling inference is the writer's opinion, conclusion, or evaluation of the subject; and it indicates the single unit of thought that will be developed. In the topic sentence the writer commits himself to supporting the controlling inference by supplying proof details in the form of facts, examples, or incidents. Usually the topic sentence appears at the beginning of a paragraph.

Your study of Stage 2 has made you aware that an inference statement always causes the listener or the reader to ask the question, "What makes you think so?" or "What do you mean by ... ?" In the cafeteria conversation, for instance, the speaker asserted his opinion about the atmosphere when he used the controlling inference *depressing*. Pressed for specific information to illustrate what he meant by the term, he had to supply proof details. When a speaker or a writer supplies proof details for an inference, he is saying to his listener or to his reader, "These are the reasons I believe what I have asserted. You may not agree with my opinion, but now you understand why I formed it." A writer's support statements, in other words, are the evidence.

When you write the controlling inference sentence for a paragraph, you need to ask yourself five questions:

1. Is my subject worth discussing (or is it obvious or frivolous)?

2. Is my controlling inference a single unit of thought (or do I actually have more than one idea here)?

3. Why am I making this assertion (what is my purpose)?

4. Who is my audience (what are their backgrounds, their interests)?

5. What method can I use to illustrate my point (what kind of support sentences will I use to back up my controlling inference)?

Here are two examples of topic sentences with workable controlling inferences. In each sentence, the controlling inference is italicized. A discussion follows each topic sentence.

Topic Sentence: Campus facilities to aid handicap students are *acceptable.*

Discussion: Test this sentence against the five criteria for a workable topic sentence listed above.

1. Is my subject worth discussing? Yes, because some handicap students need special facilities to enable them to continue their education.

2. What is the single unit of thought?
   The acceptability of the campus facilities

3. What is the purpose?
   To inform the reader of the adequacy of the handicap facilities

4 Who is my audience? Handicapped students and college officials

5 What kind of proof details will I use?
   A. The distance between parking and the classrooms
   B. Number of ramps that can be used
   C. Location of elevators
   D. Availability of drinking facilities
   E. Types of restroom facilities available
   F. Access to public telephones

Topic Sentence: *Underweight women* may have *serious problems.*

Discussion: There are two inferences in this sentence because there are two phrases which raise the question, "What do you mean by ... ?" These two phrases are underweight women and serious problems. For the purposes of this paragraph, however, it is obvious that the writer wants to focus on the idea of some women having serious problems. Therefore, this phrase is the controlling inference for which the writer will supply proof details. The student can assume that the audience would generally agree about the meaning of the term *underweight* because the condition can be determined by standardized height and weight charts.

Poor Topic Sentences

Some topic sentences that may at first glance appear to be workable cannot be properly developed in a paragraph. Two examples follow:

The Double Inference

Topic Sentence: The little half-wave rectifier buttons that attach to the bottom of light bulbs save *time* and *money.*

Discussion: The writer of this sentence cannot develop a single unit of thought because there are two controlling inferences *time* and *money.* This writer would have to give examples demonstrating how time is saved and how money can be saved. Therefore, the writer is committed to supplying two different sets of details for two distinct types of savings.

The Vague Inference

Topic Sentence: *Intruder in the Dust* is one of the most fascinating stories ever written.

Discussion: Fascinating in this sentence is an impossible inference to prove. First, the writer would have to take into consideration every story that had ever been written. Next, the writer would have to discuss all the categories of stories such as novels, novelettes, short stories, and vignettes. Next, the writer would have to take into consideration all the categories of types of stories, such as historical fiction, mystery fiction, science fiction, romantic fiction, and fantasy fiction. Finally, the writer would have to take into consideration the criteria for judging fiction, such as consideration of characterization, plot, theme, setting, verisimilitude, imagery, symbolism, and style. The writer has an impossible task and the sentence should be scrapped.

Inference from a Source

Topic sentence: Senator Jarvis Snort claims that the economy is rising

Discussion: Topic sentences are opinions of the writer. They do not come from other sources.

STEP 2 Recognizing Unsuitable Topic Sentences

You are now aware of three problems in the topic sentence: (1) a double inference, (2) an inference too vague to support with proof details, (3) a topic that is not sufficiently limited. There are three other kinds of unsatisfactory topic sentences. One is the question. For example, "Will success spoil the Dolphins?" cannot function as a topic sentence even though the sentence does contain an inference word, *success.* There is no way to supply proof details for a future possibility because the proof details cannot be verified. On the other hand, some questions converted to statements can function as topic sentences. Consider the following question: "Can inner-city schools in Atlanta keep pace with our changing urban society?" There is an inference term here, *keep pace.* But the controlling inference in the topic sentence must be an assertion of your opinion, your conclusion, or your generalization about a subject. Because this sentence is in the form of a question, there is no assertion. Revised to form a statement, the sentence would read, "Inner-city schools are having difficulty keeping pace with the changing urban society in Atlanta. "

Another type of unsuitable topic sentence to be considered is the one stated in the form of a fact. It is sometimes called a dead-end topic sentence because once the fact is stated, the writer can't go anywhere with it insofar as proof details are concerned. Consider this statement: "Absenteeism has increased 100 percent in the auto industry over the past ten years." Revised to form a topic sentence suitable for further development, this statement would read: "Absenteeism has become a growing problem in the auto industry in the past decade."

The last unsuitable topic sentence is the one which comes from a source since a topic sentence is the writer's opinion or conclusion. For example, consider this sentence: Max Holland believes that "conceptions often must be altered in mid-stream." In this case Holland's conclusion is that of an authority, not the writer's.

In summation, then, a topic sentence can be unsuitable because of one or more of six problems:

1. A double inference.

2. An inference too vague to support with proof details.

3. An insufficiently limited topic.

4. Topic sentence stated in the form of a question.

5. Topic sentence stated in the form of a fact.

6. An inference from a source.

7. No Sentence sense.

Exercise 3-1 Criticizing the Controlling Inference in the Topic Sentence

Underline the controlling inference in each statement. Then apply the five criteria for writing a topic sentence to determine how workable each statement is.

1. Aerobics can be tiring but <u>rewarding</u>. *double Inference*

    (1) Subject worth discussing? Why?

    (2) Single unit of thought? *No*

    (3) Purpose?

    (4) Audience?

    (5) Kind of proof details?
         Supply four if you can.

2. People's choices of T-shirts reveal their attitudes.

    (1) Subject worth discussing? Why?

    (2) Single unit of thought? *yes*

    (3) Purpose?

    (4) Audience?

    (5) Kind of proof details?
         Supply four if you can.

3. John's part-time job as a waiter has some advantages.

    (1) Subject worth discussing? Why?

    (2) Single unit of thought?

    (3) Purpose?

    (4) Audience?

(5) Kind of proof details?
Supply four if you can.

4. Walking is good for the heart.

(1) Subject worth discussing? Why?

(2) Single unit of thought?

(3) Purpose?

(4) Audience?

(5) Kind of proof details?
Supply four if you can.

5. The Joneses are packing their automobile for a vacation trip. Fact

(1) Subject worth discussing why?

(2) Single unit of thought?

(3) Purpose?

(4) Audience?

(5) Kind of proof details?
Supply four if you can.

STEP 3 Brainstorming

One of the first steps to writing a theme is brainstorming. First think about topics that you would like to write about and those that you feel you can easily support. One student, for example, chose several topics: events, persons. and places. She selected events and places and thought about the following subjects:

Events
Marriage
Mother's death
Finding Heidi
Returning to college

Places
Yogi Lake
Missouri farmhouse

She chose two subjects to brainstorm: returning to college and the Missouri farmhouse. As she continued to brainstorm, she thought of specific details for both subjects. She first wrote details for returning to college.

- Apprehensive
- Out of school for 20 years
- Never considered myself intelligent
- Didn't know if I would be able to keep up with the study demands
- Never was a serious student
- Felt lost, insecure
- Never performed well on tests
- Didn't know anyone
- Assessment test:
  So nervous I could hardly comprehend what I was trying to read
  Could feel heart racing
  Hands sweating so badly I could hardly hold the pencil
  Had to calm myself enough to concentrate on the test

38 years old
High school drop out
Poor mathematical skills

Poor study skills
Didn't know way around campus
Didn't know registration procedures
Felt too pressured
Didn't know how to prepare for lectures

When she reviewed the list, she realized that many of her details were generalizations and that she would be unable to find concrete illustrations. Next. she tried her second subject, the Missouri farmhouse.

The simple two story farmhouse stood at the top of a small sloping hill
From there one could see the remains of a working farm.
The barn, a small two-bedroom house built for farm hands, the pump house which
    supplied the bathing and drinking water, shed for tractors
The backyard enclosed by a sagging wire fence whose gate was worn and rusted
The familiar aroma of cold ashes resting in the belly of the old cast iron stove
The plain wooden floorboards, worn
Occasional patches of yellowing wallpaper beginning to peel
Upstairs bedrooms bulging with homemade bunk beds

There was always a symphony of sounds — Bob whites, whippoorwill, bullfrogs,
    crickets, hooting owls.
Occasionally the unmistakably foul odor of skunk hung in the air.
Idle, empty barn that served as a storage spot for abandoned farm tools
Just beyond the barnyard stood an abandoned house that had once been home to sev-
    eral farm workers.
The yard was overgrown with wild strawberries.

Terry Petrenchik

Since the student was brainstorming, her first priority was to get her thoughts written. Thus, she did not concern herself with writing complete sentences for every thought, nor did she write the ideas in any particular order, but just as they came to mind. In this case the student began with a limited subject, the Missouri farmhouse.

Step 4: Limiting the Subject in a Topic Sentence

There is, however, another type of brainstorming: limiting a broad subject and then list-ing the details. Suppose you were to select *top television programs*. You might think that the phrase *top programs* limits your subject. But when you begin to jot down your ideas for sup-porting details, you will realize that there are television shows in many categories that are considered top programs for the year. You would limit your subject even further. Your topic sentence might read "The television writers of the top soap opera *The Bold and the Beautiful* rely on past successful ideas." You may then be able to brainstorm four, five, or six ideas that happen over and over again with some character or situation variation.

Step 5: Writing the Lead-in Sentence

While a paragraph seldom has fewer than six supporting sentences, it is not longer than 250 words. However, one-paragraph themes are usually introduced by a sentence or two that lead the reader into the topic sentence. For example, the lead-in for "The Missouri Farmhouse" might be as follows:

Lead in
X   When I was ten years old, my father purchased three hundred and twenty acres of farmland situat-
    ed deep in the southern foothills of Missouri.

The writer would then add the topic sentence:

Twenty-nine years have since passed, and yet I realize that some of my most vivid memories spring
from that seemingly insignificant spot

However, in other instances, the writer may prefer to combine the lead-in with the topic sentence.

As an apprehensive forty-year old nursing student, returning to college after my children were grown, I became completely frustrated by the registration procedure.

While the topic sentence controls the subject and the supporting sentences of the paper, the lead-in gets the attention of the reader.

Exercise 3-2 Limiting the Subject in the Topic Sentence

In each of the sentences below, the subject is not specific enough to be developed in one paragraph. Revise the topic sentence so that the subject is sufficiently limited. As you do this, you may also see the need for further limiting the inference.

Example. Parents can be inconsistent.
Revision: My parents are inconsistent in their expectations about my choice of a career.

1. Elected public officials sometimes fail to carry out their campaign promises.
    Revision:

2. Just as the drug problem seems to be leveling off, people, are finding new drugs to abuse.
    Revision:

3. The ocean will eventually supply new sources of food.
    Revision:

4. Part-time jobs can be very boring.
    Revision:

5. Many fields related to medicine are now open.
    Revision:

6. New clothing fads for teenagers are appearing on the American scene.
    Revision:

7. Some mechanical tasks are frustrating.
   Revision:

8 Some customs are good.
    Revision:

9. Americans love music.
   Revision:

10.. Inflation is a world-wide problem.
    Revision:

Exercise 3-3 Choosing Suitable Topic Sentences

From each group below, select the sentence that would be suitable for a topic sentence and mark TS in the blank. Then refer to the list of topic sentence problems and identify by one of the preceding numbers the problem in each of the other two sentences (see p. 54).

Example:

___5___ A. A survey indicates that men favor women's rights organizations 44 percent to 39 percent, whereas women oppose them 42 percent to 40 percent.

___TS___ B. The New Feminism has already left its mark on the 1970s in the form of legislative changes affecting employment.

___2,3___ C. The American woman should be the happiest in history.

Group 1

_____ A. Woman Act to Control Health Care (WATCH) is a Chicago-based women's group concerned about institutional health care available for Chicago's unwed mothers on welfare.

_____ B. The Chicago Maternity Center is the only remaining institutional service in an urban area that assists women in delivering babies at home.

_____ C. WATCH is now taking an active role to insure that women in Chicago get the kind of health care they need.

Group 2

_____ A. Can the establishment of experimental schools for reluctant learners solve the dropout rate?

_____ B. The New York Schools Exchange, a clearinghouse of many "free schools," listed more than four hundred in 1972.

_____ C. Within the limits of its budget, the Ford Foundation is assisting public school experimental programs in Berkeley, California.

Group 3

_____ A. Visitors are astonished when they first meet these gentle tribespeople, the Tasadays.

_____ B. The Tasadays of Mindanao, our only link with the Stone Age, are a unique tribe.

_____ C. The wild yam is the staple food of the Tasadays although a banquet might include such foods as fat grubs, tadpoles, frogs, and stalks from palm trunks.

Group 4

_____ A. In 1991, 2,433,000 couples married but 1,168,000 ended in divorce court.

_____ B. The divorce rate in the United States is the highest in the world.

_____ C. The premarital contract, stating commitments with regard to children, work and property, may be one approach to lowering the divorce rate in the United States.

STEP 6 Supplying Support Statements

Once you have worked out a topic sentence with a limited subject and a workable controlling inference, the next step is to support your controlling inference with specific and relevant facts. You will want to avoid two types of unsatisfactory support statements. The first type is the irrelevant statement—a fact that does not relate directly back to your controlling inference. This kind of statement is sometimes called a detractor because it does not directly support the controlling inference. Read the following topic sentence with its support statements, and decide whether all details are relevant.

Topic sentence: At the 1972 Olympics in Munich, Mark Spitz, swimmer for the American Olympic team, turned in a record-setting performance.

Support Statements

A. In the 1968 Olympic Games, Spitz hoped to win six gold medals.
B. In Munich, he won the 200 yard butterfly and anchored the 400 yard freestyle relay, both in world record time.
C. *Time* magazine quoted Spitz as saying that he swam because he wanted to be recog-- nized as the best in the world.
D. Mark surpassed the record for gold medals of five set in 1920 by an Italian fencer.
E. During the 1972 Olympic Games, Mark won seven gold medals.
F. In Mexico, in 1968, Mark won only a silver and a bronze medal.
G. Mark trained hard for four years before going to the Olympics.

The writer of this paragraph got off the track with several details. Two of the sentences, A and F, are irrelevant because they do not refer to the subject of this paragraph, which is the 1972 Olympics. Two of the sentences, C and G, are irrelevant because they have nothing to do with the controlling inference. Only three statements, B, D, and E, support the controlling inference, *record-setting performance.* When the detractors are eliminated, the paragraph has too few support statements. The writer should have included the other records set by Spitz at the 1972 Olympics to support his controlling inference adequately.

The second type of unsatisfactory support statement is the inclusion of another inference. Known as a minor inference, this kind of proof detail does relate to the controlling inference; but because it is another inference, it must have a fact attached to it to serve as a supporting detail. Notice how the minor inference works in the following example:

Topic sentence: My landlord is charging excessive prices for his rental units.
Supporting detail in the form of an inference:
 A. The rent for a one-room efficiency is outrageous.

Discussion: Outrageous is a minor inference. The writer can make his minor inference sentence serve as a supporting detail if he cites a specific instance or example that illustrates what he means by *outrageous.* He can incorporate a fact within the sentence, or he can follow the minor inference sentence with a fact sentence. Here are two possibilities for revision:

> *Fact incorporated in sentence:* The rent for a one-room efficiency apartment, $550, is outrageous.
> *Minor inference sentence followed immediately by fact sentence:* The rent for a one room efficiency apartment is outrageous. My landlord charges $550.

Here is another example of how a minor inference sentence is revised so that it functions as a specific detail supporting the controlling inference.

Topic sentence: Alcohol was involved in the two-car accident at Twelfth and Pine Avenue.

Supporting detail in the form of a minor inference sentence:

> The alcohol content in the blood of the driver of the compact car was high.

Revision The alcohol content in the blood of the driver of the compact car was high—15 percent.

Exercise 3-4 Working with Supporting Statements

Following are four topic sentences with the controlling inference in italics. Each topic sentence is followed by a minor inference sentence.

A. In the first blank, make the minor inference specific by attaching a fact or by writing another sentence of fact to follow the minor inference sentence.
B. In the second blank, supply a second supporting statement sentence that is strictly relevant to the controlling inference in the topic sentence.

Example: There are a *variety of shops* at the mall.

A. Small craft shops dominate the Collegian Mall.
Revision: Rawhide designs, leather belts, and purses for individual customers.
B. Second support sentence: Wax Wick allows customers to create their own candles for special occasions.

1. Registration for first time in-college students is *frustrating.*
    A. Students have to wait in line for a long time.
        Revision:

    B. Second support sentence:

2. Graffiti is a visual form of the artist's visual emotional
    A. Rod Warring depicts his desire for a better life:
        Revision:

    B. Second support sentence:

3. Computers save time for students.
   A. John's Zeno computer helps him to save time in revision of themes.
      Revision:

   B. Second support sentence:

4. Mechanics perform many important tasks with the latest electronic equipment.
   A. They are are using electronic devices to check malfunctioning pans.
      Revision:

   B. Second support sentence:

Up to this point you have been examining supporting details in isolated sentences to determine if the statements were relevant or irrelevant to the controlling inference in the topic sentence. You will need to develop your skill in criticizing proof details in paragraph form. Here is a paragraph written by a student involved with a civic theater group. The assignment was for the student to select as his subject his special field of interest and to construct a controlling inference sentence followed by at least five proof detail sentences to support the controlling inference. Read the paragraph and the discussion which follows it.

A WAY TO THE FOOTLIGHTS

(1) The amateur actor who wants to win a role in a play produced by a civic theater group must put a five-point plan in operation. (2) At some time in our lives, the suppressed Walter Mitty escapes into our consciousness and we imagine ourselves projected on a silver screen or parading before a Broadway audience. (3) Since the world of professional theater will remain only a dream to most people, an aspiring actor can fulfill his desire to act by trying out for a role in a local civic theater group. (4) He should first arrange his schedule to see if he can fit in rehearsal hours. (5) Then he needs to read the play. (6) He should select a character he might like to play; but while he is reading the play, he might keep in mind other jobs related to the production of the play. (7) For instance, if he doesn't win a role in the play, he might consider working on lights or stage props. (8) Much could be learned about stagecraft and costume design just by working with the technical crew. (9) In fact, he might decide that a career in the theater can be his and that his dream of working on Broadway can be fulfilled.

Discussion: The topic sentence in this paragraph is very workable. The subject is clearly limited—the amateur who wants to win a part in a play produced by a civic theater group. The controlling inference is clear-the actor must put a five-point plan into operation. The writer's commitment is to state as clearly as possible what these five points are. In the paragraph, however, the writer has strayed far afield; only sentences four and five and half of sentence six have any relevance to the commitment of his controlling inference. If these two and a half sentences are the only relevant ones, then what do the others contribute? Sentence two might serve as an interesting opener for a longer paper. Here, however, it is not only another inference sentence, but one which has no relation to the five-point plan. At first glance, sentence three seems to be relevant; however, it, too, is an inference and is irrelevant because it concerns professional, not amateur theater. The writer could possibly combine the ideas from sentences two and three into his topic sentence in order to enlist interest in his paragraph. The topic sentence then would read like this:

> Since the world of professional theater remains only a dream to most people, an aspiring actor can fulfill his interest in the theater by following a five-point plan for winning a role in a play produced by a civic theater group.

The writer would then be ready for his supporting details: (1) arranging his schedule, (2) reading the play, (3) selecting the character he wants to play. He got into trouble in sentence six because he wandered off into related jobs in amateur theater. Thus, the second half of sentence six together with sentences seven, eight, and nine are all detractors. The confused reader is still waiting for points four and five, but they never do materialize. As the paragraph stands, it fails to fulfill the commitment of the controlling inference, and the reader remains uninstructed. Following is a rewritten version of the paragraph.

A WAY TO THE FOOTLIGHTS

Since the world of professional theater remains only a dream to most people, an aspiring actor can fulfill his interest in the theater by following a five-point plan for winning a role in a play produced by a civic theater group. First, he should study the rehearsal schedule set up by the director and the dates the play is to be presented to make sure that he has enough time to attend rehearsals and to be present at all performances. Second, assuming that he has already read the play, he should select the character he thinks he would like to play. Third, he should interpret the part and practice it aloud so that he will read well for the tryouts. In addition, he should be prepared to read other parts. Fourth, he must come to the tryout on time and be prepared to stay for the duration, since he may be called again by the director to read for another part or to read his part with other characters. Fifth, he must be willing to accept any role the director may ask him to play. Although this five-point plan will not guarantee him a part, it will certainly improve his chances of winning a role.

Exercise 3-5 Criticizing Supporting Details in the Paragraph

Read the following paragraph and determine the effectiveness of each supporting detail. Are there any irrelevant sentences? Underline the topic sentence.

EXPOSITORY WRITING

It is now four o'clock in the morning, and my second English writing assignment. which is due in five hours, is still not finished. It is not as if I haven't devoted myself to the task. It is simply that I find expository writing a frustrating process. Most of my writing finds its way into the nearby trash pile whose size grows with each of my contributions. Each discarded paper represents two to four hours of work which I deem unfit for my English professor's evaluation. It is aggravating to feel so inept at such a deceivingly simple assignment—write one paragraph; and yet the moment my thoughts are translated into writing, they seem to lose much of their original depth and meaning. Thoughts that once seemed worthy of being expressed are reduced to awkward, childlike scrawl. Another obstacle is protocol. I am unaccustomed to using formal English in my communications, and I find the transition from slang and informal English tedious and cumbersome. Furthermore, I have encountered a problem which I am certain every would-be writer experiences. At times my mind is so flooded with ideas that I barely have time to capture one thought before another is hurled at me. On the other hand, there are moments when my thoughts are as dry and empty as an old deserted well. Still, I can almost imagine the thrill of producing an expository paper which embodies grace and elegance. Then again, having read excerpts from Ernie Pyle's book entitled *Brave Men*, it is difficult to hope of ever being satisfied with one's own work. Nevertheless, I am relatively certain that with discipline, practice, and an ample supply of paper, I will someday be capable of producing a paragraph that adequately conveys my meaning. Although I find the process of expository writing somewhat tedious and laborious, I can imagine no greater satisfaction than developing the ability to express oneself with clarity and eloquence.

Terry Petrenchik

STEP 7   Criticizing Support Statements

Students from an art appreciation class went to a museum of art to view the collection of Lisa Hyatt, an artist from Florida. Notice the difference in the topic sentences and the details used in the two paragraphs written by different students and the explanation that follows.

Paragraph One

Of the paintings by Lisa Hyatt, there is one that creates a feeling of tension. This feeling is created through a repetition of doors. There are four doors with the first door partly showing. The artist drapes the second door by using gradual shadowing to form the folds in the drapes. A window in this door allows the local blue sky to show through. Although the third door has no window, it has a drape covering part of it. In contrast, this door is painted a deeper red than the others. At the edge of this painting, the artist depicts only a sliver of the last door. It is not only the repetition of doors but also the deep red of the four doors contrasted with a negative peach background which creates for the viewer a feeling of tension. This feeling is intensified by the fact that all the doors are tightly closed.

Paragraph Two

The subject matter in every large painting on display seemed to evolve around doors, doors that were always open and led somewhere beyond, in some cases, to other open doors. This was my only disappointment when viewing Hyatt's work. The subject matter was always the same, repetitious shapes that were almost always geometric in structure with fine lines separating these shapes. In one or two paintings some organic shapes could be seen but they were not proportionally large enough to soften the hard, geometric shapes of the doors.

In the first paragraph the student has a unified, coherent paragraph because every sentence relates to her topic sentence: "This feeling is created through a repetition of doors." In the second paragraph, the topic sentence involves too many ideas: "The subject matter in every large painting on display seemed to evolve around doors, doors that were always open and led somewhere beyond, in some cases to other open doors." The writer promises the reader that he/she will discuss what lay behind the open doors and what the other doors were. The topic sentence should have only one controlling inference. However, after the topic sentence, the writer does not give one single detail to support it, which is after all, only the writer's opinion. The paper must illustrate to the reader that the writer arrived at his/her opinion after observing specific details of the paintings.

STEP 8   Providing Transition

Now that you know how proof details are enumerated to support the writer's controlling inference, you need to know how to connect these details to make your paragraph read smoothly. Writers refer to the relevance of proof details as unity. They refer to the way the details are connected as coherence. The connecting words and phrases that give coherence to the details of a paragraph are called transitions. There are several ways to achieve coherence in a paragraph:

1. Repetition of a key word.
2. Use of a synonym for a key word.
3. Use of a pronoun to refer to a noun used in the previous sentence.
4. Use of a transitional word or phrase.

In order to choose an appropriate transitional expression, you should ask, " What is the function of this transition?" For example, if you had a series of facts that you were adding up to prove a point, you could use such expressions as *also, another example, in addition, and furthermore*, to name only a few. The following chart lists transitional expressions according to their function.

Transitional Expression

To Mark Addition: and, again, also, moreover, first, second, third, equally important, in addition, then too, furthermore

To Indicate Time: in the beginning, at the outset, at the start, first, next, then, before, during, while, at the same time, concurrently, again, subsequently, at last, finally

To Indicate Spatial Order above, below, beyond, near, far from, over, under, in the distance, on top of, nearby, to the left to the right, straight ahead, opposite to, behind, adjacent to, at right angles to, perpendicular to, parallel to, to the east, to the west, to the north, to the south, further away

To Indicate Comparison and Contrast: similar to, like, similarly, in a like manner, just as, identical to, likewise, but, or, nor, however, yet, on the other hand, in contrast, conversely, on the contrary, unlike

To Indicate Cause and Effect: therefore, as a result, accordingly, consequently, after, hence, thus, subsequently

To Indicate Conclusion: therefore, thus, then, in conclusion, last, consequently, as a result, in the last analysis, in summary, in other words, to conclude, to summarize

The paragraph below illustrates the various transitional devices a student used to link his proof details about a political candidate. The devices are underlined. Identification of the devices by number appears before each one: (1) repetition of a key word; (2) use of a synonym for a key word; (3) use of a pronoun to refer to a noun used in the previous sentence; (4) use of a transitional word or phrase.

ROBERT WEAVER FOR CONGRESS

Robert Weaver is a highly qualified Democratic candidate for the Tenth Congressional District. [4]First, [3]he has had two years of International Law at Yale University, and he has earned a Bachelor of Arts and Master of Arts degree. [4]In addition, [3]he assisted in the framework of the United States Government services as a diplomat for fifteen years with assignments in Europe, Asia, and Latin America. Two of this candidate's diplomatic titles were Vice Consul and Attache. [4]Furthermore, [3]he was named twice for the Pulitzer Prize. [4]Not only has [3]he written three books on international relations and defense, [4]but [3]he is [4]also an editor for *People to People* in Washington, D.C., and has been syndicated by United Features in New York. Mr. Weaver is bilingual; [3]this allows [3]him to communicate with both the Spanish and the English speaking citizens of this city. [3]He is [4]also a member of the Senate Subcommittee on International Security. [4]Therefore, because of his outstanding qualifications, [1] Mr. Weaver should be elected.

When you are working at providing transition, you could think of the paragraph as a folding fan. A fan has webbing. All of the parts are attached to a pivot so that the fan can open and be operated.

Look at the illustration of the paragraph "Weaver for Congress" on the following page. Just as the paragraph has the topic and the summary sentence to frame it, the fan has the end ribs which serve as anchors. The proof details of the paragraph are like the intermediate ribs of the fan. In a similar manner, the transitional devices link the details much like the webbing of the fan links the ribs. If the webbing is cut at any point on the fan, the fan will no longer function. Similarly, if the proof details are not linked together, the paragraph loses it coherence. Finally, the controlling inference functions in the paragraph much as the pivot functions on the fan: both control the entire operation.

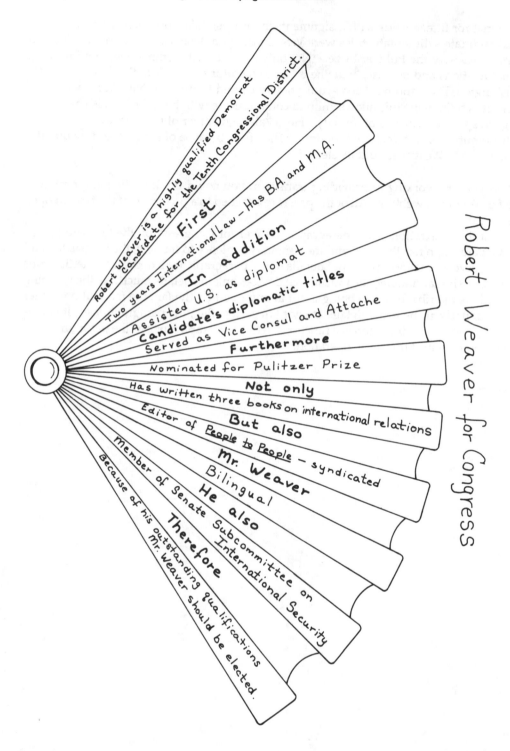

Robert Weaver is a highly qualified Democrat Candidate for the Tenth Congressional District.

First

Two years International Law – Has B.A. and M.A.

In addition

Assisted U.S. as diplomat

Candidate's diplomatic titles

Served as Vice Consul and Attache

Furthermore

Nominated for Pulitzer Prize

Not only

Has written three books on international relations

But also

Editor of People to People – syndicated

Mr. Weaver

Bilingual

He also

Member of Senate Subcommittee on International Security

Therefore

Because of his outstanding qualifications Mr. Weaver should be elected.

Robert Weaver for Congress

Exercise 3-6 Recognizing Transition

A. Underline the transitions in the following paragraph.
B. Identify the type of transition by number as in the preceding paragraph

ABI DAY

    In Finland, graduating from one class to another is much more important than passing final examinations. Because classes at Finnish high schools are very difficult, completing a grade is considered a major accomplishment. This is especially true between the second and third grade classes (the junior and senior year). In February, after the third graders have completed their last examinations, they are still not ready to graduate from *lukio*, the high school. It is at this time that they must study for several more months before taking their final matriculation examinations. Now the teachers and other classmates say goodbye to the third graders and welcome the second graders as the reigning seniors. This event is not taken lightly at the school, for it is time for festivities, costumes, and celebrating the end of three long years of hard work. First, the third graders, now called *abis*, get to parade their accomplishments. With their bright costumes and painted faces, it is like Halloween in February. There is singing and music, also. But because the Finns believe that all good times must be shared, all of the *abis* pile into huge trucks and drive to the village to parade around the market square. Stores are closed for the afternoon, for all shop owners are also at the market square to cheer on the students and wish them luck. Hundreds of people gather for this affair, along with the second graders who know that their time for festivities is next. Since the second graders are now the oldest students at the school, they are given a day to dress up in Finnish clothes from the 1920's and 30's and also to parade around the town. In the morning, when all of the festivities have died down and the *abis* are at home studying intensely for their finals, the second graders begin their ceremony. Dressed in authentic clothes that their parents or grandparents once wore, they perform Finnish folk dances in the snow while onlookers applaud them. After the dance, there is a celebration at an elegant hotel where dinner is served and teachers give speeches to the second graders, telling them of their responsibilities and enumerating the steps that they must follow as third graders. After the dinner, there is a disco dance at the nearest school. The next morning, classes resume for all students, especially for the second graders, who now have a cool and aloof attitude. In the months that follow, they work very hard, for they are sure that next year, their *abi* day will come.

Susan Swails

STEP 9 Writing the Summary Sentence

The last sentence in a paragraph is usually the summary sentence or conclusion. It signals your reader that you are coming to an end of the development of your single unit of thought. The summary sentence is often stated in the form of a conclusion which reasserts your controlling inference. For instance, in a paragraph about children's views of religion, the writer's controlling inference was that children's religious discussions can be amusing. The writer had provided enough convincing evidence (support sentences) to conclude with this sentence, which reasserts the controlling inference "children's religious discussions can be amusing."

A four-year-old's view of religion can provide adults with an hilarious collection of verbal misconceptions.

In another paper about the uses an abandoned refrigerator has had over the years, the writer's assertion was that "an ancient refrigerator has become a final resting place for unwanted and unusable articles." He concludes his paper with this sentence:

As I turn to walk away, I am saddened by what I see; once the storer of all of our perishable foods, the aged refrigerator is now the grave for idle, undesirable materials.

Other summary sentences draw logical conclusions. In a paragraph about the parallel that exists between the comic strip character Cathy and today's career girl, the writer concludes with:

"Cathy" is a way of laughing with ourselves as well as at ourselves, an extension of our every day life, put down on paper to make us smile.

STEP 10 Writing a Title

The last step in writing a paragraph is to pick an appropriate title. Keep in mind the four points for a title:

1. It should be short.
2. It should reflect the subject of the paper.
3. It should not be the topic sentence.
4. It should catch the reader's attention.

Here are a few titles that writers chose for their paragraph:

FIRST IMPRESSIONS, about the J. W. Corbet Wildlife Preserve in the Everglades; TAKE ME OUT OF THE BALL GAME, by a Little League father; AND ON THE SEVENTH DAY, by a student working as a mother's helper six days a week; FLYING HIGH, by an amateur kite designer; HIGH IN

THE SADDLE, a paragraph about movie actor John Wayne's career; THE PORCELAIN TOMB, about abandoned refrigerators; TEDIOUS TROUBLESHOOTING, about finding a discrepancy in the automatic fight control system of a helicopter.

Stage 4 | Writing the Paragraph

1. Understanding the Organization of a Paragraph
2. Understanding Methods of Development
3. Developing a Paragraph with Details
4. Writing the Paragraph

STEP 1 Understanding the Organization of a Paragraph

A paragraph is made up of a group of sentences that develop (support with concrete evidence) one central idea stated in the Topic Sentence, the writer's opinion (inference) about a topic. Every sentence in the paragraph must contribute to the development of that central idea with verifiable statements (facts) made by the writer or gathered from another source, such as a periodical, an authority on the subject, another person, and so on. A graphic model of a paragraph might he outlined this way:

TITLE

(Lead-in Sentence)

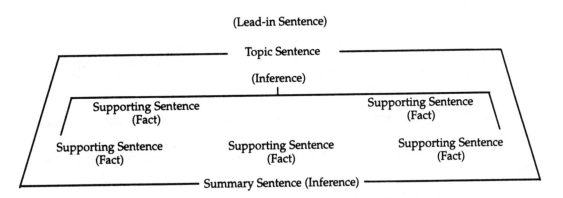

Topic Sentence

(Inference)

Supporting Sentence (Fact)   Supporting Sentence (Fact)

Supporting Sentence (Fact)   Supporting Sentence (Fact)   Supporting Sentence (Fact)

Summary Sentence (Inference)

The *Topic Sentence* of a paragraph has two important elements. It has the *limited subject* and the *controlling inference,* sometimes known as the key term, the writer's opinion, viewpoint, or generalization about the subject. For example, in a paragraph about a Fire department, a firefighter wrote this topic sentence:

> The Ladder Company of the Lauderhill Fire Department is very diversified in the job it performs.

Another topic sentence expressed this writer's opinion:

> Children's religious discussions can be very amusing to adults.

Thus, the topic sentence expresses the idea to be developed by the other sentences in the paragraph. and while the topic sentence may be in the beginning, the middle, or at the end of a paragraph, it is usually placed at the beginning.

The specific details that the writer uses to develop the controlling inference are the supporting sentences, and an expository paragraph must have a sufficient number (six to eight) to support and develop the topic sentence well. For example, in an article on the Duchess of Alba, the writer wanted to convey the idea that the duchess is measured in superlatives.

> Almost everything about her is measured in superlatives She is the most titled woman in the world-six times a duchess, 10 a countess, 24 a marquess. She is the grandest of grandees—uniquely Spanish anachronism entitling her to sit and wear her hat in the presence of the king. It is said that her land holdings would stretch all the way across the Iberian peninsula if laid end to end. Her masterworks by Rembrandt, Rubens, Velazquez, El Greco and Goya comprise what may be the world's most spectacular private collection. Her blood is the bluest; Mary, Queen of Scots, Christopher Columbus and Winston Churchill are all among her forebears. Her wealth is reckoned at "billions of dollars" by an aristocratic friend.
>
> Barbara Barker, "The Marriage That Astounded Spain—
> The Duchess of Alba and Her Ex-Priest—Is Now a Year Old,"
> *People,* April 29. 1979. pp. 119-121.

The Lead-in Sentence

You will recall that one-paragraph themes are usually introduced by a sentence or two that lead the reader into the topic sentence, or in some instances the writer may prefer to combine the lead-in with the topic sentence. For example, the lead-in for "Abi Day" is one sentence:

> In Finland graduating from one class to another is much more important than passing final exams.

On the other hand, the lead-in for "A Way to the Footlights" is combined with the topic sentence:

> Since the world of professional theater remains only a dream to most people, an aspiring actor can fulfill his interests in the theater by following a five-point plan for winning a role in a play produced by a civic theater group.

Exercise 4-1 Analyzing the Paragraph

1. On a separate sheet of paper, write the controlling inference.
2. List the specific sentences that support the controlling inference.
3. Are there any inferences in the paragraph? If so, list them. Are any of them unsupported? If so, which ones?

Exercise 4-2 Analyzing Paragraphs

Read the following paragraphs. Then complete the exercise.

A.

Sunday is my favorite day of the week. It's not because of the extra sleep I enjoy without the knowledge that the alarm will ring, nor is it the special mouth-watering breakfasts of hot, golden waffles covered with rich yellow butter and sweet maple syrup. Neither is it the joy of reading all of the Sunday newspaper while I am sprawled on the living room couch. To me Sunday is a day of rest, one in which I can just saunter through the house. It's a day that means serenity and peace—peace within myself, perhaps created by the hour spent in church surrounded by the quiet tones of an organ and the rhythmic chants of the satin-robed clergy. Sunday is a day for visiting friends, cheering relatives, or just watching television. Maybe I like Sunday because it is really my day.

B.

The south end of Fort Lauderdale beach is full of activities on a sunny, clear day. Flying up near the white fluffy clouds are kites in every shape from square to round and in every color of the rainbow. Sometimes it is possible to hear the kites ripping through the wind when a gusty breeze blows. At the picnic grounds to the right, there is not one available picnic table or charcoal barbecue grill. The delicious aroma of hotdogs and hamburgers grilling is one very good reason why. There is not a half foot of shade to be found under any of the twenty palm trees that line the outside edge of the public picnic area. To the left, the screams of laughter can be heard from the lungs of deeply tanned children playing in the weather-beaten wooden playground. Straight ahead, a group of six boys and girls is frantically trying to save a sandcastle from being washed out to sea by two-foot waves. Beyond them, four teenage boys are attempting to surf the four-foot waves before the waves completely disappear into the ocean. At the very edge of the horizon, a United States naval aircraft carrier appears to be gliding out of sight. On a clear. sunny day, Fort Lauderdale beach is an excellent place to avoid boredom.

Debra Dolphin

C.

As I look back on my childhood, one of my happiest memories is of staying at my grandparent's house with my cousin Lynn. Here one of our favorite activities was playing dress up in the walk-in closet of an upstairs bedroom. This closet held an abundance of old, discarded clothing, which through our eyes looked like Paris originals. For example, there were dresses of various fabrics-silk, organdy, linen, satin, even a few bridesmaid's gowns our aunts had worn. Also, there were hats of every size and color, many with feathers, sequins, or ribbons. Along one wall, the floor was filled with rows of spike-heeled shoes and with shopping bags overflowing with purses to match the shoes. There were also a few cast-off umbrellas which, in our minds, became lacy parasols to be twirled over one shoulder. In addition. there was a large. black lacquered jewelry box filled with what we thought to be precious gems. But, by far, the most elegant item was an old fox fur piece which had lost its luster and which was slowly shedding its hair. The moment we put on this stole, we were transformed into elegant sophisticated ladies on our way to tea: for this is where such women went. We enjoyed this special world of fantasy for several hours, then tucked it back into the closet to be discovered again another day.

Susan Owen

D.

In the past my sister had difficulty keeping her room neat, but she was determined that her new apartment would be an immaculate success. It was not. It was a disaster. As soon as she opened the door for me, I knew that her determination was lost under all the rubbish. There was not a vacant seat in the living room. The sofa and armchairs were buried beneath layers of jeans, skirts, blouses, and jackets. A stray pillow lay on the floor next to an end table on which an ashtray had overturned; the ashes and cellophane candy wrappers were still trapped underneath it. I hardly noticed the thick brown shag rug was infested with popcorn because both were covered with the past ten issues of *Good Housekeeping* magazines. Nothing was in place in the kitchen. There were dirty dishes everywhere except in the empty cupboard. Pots soaked in the sink while pans, with what looked like baked-on tomato sauce, still rested on top of the stove. Over on the table remained two slices of shriveled pizza, a jar of grated parmesan cheese, and a nearly empty bottle of wine. I walked down the hall. The bathroom was no improvement. Make-up spills were on the counter top, toothpaste drippings were in the sink, and pink and blue hairpins littered the floor. Convinced that my sister had not turned into a zealous housekeeper, I smiled and began to pick up the hairpins.

Robin Kessler

1. Which paragraphs are written using informal standard English? Which are more formal?
2. Write the topic sentence from each of the paragraphs. Then underline the limited subject and the controlling inference from each. What is the lead-in sentence?
3. List the specific details that support the topic sentences. Are there any irrelevant sentences? Are there any minor inferences that need support?
4. Write the summary sentence for each. Is it a reassertion of the topic sentence or a logical conclusion drawn from the supporting sentences?

Length of a Paragraph

The length of a paragraph varies according to the subject matter and the writer's purpose. In general, however, an average expository paragraph is approximately 150 to 200 words. Regardless of the length or its function within a given composition, a paragraph is a fundamental unit of a composition, one of the basic building blocks in writing.

Types of Paragraphs

The topic sentence of a paragraph may be developed in several ways. It can be developed by the use of specific details, examples, or illustrations; by comparison and contrast; by reasons and results (cause and effect); by definition; by enumerating statistical data; by classification or division; or by a combination of the various methods.

Unity and Coherence

Nevertheless, whatever method the writer chooses to develop the topic sentence, the paragraph must have two other important elements: unity and coherence. A paragraph is unified when all sentences relate to the topic sentence, and there are no irrelevant ideas. That is, the writer must stick to the subject from the first specific idea to support the topic sentence to the summary sentence. Coherence shows the logical relationship between sentences by linking one idea to another with transitional devices. If all sentences are unified and related, the paragraph is said to have unity and coherence.

STEP 2 Understanding Methods of Development

By Example and/or Illustration

At times the writer may use a list of specific details, a specific illustration or a brief narrative to explain the topic sentence. For example, one paragraph illustrates the damage to an airport following winds of hurricane force.

Hurricane-force winds, which struck International Airport last night, left the airport looking like a junkyard. Most noticeable was the damage done to the roof of the Eastern Airlines' baggage terminal. Here one could see torn tar paper hanging in strips. Along with the paper were pieces of aluminum stripping and pieces of wood dangling from the roof also. At the southwest end of the field were three planes crunched together. Nearby, a DC-4 was blown by the wind into six parked cars. To the left of this scene were two small planes that were hurled into a larger craft owned by L & H Airmotive, Incorporated. Just beyond those planes, two workmen worked for several hours separating a Lodestar from a palm tree, which had cut the plane's wing. According to John Judd, local air coordinator for the Federal Aviation Administration, 75 of 600 planes based at the airport were damaged beyond repair. For example, one DC-4 had remains of four other smaller planes of various colors and sizes which jutted out from the body of the larger plane. Furthermore, tar paper which had blown from the roof of the larger terminal could be found on cars parked in the lot. In addition, the tires of two dozen cars were punctured, and the owners of ten other cars reported that pieces of flying glass and metal broke windows of their cars.

Moreover, uprooted signs, broken pieces of glass, and pieces of shrubbery were lying in the terminal as well as in the parking lot. Airport Director Brenton Lonigan said that there appeared to be $20,000 to $30,000 in damage to the airport. From the scene observed, it appears as if International Airport will not be restored to normal operations for several months.

By Cause and Effect

In an effort to explain an incident or a situation, we look for causes (reasons), or seeing an effect (a result), we look back on the events preceding the effect to determine the causes. When we begin with a generalization that we assume to be true and look for reasons, we use deductive reasoning. When we gather evidence or reasons and then draw a valid conclusion or generalization about those reasons, we use inductive reasoning. Paragraphs developed by cause and effect give the reasons or results for a particular event. In the following paragraph, a college student, recalling an incident, explains the results of her habitual procrastination.

As a flute player of the South Plantation marching band, commonly known as the Paladins, I recall anxiously preparing for the most important event of the marching season—the annual band concert. Unfortunately, I learned that being late to a band contest can have disastrous results. Every November, the Band Parents Association sponsors and judges the contest in which each of the participating bands is evaluated and rated according to its musical ability, marching skills, and uniformed appearance. Before the contest, the Paladins were given thirty minutes in which to put on their uniforms and to make sure that the white shoes and gloves were spotless. However, due to my habitual lack of punctuality, I showed up late, allowing myself only ten minutes in which to dress. In my haste, I scuffed one of my shoes, dropped my clean gloves in the dirt, and broke my suspenders. After the band director rescued me by pinning up my trousers, dusting off my gloves, and trying to clean the shoe at the water fountain, I lined up with the other band members for the first stage of the contest: inspection. Under the bright spotlights, the white gloves and the shoes shone against the dark purple uniforms. However, the judges could see a silver glimmer of light coming from one of the uniforms. After inspection, I learned to my dismay that the band had received a demerit. In my scramble to get ready on time, I had overlooked closing the front twelve-inch silver zipper on my trousers.

Rebekah Malloy

By Comparison and Contrast

In paragraph development, when two or more items are shown to be alike or different, the development is said to be by comparison or contrast. Paragraphs can be developed by either comparison or contrast, or the methods can be used together. In this paragraph the student writes of the differences of doing laundry in California and in Germany in the 1970's.

Although I am a born homebody and a "ground" person, I made an overseas trip by air to join my husband who was stationed at Bitburg Air Base, Germany. It was there that I discovered that life in Bitburg differs greatly from life in Oxnard, California, especially in respect to doing the laundry. First, I would fill several buckets with water to be emptied into a large caldron. Beneath the iron caldron was an opening where a fire of wood and coal had to be started. When the fire was very hot, the clothes were placed inside the caldron for a half an hour to be boiled. After the boiling procedure, only one towel and one sheet could be placed into a small washing machine. When finished in the machine, each article would be hung on lines which were located on the side of a steep hill. To do four days' laundry for my family of three, which included our three-year-old son Gary, took approximately six hours of steady work. However, in Oxnard, I had a modern dryer and washing machine which made my work easier and helped me complete it in very little time. I only needed to set the dials to the wash cycle and then go about my household chores, such as vacuuming the floors. Within a period of thirty minutes, my wash was ready to be placed in the dryer, and twenty minutes later my clothes were fluffy and dry.

Suzanne Driscoll

By Process

A paragraph that explains how an item is made, used, developed, organized, or operated is developed by process. **Directional process** gives the reader directions so that the action may be completed. **Informational process** simply informs the reader about a specific method. In the following paragraph, the student informs the reader about one way of preparing artichokes.

An enticing, savory dish can be achieved through the creation of a well-prepared artichoke in several easy steps. The first step is for the cook to remove the thorny edges of each leaf; this is done by one of two methods; either cutting off one inch of the top with a sharp knife and trimming the stem, leaving a one-half inch stub; or by holding the artichoke with the stem-end in the palm of the hand and pounding the top in the sink or on a board to break off the thorny edges. At the same time, the leaves separate, making it easier for the washing and stuffing of this vegetable. Once the artichoke is prepared, olive oil is then poured between the leaves; the artichoke is set aside, giving the oil time to seep into the core. Meanwhile, the bread crumb stuffing is prepared by adding garlic, salt, parsley, oregano, black pepper, chopped basil leaves, and grated parmesan cheese. These ingredients are mixed thoroughly with a beaten egg and some warm water to moisten the crumbs. The center of the artichoke is then stuffed; the artichoke is wrapped in foil and baked in a 350° oven for forty-five minutes or arranged in a pan of lightly salted water, covered, and left to simmer on the range for an hour. The artichokes can be served either as a hot vegetable, with a side dish of lemon butter in which to dip the leaves, as a chilled appetizer, or as a salad. In any case, as the diner pulls the artichoke leaf between his teeth, he can appreciate the delicious taste of the soft juicy pulp and the savory stuffing.

Lorraine Commerford

By Definition

When a writer explains in more detail what the dictionary definition of word means, he develops a paragraph by **extended definition,** that is, by using other means to define the word. For example, one student learned that the word **camera** meant more than an instrument for taking pictures.

The camera is an amazing instrument. In a blink of an eye, it can record intricate details of landscapes, people, and other objects. However, the word *camera* has had many other meanings in its history. Most people know the camera to be a plastic or metal box that regulates light in order to make graphs or objects in a life-like form on a light-sensitive paper. However, originally, the Greek word *kamara* meant "an arched chamber." In 1708, the definition of camera was extended to a locked building with an upper room, and in 1730 it was first used in the title of music referred to today as chamber music. The Latins adopted the term in 1863 to mean a judge's chamber, and our common expression *in camera,* meaning "settled in the judge's private room," came from this usage. However, the word *camera* came to the United States first as the name of a small optical child's toy. Later, when the device that took pictures was invented, an appropriate name "camera obscura" was borrowed from the original meaning, for the term literally means a "dark optical chamber." As the black box became more popular, the term was shortened to *camera.* Today, we find that the camera has taken on many new forms, for we now have video cameras, disk cameras, underwater cameras, and even miniature cameras used in undercover work. Certainly, the evolution of the word is an interesting piece of history.

Amy Brown

Paragraph Order

In addition to various types of paragraph development, details of a paragraph may be presented in a particular order, such as geographical settings or room arrangements. Spatial order describes the placement of objects as they are arranged in a given space. The writer uses expressions, such as *on one side, above, below, to the left, beyond, in the distance,* and *farther along.* The student writing of her first impression of the Florida Everglades begins her walk at a specific wildlife preserve.

I had always thought of Florida's Everglades as being dismal; but after a recent backpacking trip, I could see that my first impression was not correct. Shortly after beginning my walk at the J.W. Corbet Wildlife Preserve in Palm Beach, Florida, I discovered that the Everglades was alive with color. Before me the cypress trees stood like towering gray sentinels trimmed with foliage as green as spring grass. Below the trees the bright red flowers of the bromeliads provided a startling contrast to the stone gray color of their tree trunk perches. To the right here and there the trail was spotted with tiny bright yellow orchids, growing wild in the cool, damp mud. In the distance I could see the sunlight, filtered through the trees, dancing upon the water showing off a rainbow of colors. To the left, farther along the route, I saw a multitude of life forms. Just ahead, alligators, with wary eyes, watched me trudge by. Adjacent to them, snakes glided carelessly across the water. As a result of a portion of the trail being submerged in water near me, I was able to observe, first hand, fish swimming to and fro. Of even greater appeal I was fortunate enough to pass on one side through a neighborhood of red headed wood-packer nests, a rare sight to see. Under these conditions, the Everglades can be called many things, none of which should be dismal.

Joanne Salters

Chronological Order

In this pattern, the writer describes the events in the order as they happen. Transitional words such as *first, next, later,* and *last* are used. In the paragraph that follows, the student begins the order by stating the time of the flight, eleven thirty in the morning.

Each weekend, I fuel airplanes at the North Perry Airport in Pembroke Pines, Florida. But one particular time, I was witness to an unexpected crash. The twin engine Beechcraft departed from the airport at approximately eleven thirty in the morning with favorable weather conditions. After takeoff, the airplane reached four hundred feet above the ground and then proceeded to make a right turn west. Immediately after the turn, the aircraft began to lose altitude rapidly; and then without delay, it began to spin until it hit the ground. On impact the multi-engine plane exploded and instantly sent up a frightening black stream of smoke into the sky. I rushed to the site, but I realized I was too late; as I watched helplessly, the fire engulfed the old World War II airplane with the pilot and three passengers trapped inside. Although the accident happened years ago, I shall never forget the date, September 23, 1979.

Terry McCullough

STEP 3 Developing a Paragraph with Details

It is not difficult to train yourself to think in specific terms. For example, suppose that you decided to return to your hometown after being away for a decade or more. One of the places you wish to see is the elementary school you had attended many years before. You remembered it as it was then. However, when you see it now, you realize that the building has deteriorated considerably. If you were to tell someone that your elementary school had deteriorated considerably since you last saw it, you would not be communicating to your listener, for he would lack the information necessary to arrive at the same opinion you had. After all, you saw the building and thus were able to arrive at a logical conclusion. Suppose, however, that you wanted the person to see what you had; you would then have to think and speak in specifics. You might mention some of the following specific details:

1. The exterior was cracked.
2. Bricks had been chipped out.
3. Pieces of the wooden frames and doors were missing.
4. There were drawings on the walls.
5. The bulletin board did not have a single spot that had not been scarred by a thumb tack.
6. There were crude drawings of animals and people on the bulletin board.
7. The walls had dirty fingerprints on them.
8. The walls had spots where the Scotch tape had held a poster or a drawing.

STEP 4 Writing the Paragraph

If you can think in specific terms, writing them in a paragraph is not difficult. After all, you do have the controlling inference for the topic sentence—*"deteriorated considerably"*—and you do have the limited subject—*your elementary school in Springton Valley.* You need only combine those two elements in a sentence.

As I stood in the school yard, I could see that the elementary school had deteriorated considerably.

However, in order to be even more specific, you will need to tell your reader a little more so that he can understand completely your point of view. One way is by introducing the Topic Sentence or the subject of the paragraph with a lead-in sentence or two, which will introduce the topic and lead the reader gradually into understanding your point of view or opinion. In this case, you might begin with this lead-in:

> Returning to my elementary school was the one event I looked forward to when I decided to take my family to visit my hometown in Springton Valley, Pennsylvania.

Now, by combining the lead-in and the topic sentence, you have begun the paragraph. Follow the topic sentence with the specific details you remembered, and, then, conclude the paper with a summary and a concluding sentence that sums up your feelings about the school.

> The school I had remembered was not at all like this one—shabby, run down, and poorly cared for.

Writing the Paragraph

Once you have organized all of the details, revised and corrected the first draft, you are ready to write the paragraph in its final form. Place the title above the paragraph.

SPRINGTON VALLEY ELEMENTARY SCHOOL

Returning to my elementary school was the one event I looked forward to when I decided to take my family to visit my hometown in Springton Valley, Pennsylvania; but as I stood in the school yard, I could see that the school had deteriorated considerably. Once the building was quite attractive with its red brick exterior and wooden framed doors and windows. Now, however, the exterior was cracked beyond belief. Bricks had been chipped out; and although the wooden frames had been painted, pieces of wood were missing from doors and window frames. As I walked into the building and down the hall, I noticed that the bulletin board no longer had a single spot that had not been scarred by a thumb tack. On both the bulletin board and the wall that surrounded it were writing and crude drawings of animals and people. I stopped in front of my old fourth grade room, Room 106, and there I looked into a room that once was very attractive. Now the beige walls had dirty fingerprints, and I could see the spots where the Scotch tape had held some poster or drawing. Not wanting to continue with my tour, I left the building, saddened by the fact that the school I had remembered was not at all like this one—shabby, run down, and poorly cared for.

Exercise 4-3 Writing a Paragraph by Details

Write a paragraph using details. You may describe a place, an event, a person, or an article. Begin by writing a topic sentence. Then, list at least six specific details that will support the controlling inference. This list will serve as a "blueprint" (outline) for your paragraph.

Writing Suggestion: The Paragraph

Your source material for the first writing assignment will be personal experience Get your idea for a limited subject from one of the following suggestions; then, following the steps of Stage 4, write a paragraph. Use the rating sheet on page 97 as a guide for writing your paragraph.

Suggestions

1. Use as the basis for your subject one of the following: the most controversial. frightening. frustrating, humorous or thought-provoking experience, observation, or idea that you have recently encountered.
2. Select as your subject one person currently in the public eye. That person may be in sports, politics, law, medicine, theater, films, television, arts, science, education, the Armed Forces, law enforcement, or social service. Explain in your paragraph why you admire or disapprove of this person.
3. Select one of the following topics: college registrations, current technology, old people, television commercials, current music, a special place, modern art.
4. Select a proverb and support it with specific illustrations: for example, "Two captains sink a ship," "Deeds talk louder than words," "He who dies with the most toys wins nothing," "Money talks. Mine says 'Goodbye.'"
5. Use the following photograph as your subject. There are many possibilities for a controlling inference and many support sentences that can be supplied.

Photograph 4.1 (Photo by Stephen Grasso)

PARAGRAPH RATING SHEET

	Unacceptable	Weak	Fair	Good	Excellent
Topic Sentence Introduced by a suitable lead-in Subject suitable controlled Controlling inference clear	____	____	____	____	____

Body (Content)
Minimum five support statements
All proof details relevant to the
    Topic Sentence
Any minor inference includes fact
Shows quality and good development
    of ideas
	____	____	____	____	____

Transition (Organization within the Body) Adequate number of transitions Transitions appropriate to function	____	____	____	____	____
Title Enlists reader interest Reflects subject of paragraph Is short	____	____	____	____	____
Language Has appropriate language level Uses effective word choice Shows individuality	____	____	____	____	____

	Unacceptable	Weak	Fair	Good	Excellent
Summary Sentence					
Uses appropriate transitions					
Restates assertion of controlling inference					
or					
Draws a logical conclusion from proof details	___	___	___	___	___
Mechanics					
Spelling					
Grammar (correct usage, agreement, etc.)					
Sentence structure					
Punctuation					
Manuscript form					
Correct use of capitals					
Neatness					
Numbers, abbreviations, signs and symbols properly written	___	___	___	___	___

Stage	
5	# Rewriting

1. Getting Your Paper Back
2. Understanding Correction Symbols

STEP 1   Getting Your Paper Back

When you hand in your first paper, you may say, "Well, I think I've done a good job." You followed all the steps for writing a paragraph, you worked hard to express yourself, and perhaps a friend or two looked at the paper and thought it was good. Now you have nothing to do but to wait for your paper to be returned with the grade on it.

You may find, however, that the paper is returned to you with a grade lower than the one you had expected and that the instructor has made comments and corrections. Your first reaction may be one of disappointment. Keep in mind, however, that a grade reflects three considerations:

1.   Content (the quality of your ideas and how well you have developed them)
2.   Method (the organization of the paper)
3.   Mechanics (grammar, sentence structure, spelling, punctuation, manuscript form)

Working through the seven steps to paragraph writing, you learned how to form suitable inferences, how to support them with adequate proof details, and how to organize the details into a coherent paragraph. Now you need to combine these three skills with acceptable mechanics; because if the mechanics aren't correct, the meaning will not be clear. Consider, for example, these sentences written by a student attempting to describe the scene on entering a discotheque: "Directly ahead is the bandstand with red and purple lights and five musicians lit up." He compounds the confusion by adding: "Going backwards by the bar, comfortable sofas welcome couples to the left and right." By the time the reader has had to deal with incapacitated musicians and animated sofas, he's not sure what scene he's in.

What may have happened here is that the student was so concerned with content and organization that he overlooked problems that occur in grammar, sentence structure, spelling, and word selection. Another problem may have been that when the student submitted his final draft, he did not proofread it carefully, or he submitted his first draft.

Even professional writers, although they are highly trained in all the communication skills, often write three or four drafts of a paper, and sometimes even of a letter, before they are satisfied. You too will need to rewrite. You will need to make at least two drafts before submitting any paper. Even with this rewriting, you may still overlook some points concerning content, organization, and mechanics. The time and effort your instructor takes in reading your paper and marking it is of no value unless you take the time to interpret those marks and comments and to make the necessary revisions. This effort on your part will help you to avoid making the same mistakes on your next papers.

STEP 2   Understanding Correction Symbols

Here is the original and revised version of a paragraph written by a student who selected as his subject "a special place." The original is shown with the instructor's correction symbols and comments. The student's revised version follows. First, read the original paragraph just for content and organization. Then read it again, and as you come to each correction symbol, refer to the correction symbol list in the "Mechanics Guide" to determine what that symbol means. If the explanation for the correction symbol is not clear or if you are not familiar with the particular problem indicated by the symbol, turn to the basic review sheets in the Mechanics Guide. These review sheets group the basic mechanical errors according to their types. You will notice that the symbol is not only defined, but that a sentence illustrating the particular type of error is given along with the correction for the error.

Original Paragraph with Instructor Corrections

title?   **MY BOX HAS SENTIMENTAL VALUE**

combine   Beneath my bed is a gray tin box with a lock and key. The box used to
belong to my mother. She used it to keep money in from the used furniture store
that she owned while we were living in the North. The box, now mine, and its
unn rep. contents have much sentimental value to me. My five diaries are the main *org.*
reason I keep the box locked, as my very intimate feelings are recorded on each
p. priceless page. In one corner of the box sleeps Clinger, a small stuffed raccoon
where is that Andrew a former boyfriend, bought me when we were going steady. Under
the Clinger is the box of chocolates that Andrew gave me at Christmas. The box is
*cellophane*empty, except for the carefully folded cellophane wrapping. One evening a *p.*
group of us went to eat pizza and Andrew picked up the dinner mints and gave
p. them to me. Although we were no longer going steady I still liked him, and I
keep the mints in another corner of my tin box. There are also two letters which *sp. agu*
I recieved from an admirer while I was attending school in Jamaica. Along with *pro. ra*
these is a "get well" card that Andrew sent me when I had a cold. The greatest
sentimental value that my box holds is that it is a remembrance of my mother

who died two years ago. I hope to keep my box forever, or at least until I have a daughter to pass it on to.

you have a good I.S., but the paper lacks good organization. What other details can you supply? Where in the north were you living?

Revised Version Incorporating Instructor's Suggestions

THE GRAY TIN BOX

Beneath my bed is a gray tin box with a lock and key that used to belong to my mother. She kept the box in her bedroom, and each evening when she came home from the used furniture store my family owned in Canada, she would carefully place in it the money from the day's sales before locking the box and placing it under her bed. The next day, she would unlock the box, take the money, and deposit it in the bank before she opened the store. The box, now mine, and its contents have much sentimental value. I keep the box locked for reasons which differ from my mother's. My five diaries with all of my intimate feelings recorded on each priceless page are the main reason. But I also keep the box locked because it holds many memories of my first boyfriend, Andrew. In one corner of the box sleeps Clinger, a small stuffed raccoon that Andrew bought me when we were going steady. Clinger rests on a small box that held chocolates. The box was given to me by Andrew the last Christmas we were together. Inside the box is the carefully folded Christmas wrapping and red and green ribbon, which now have the odor of chocolate. In another corner of the box is a package of two white dinner mints still in their cellophane wrapping. One evening a group of us went to eat pizza, and Andrew picked up the dinner mints from a bowl near the cashier and gave the mints to me. Although we are no longer going steady, I still like him; and I keep the mints as a reminder of that evening. On the top of the package of mints are two letters I received from an admirer while I was attending school in Jamaica. Along with these letters is the "get well" card that Andrew sent me when all I had was a cold. From time to time, I unlock the box, place all of its contents on my bed, and spend a nostalgic hour examining each item. However, the greatest sentimental value that my box holds is that it is a remembrance of my mother who died two years ago. I hope to keep my box forever, or at least until I have a daughter to pass it on to.

Aundrea Plummer

Exercise 5-1 Evaluations and Revisions

Part I: Using Correction Symbols and the rating sheet, evaluate the paper.

A LATIN BUS RIDE CAN BE FUN

A bus ride through the Andes can be fun and exciting. It's a small thing like maybe a fourteen-hour trip. This could turn into a day and a half, dirt roads winding along cliffs with a 2,000 foot drops, 2 busses dueling for the lead along a typical stretch of perpetually blinding curved highways, the landslides and the thieves is what makes a memorable trip. Breath-taking scenery is a common occurrence. You might be riding with anyone. From the poorest Indian to the richest spanish. Watching every last movement that's being made with your backpack, trying to get the best seats, being aware of your passport and your money even when you're asleep, writing down your name, meeting friends; writing down other details at different police road blocks during one trip, pulling into towns and having scores of people surround the bus to sell you every kind of food and gifts you can imagine. But it's alright because you can have fun on any bus trip in Latin America. (Source unknown)

Part II: Revision

Directions: On a separate sheet of paper, rewrite the following paragraph by using suitable linking words or phrases, by using coordinate or subordinate conjunctions to join ideas together and by breaking down stringy sentences into more than one if necessary so that the paper is more coherent. Make all other necessary corrections, such as correcting all errors or writing the paragraph in formal standard English. Make sure all minor inferences have adequate support. If not, add a few details that would be suitable.

Suggestions:

1. Where are the Andes?
2. Explain what details must be written down?
3. Be specific. Name various foods and gifts.
4. Do all the details support one controlling inference?
5. Write a lead-in statement if one is missing.

From Part to Whole

1. Looking at the Whole Theme
2. Looking at the Pattern for the Whole Theme
3. Considering the Word Count for a Theme

You have seen that the paragraph, the basic unit of exposition, develops a single unit of thought. You know that the purpose of expository writing is to explain an idea, an organization, a system, a process, or an object. These explanations frequently involve more than a single unit of thought. Also, there are two main types of essays: the **formal** essay and the **informal** essay.

The **formal essay** deals on a thorough, objective level. The subject is usually a serious one, such as the housing problem for low income families, the control of drugs, and the control of nuclear energy. The writer presents his views on the subject that have been based on a careful examination of the facts; on personal observation or experience; and, in the case of a documented paper, research in the library. The paper may take the form of an investigative report; a summary; an argument; or a critique of a film, a literary work, a musical composition, or a work of art. Whatever the form and subject, the writing is based on logical thinking.

The **informal essay,** in contrast, leaves the writer free to say almost anything he wants in any form he prefers. Such an essay, usually an expression of an individual's personality, may be humorous, fanciful, emotional, or sentimental, or individualized in some other way.

Since both the academic and business worlds require the writer to explain a process, to analyze a problem, to interpret information, to criticize a work, to report an incident, to debate an issue, or to summarize events, you will write formal essays in college. In any case, however, to improve your own writing style, you must choose your words correctly, organize your thoughts logically, revise and correct your material to avoid grammatical and technical errors, and support your opinions with specifics, which include facts, illustrations, examples.

Suppose that you were in a work-study program in early childhood education, and your assignment for the term was to develop a plan for a day care center at Brownsville College for the children of students, faculty, and staff because there has been a demand for such a center. Your advisor has asked you to conduct a survey and to submit a written explanation of your findings to determine first whether there is a need. You obviously have to look into several areas: the number of people who would use the center, the availability of space for both a classroom and a playground, then the number of employees needed, and the cost to the college. Because you would draw a conclusion about each of these areas after completing your survey, your report could begin with a thesis that would have **multiple inferences,** rather than a single controlling inference. Based on your findings, your **thesis** might begin like this:

> Plans for a day care center at Brownsville College can be implemented because there is a need, there are adequate facilities, there is an adequate number of qualified personnel at the college, and there is a relatively low cost for the college.

Your advisor would expect you to supply specific details to support each of your inferences because only then could he take steps to present the information to the administration. Because your report involves a number of units of thought, it would involve several paragraphs. A multi-paragraph is commonly referred to in a composition course as a **theme.**

The Introductory Paragraph

The introductory paragraph for the theme is composed of two parts: the lead-in and the thesis statement. The lead-in is an introduction to the paper. The number of sentences may vary, depending upon the writer's purpose. The lead-in has two purposes. First, it gets the reader's attention; and, second, it introduces the subject to the reader. Furthermore, it must be relevant to the thesis statement.

The Thesis Statement

The multiple inference sentence for the theme is called the *thesis statement*. The thesis statement serves the same function for the multi-paragraph theme as does the topic sentence for one paragraph. The thesis lets the reader know what the limited subject is, what assertions the writer is making about the subject, and what support sentences to expect. The thesis statement is more involved than the topic sentence because of the multiple inferences.

Alternate Thesis Statement

However, not all thesis statements list the minor inferences or subordinate ideas. An alternative to the thesis statement on child care centers might be written as follows:

> Plans for a day care center at Brownsville College can be implemented because of a number of reasons.

Another example would look like this:

> **Thesis with inferences**: There are many factors that contribute to the alarming social problem of teenage pregnancy: the steadily decreasing age of unwed mothers, the number of teens who choose to

keep their babies, and the lack of education on moral values.

Alternate thesis: There are many factors that contribute to the alarming social problem of teenage pregnancy.

Placement of the Thesis Statement

Just as the placement of a topic sentence can vary, so may the thesis statement, depending upon the organizational pattern and purpose of the paper. However, a good rule for freshman composition students to follow is to place the thesis at the end of the introductory paragraph. The reader needs to know early what direction the paper will take.

The thesis statement begins the organizational pattern for the paper because it determines what direction the paper will take and the points that will be discussed. A good thesis statement gives both the scope and the purpose and has a narrowed major inference.

Regardless of which thesis statement the student wishes to write, the organizational pattern of a theme demands that each of the minor inferences, either stated or implied, be discussed within the body of the paper.

Body of the Paper

Each minor inference from the thesis statement becomes the controlling inference of the topic sentence of each developmental paragraph. In a short theme (five hundred to eight hundred words), if you have three minor inferences in the thesis statement, you will have three developmental paragraphs. Each paragraph will give supporting details to illustrate, explain, describe, or prove the inference terms from the thesis statement. If it stands by itself, each developmental paragraph with its topic sentence, supporting details, and summary sentence can be considered a one-paragraph theme. Taken together, however, these developmental paragraphs are unified and related to the thesis statement with the aid of transitional sentences or expressions, just as sentences within the paragraph are unified by transition.

The Concluding Paragraph

Just as the introductory paragraph is composed of two parts, so is the concluding paragraph. It usually begins with a transition sentence that links the developmental paragraphs with the concluding statement, which may consist of one or several sentences, summarizing the entire paper or drawing a logical conclusion from the evidence presented. The concluding statement for the theme serves the same function as the summary sentence for the paragraph. Thus the concluding paragraph should tie together the ideas that you have been developing and emphasize the main points of the paper so that your reader will have a clear understanding of your subject. Avoid, however, the following conclusions:

An Apology
This is only my opinion, and I am not well qualified to write about it.

A Warning
If you do not vote, you will be responsible for higher taxes.

Don't Threaten

Editorializing

Yes, America, keep reading the comics and learn a little about yourselves.

The Excuse

There is a lot more that I could write about this subject if I had more time.

The Trite Conclusion

Last but not least, we need to consider these ways of controlling child abuse in America.

Don't say 'in conclusion' or 'in summary'

STEP 1 Looking at the Whole Theme

Here is a theme written by a student who decided to write more than a single paragraph about a person he admired. The theme is annotated in the margins so that you can see how the various parts work together. Notice that the paper begins with a lead-in statement. Its function is to interest the reader in the subject and to lead into the thesis statement. The thesis statement and the topic sentences are underlined; the inferences are underscored with a wavy line. Following the annotated theme is a diagram which shows the pattern of order for writing the theme.

JACQUES COUSTEAU

Lead-in statement Many Americans might never have known of the French scientist Jacques Cousteau if it had not been for his documentary series The Undersea World of Jacques Cousteau. At first television viewers were interested only in the underwater explorations which introduced them to unique marine habitats and inland areas that had never been seen before. But as the viewers continued watching these documentaries, they became interested not only in the subject matter, but also in the background of this unusual man. *Thesis statement* Jacques Cousteau is to be admired because of his inventiveness, his contributions to marine science, and his dedication to his field.

Transition Of these admirable characteristics, *Topic sentence* Cousteau's inventiveness has assisted him most in his desire to explore the new world of inner space. First, the Aqua-Lung which he co-invented in 1943 has proved to be a valuable piece of marine *Supporting Details* equipment which revolutionized exploration of the undersea world because it enables underwater explorers to breathe without the assistance of air hoses from the surface. The Aqua-Lung, carried on the back of the diver, allows more freedom of movement than did the underwater devices of the past. With the Aqua-Lung and a water-tight camera, Cousteau has been able to explore the ocean depths that had not been previously explored. He has also designed other types of undersea craft, such as the mini-sub and personal diving equipment. In addition, he was the first to use underwater television cameras to maintain contact between divers in the water and scientists aboard the ship and to use the bathy-*Summary Sentence* scaphe which enabled divers to make observations two miles below the surface of the sea. Cousteau's inventiveness has really made inner space a new frontier.

transition

Topic Sentence   Cousteau is to be admired not only for his inventiveness, <u>but also for his many contributions to marine science.</u> One of his books, <u>The Cousteau Almanac: An Inventory of Life on Our Water Planet,</u> helps people find their place on the planet and explains the developments that are changing the world so rapidly that ordinary people may make sound decisions about environmental issues.

Supporting Details   Two of his other books, <u>The Silent World</u> and <u>The Living Sea,</u> describe his experiences exploring the ocean depths and made millions aware for the first time of the importance of marine science in our modern world. In 1976 he made a journey in search of the legendary Atlantis, and in 1982 he made a trip up to the Amazon River. He also made a film documentary on the Galapagos Islands and one of its inhabitants, the marine iguana, important to marine science because of its ability to slow down and even to stop its own heart beat. Another film documentary explains some of the behavioral characteristics of the sperm whale, such as its grouping and mating habits and its migration patterns, to help prevent this mammal from becoming extinct. Other fascinating film documentaries produced by Cousteau which help to explain the undersea world are those on the sea otter, the bottle-nosed dolphin, octopi, and the ecology of reefs around

Summary Sentence   the world. The diversity of his many contributions to marine science is an indication of why Cousteau is a leader in the field.

Transition

Topic Sentence   Cousteau's inventiveness and his contributions to marine science are matched <u>by his dedication to the field.</u> For example, when all research money

Supporting Details   was diverted to armed defense during World War II, Cousteau continued his research using his own financial resources. Following World War II, Cousteau, with the help of a financial backer, purchased a ship, the <u>Calypso,</u> to further his research. With this 141-foot research vessel he has introduced a new research project called Project Ocean Search, in which amateurs, along with marine scientists, explore the ocean depths. At times they assist Cousteau in studying various schools of fish. In August of 1986, Cousteau set sail on a five-year odyssey that took him to New Zealand, China, the Indian Ocean, and the Congo River. On some of his past voyages, using the <u>Calypso</u> as a sea base, Cousteau dedicated himself to the field of underwater archaeology. From one of these sites, divers found a 2,100-year-old wine jar still sealed. On other expeditions he has found coins, dishes, silverware, and jewelry. Instead of merely selling the cargo, however, Cousteau carefully catalogs the various pieces of sunken treasure and notes the sea's effect on them, adding to historical knowledge. Director of the Monaco Oceanographic Museum and president of the world-wide Cousteau society, he plans to build an ocean center in Norfolk, Virginia, to monitor and evaluate marine ecosystems. Through the non-profit Cousteau Society, Cousteau keeps the public informed about the state of the environment through films, books, and lectures. For over four decades Cousteau has given people a sense of the

Summary Sentence   beauty of the oceans and its importance to the world. His unselfish devotion to his field is an admirable quality.

Concluding Statement   At a time in life when most men are retired, Jacques Cousteau, who is in his eighties is still with his men, diving and researching. <u>This oceanographer and</u>

scientist, physically and mentally active and still contributing to the marine world, is truly a man who deserves admiration.

STEP 2 Looking at the Pattern for the Whole Theme

JACQUES COUSTEAU

Lead-in statement:
Thesis statement: Jacques Cousteau is to be admired because of his inventiveness, his contributions to marine science, and his dedication to his field.

Introductory Paragraph (102 words)

Transition:

Topic sentence I. Inventiveness
A. Invented aqua-lung B. Invented mini-sub C. Invented other types of gear D. Used underwater TV E. Used bathyscaphe
Summary sentence:

First developmental paragraph (183 words)

Transition:

Topic sentence II. Contributions to marine science

A. Wrote books
   1. The Cousteau Almanac
   2. The Silent World
   3. The Living Sea

B. Made two journeys
   1. In search of Atlantis
   2. Up the Amazon River

C. Produced documentaries
   1. On Galapagos Islands
   2. On the sperm whale
   3. On others

Summary sentence:

second developmental paragraph (240 words)

Transition:

Topic sentence III. Dedication to his field

A. Used own money for research

B. Purchased ship for research
   1. Introduced Project Ocean Search
   2. Set sail for a five-year odyssey

C. Opened field of underwater archaeology
   1. Catalogued salvaged cargo
   2. Noted sea's effect on treasures

D. Began plans to build an ocean center

E. Contributes time
   1. As Director of Monaco Oceanographic Society
   2. As President of the Cousteau Society

Summary sentence:

third developmental paragraph (280 words)

Transition:

> Concluding statement: This scientist, physically and mentally active and still contributing to the marine world, is truly a man who deserves admiration.

Concluding paragraph (49 words)

STEP 3 Considering the Word Count for a Theme

You will notice that the word count for each paragraph has been noted on the pattern for the theme. Expository themes for the first semester of English are usually between five hundred and eight hundred words. Thesis statements with three or more inferences cannot be adequately developed in fewer than five hundred words. The introductory paragraph for this length theme is brief; the conclusion is even briefer. The developmental paragraphs, however, known as the body of the paper, follow the regular principle of paragraph development—that is, each controlling inference seldom has fewer than four proof detail sentences to support it.

The diagram you have seen is only a basic pattern for expository writing. However, if you did nothing more than follow this pattern, you would have a well-organized, adequately-developed paper. Once you have mastered this basic pattern, you will be able to develop variations on it and to learn more sophisticated techniques of writing.

You have now seen the basic component of the theme, which is the paragraph, and the whole theme in pattern form. Stage 6 will show you how to limit a subject, how to develop a thesis statement by analyzing the subject, how to write a lead-in statement, and how to arrange the paragraphs of the paper to support the thesis.

Stage	Analysis: Classification
7	and Division

STEP 1   Analysis as a Method of Organizing Thought

Analysis is a method of developing and organizing a subject by breaking it down into its parts. Through analysis, you convey to your reader a discovery about your subject. This breakdown helps to explain how the parts relate to each other and to the whole. There are two methods of analysis: classification and division.

Take a typical day in your life—a twenty-four hour period packed with a chaotic jumble of activities. You might have to grab breakfast, drop the dog by the veterinarian's for shots, research your sociology project, pick up the television from the repair shop so you can watch the documentary assigned for anthropology class, type up your process report for English class, give your friend a promised tutoring session for tomorrow's mathematics test, put in at least two hours on your student workship, get a good meal tonight because you skimped last night, and get some sleep. You have so much to do that you haven't even found a half hour for fun.

Almost instinctively, you begin the first logical operation in any analysis, because to make sense out of your day, you must classify and divide all of your activities to give them some order. Classification means grouping: it means sorting and putting together

113

items, activities, or ideas that have something in common. Thus, to plan your day, you start classifying what you must do according to types of activities: survival needs, studies, work, errands, and hopefully, recreation. Then, in order to get a complete picture of what you must accomplish during the day, you divide each general activity into its component parts. This classification and division operation makes your day look something like this:

Survival	**Errands**
eating	dog to vet
sleeping	TV from repair shop
Studies	**Workship**
sociology research	photocopies for debate coach
English paper	collating speech test
math tutoring	**Recreation**
TV documentary	concert at music hall (?)

You may not do all of these things in sequence. However, in order to remember all of the things you must do and in order to save yourself time and energy, you need analysis to plan your day; without it you will conclude (and with good reason) that you should have stayed in bed.

Look at the way analysis works in another situation. Your college would not make sense without classification and division. College personnel, for instance, have to be classified by duties: administration, instructional personnel, non-instructional personnel, and maintenance staff. Each of these classes of employees is then sub-classified, usually by the type of work each group does. Thus, non-instructional personnel breaks down into counselors, academic advisors, paraprofessionals, and clerical workers. Think about another instance where classification and division are necessary; you would have a hard time finding your way through the college catalog if it were not classified according to major areas of instruction. A college catalog, for example, usually classifies its areas of instruction as Business Administration, Communications, Fine Arts, Physical Education and Recreation, Mathematics and Science, Social Science, Pre-professional Programs, and Technical Education. Each major class of studies is then subclassified into separate subject areas. Communications, for example, comprises English, Speech, Reading, Foreign Languages, Journalism, and English as a Second Language. Each one of these subject areas is then further subclassified into courses by type. The two subclasses under English are Composition and Literature and these areas are in turn subclassified. Literature may be divided into American literature, English literature, world literature, and special interest literature. These subclasses are finally divided into individual course offerings. American literature, for example, might be divided into American Literature before 1900, Contemporary American Literature, The American Short Story, The American Novel after 1920, or Modern American Poetry. When you stop to think about it, almost everything is classified and divided—stores, athletic teams, libraries, geographical areas—even your own home.

STEP 2 Using Analysis for a Subject Limitation

Just as fact enumeration is a way to support your inferences, analysis is a way of limiting and organizing expository writing. Assume that you are given as a possible subject for one of your first themes your home town or city. Analysis will help you with the first requirement of expository writing, suitable limitation of your subject. For example, you might make a quick analysis of your city or town in terms of areas classified on the basis of function. Your analysis would look like this:

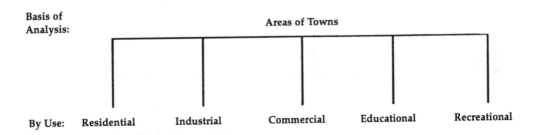

Since your first themes, however, are probably going to be only about five hundred words, you can quickly see by studying your analysis chart that you cannot handle all of these areas in a short paper. You must, therefore, think about limitation. Assume you are a business major. You focus on the commercial area of your town. You think about the office buildings, the various shopping centers; and then a picture of the new shopping mall that took three years to complete comes into your mind. You think about the "everything under one roof" concept of planned shopping centers as an improvement over the older, random growth types of shopping centers. At this point you decide that the subject for your paper will be shopping malls—a new concept in city planning. Your extended analysis chart would look like the diagram on the following page.

STEP 3 Supplying Supporting Details for the Subject

In order to determine what you are going to say about your limited subject, you now start a list of ideas, which are the supporting (proof) details. Your list might look something like this:

clothing stores	art galleries
gift shops	barber shops
department stores	shoe stores
cold drink stands	banks
snack bars	bakeries
book and record shops	telephones

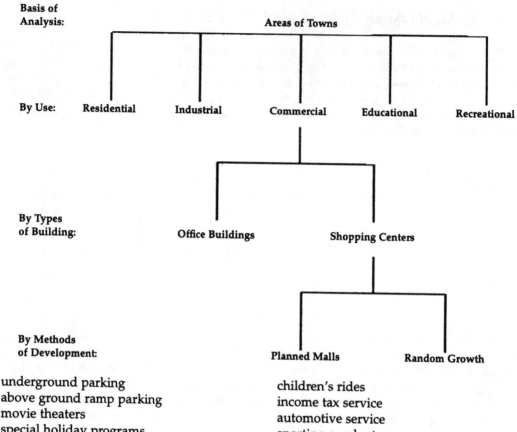

Basis of
Analysis: Areas of Towns

By Use: Residential   Industrial   Commercial   Educational   Recreational

By Types
of Building: Office Buildings   Shopping Centers

By Methods
of Development: Planned Malls   Random Growth

underground parking   children's rides
above ground ramp parking   income tax service
movie theaters   automotive service
special holiday programs   sporting goods stores
fountains   drug stores
art shows   lower gardens
benches to sit on   sculptures
hobby shops   celebrity visits (sports figures, etc.)
hobby shows   politician's visits
toy stores   Santa Claus
specialty shops   Easter displays (lower shows)
specialty food shops   television in rest areas
specialty restaurants   choir and band performances
rest rooms   art shows
furniture stores   hobby displays

STEP 4 Classifying the Proof Details

When you look over your list, you can see that the supporting (proof) details fall into four main categories: (1) stores for every purpose, (2) service facilities, (3) parking areas, (4) rest and recreation facilities. With these categories the analysis chart for the limited subject or planned malls would look like this:

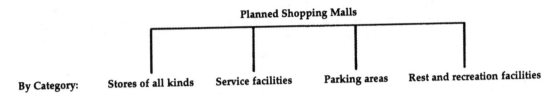

Planned Shopping Malls

By Category: Stores of all kinds   Service facilities   Parking areas   Rest and recreation facilities

STEP 5 Writing the Tentative Thesis Statement

After you have limited your subject by analysis, you can write a tentative thesis statement. The first part of a thesis is a general statement called the major inference. The major inference asserts your opinion, judgment, conclusion, or generalization about your subject. The major inference for a theme about shopping malls might be

> The mall concept of planned shopping centers offers the buyer everything under one roof.

Your reader, however, needs more of an idea about where your exposition will take him. If you examine the bottom of your analysis chart, you can add to your general statement the main categories or classes of your discussion. These categories are called the minor inferences. Your complete thesis statement will then look like this:

> The mall concept of planned shopping centers offers the shopper everything under one roof by providing stores for every purpose, varied service facilities, unlimited parking, and unusual rest and recreation facilities.

The thesis statement, then, consists of three parts:

1. The limited subject:
   mall concept for planned shopping centers

2. The major inference:
   offers the buyer everything under one roof

3. The minor inferences:
   provides stores for every purpose
   provides varied service facilities
   provides unlimited parking
   provides unusual rest and recreation facilities

The categories of the discussion are called minor inferences because each of them is a generalization which must be further supported with proof details in the form of facts and examples.

STEP 6 Writing the Introductory Paragraph

The thesis statement controls your paper; it gives the major and minor inferences which will be developed in the body of your paper. While the thesis begins the paper, it is only one part of the introductory paragraph. The introductory paragraph consists of two parts: the lead-in statement or statements, and the thesis statement.

The Lead-In

The thesis statement contains the limited subject. The lead-in introduces the general subject and narrows it to the specific subject. The purpose of the lead-in is to arouse the reader's interest in the subject and to focus his attention on the thesis. The lead-in, in other words, is the attention-getter for your theme, while the thesis is the control center for your theme.

You saw the analysis of the subject of shopping malls presented graphically in chart form. It is often helpful to see how an introductory paragraph looks in graphic form; it is much like an inverted triangle because it begins with the general subject and narrows to the specific thesis.

General subject:
    commercial areas
Narrowed subject:
    shopping centers
Specific subject:
    malls
Thesis:
    major inference
    minor inferences

American cities are often notable for the inefficiency and ugliness of their *commercial areas*. Most *shopping centers* have developed without adequate planning for function or attractiveness. The mall concept of *planned shopping centers offers the shopper everything under one roof by providing stores for every purpose, varied service facilities, unlimited parking areas and unusual rest and recreation facilities.*

STEP 7 Setting Up the Tentative Framework

Now that you have written the introductory paragraph, you are ready to set up the framework of the theme:

General subject: commercial areas of cities
Narrowed subject: shopping centers
Limited subject: the mall concept
Title: THE SUPERSHOP
Thesis: The mall concept of planned shopping centers offers the buyer everything under one roof by providing stores for every purpose, varied service facilities, unlimited parking areas, and unusual rest and recreation facilities.

I.   Stores for every purpose

II. Varied service facilities

III. Unlimited parking areas

IV. Unusual rest and recreation facilities

Notice that the lead-in sentence, while it will appear in the theme, is not part of the framework, which begins with the thesis. The minor inferences, pulled down from the thesis in order as they are written, indicate the major categories of the discussion that will form the body of the paper. Each minor inference from the thesis will function as the controlling inference in the topic sentence of each developmental paragraph.

STEP 8 Limiting the Subject Further

Now that you have set up a framework by presenting the thesis and listing the minor inferences, you are ready to study your list of proof details and to place them under the appropriate minor inferences. However, given the number of details you already have listed, together with additional information you will want to add to support the minor inferences, you realize that you will have far too much to handle in a five hundred to eight hundred word theme, which is only about two to four typewritten pages of double-spaced text.

Once again you must limit your subject and rewrite the thesis according to the new limitation. Which of the four categories should you choose for discussion? You may decide that one of the mall ideas—the rest and recreation facilities—is a distinct innovation. This innovation is absent from the older, random growth type of shopping center, so you select this for your new limited subject. It is time to review your list again and to sift out only those details which pertain to the rest and recreation facilities of a mall. You might select these proof details.

children's rides

snack bars

juice bars

benches

fountains

flower gardens

sculptures

special holiday programs

art shows

hobby exhibits

visits by sports figures

garden shows

visits by TV and movie stars

visits by politicians

Santa Claus

television viewing areas

choral groups

telephones

rest rooms

specialty restaurants

Once again the problem is to bring order out of this random assortment of details. Again you use the logical operation of classification by grouping these details according to some basis of similarity. The rest and recreation facilities of a mall can be classified into six main categories:

1.   Landscaped areas for relaxation

2. Restrooms

3. A variety of eating experiences

4. Play facilities for children

5. Displays for special interests

6. Shows for special events

As you look over these six categories, you realize that there is still too much information to handle in a five hundred to eight hundred word theme. The next question is, which of the categories can be eliminated by the writer and still let him get across the idea that a mall is an innovation in shopping centers? Upon reflection you realize that shopping areas other than malls offer conveniences and some recreation facilities for children. It is the other four categories that really make a mall distinctive.

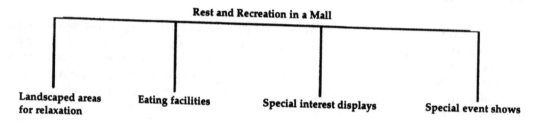

Revising the Thesis

The thesis statement revised in accordance with your further limiting of the subject will look like the following:

A special attraction in the new shopping malls is the rest and recreation facilities, which provide landscaped areas for relaxation, a variety of eating experiences, displays for special interest groups, and shows for special events.

Here is an analysis of the new thesis:

1. Limited subject:
   the rest and recreation facilities of malls

2. Major inference:
   they are a special attraction for shoppers

3. Minor inferences:
   provide landscaped areas for relaxation
   provide a variety of eating experiences
   provide displays for special interest groups
   provide shows for special events

Reviewing the Lead-In

Now that you finally have limited your subject so that you know you can handle it in a short paper, you will want to look over the lead-in you wrote in order to make sure that it is still appropriate for the newly revised thesis statement and to make sure that it leads directly into the thesis. The first two sentences are still suitable:

1. American towns are often characterized by the inefficiency and ugliness of their commercial areas.
2. Most shopping centers have developed without adequate planning for function or attractiveness.

But now you really need another narrowing sentence to lead into the new thesis. You could add:

3. The new mall concept for planned shopping centers offers the shopper everything under one roof.

You are retaining your old major inference and using it now as another narrowing sentence in the lead- in. The inverted triangle for your revised introductory paragraph will look like the following:

General subject

Narrowed subject

Specific subject

Thesis

American cities are often notable for the inefficiency and ugliness of their commercial areas. Most shopping centers have developed without adequate planning for function or attractiveness. However, the new mall concept for planned shopping centers offers the shopper everything under one roof. One of the special attractions in any mall is the rest and rec-recreation facilities, which provide landscaped areas for relaxation, a variety of eating experiences, displays for special interest groups, and shows for special events.

STEP 9 Setting up the Framework for the Analysis Theme

The framework for your revised theme sets up like this:

General subject: Commercial areas of cities

Limited subject: The rest and recreation facilities of a mall
Title: THE PAMPERED SHOPPER
Thesis: One of the special attractions in any mall is the rest and recreation facilities which provide landscaped areas for relaxation, a variety of eating experiences, displays for special interest groups, and shows for special events.

I.   Landscaped areas for relaxation

II.   Variety of eating experiences

III. Displays for special interest groups

IV. Shows for special events

STEP 10 Understanding How Classification and Division Work Together

You have seen from the analysis of the shopping mall topic that classification and division operate together. Notice that the writer, in order to make a logical analysis, had to classify and divide his subject on only one basis at a time. First, he classified the areas of his home town on the basis of function. When he decided to write about the commercial area, he then classified this subject on the basis of **type of activity.** When he selected shopping centers as a further limitation, he then subclassified this subject on the basis of **type of planning.** Finally, when he decided that planned shopping malls would be the subject for his paper, he subclassified malls on the basis of **types of service** provided for the shopper. In order to further analyze his subject, he then divided each type of service into its **component parts.** On each level of analysis, then, he classified, subclassified, and divided on only one basis at a time.

The reason for classifying and dividing a subject is to help the student to limit the subject, thus making an abstract subject concrete. For example, a student cannot write on the subject of bicycles because the subject is too broad. First, he needs to classify and divide on one basis at a time. Bicycles may be classified into four categories: Specialty Cycles, Lightweights, ATB Terrain, and 20 inch Wheels. Thus if the topic were bicycles, it might be analyzed in the following manner:

Subject: Bicycles
Basis of analysis: Lightweights
   (By Type)   Touring Cruisers
                             Sports
                             Racing
Basis of analysis: Specialty Cycles
                             Unicycles
                             Big Wheels
                             Recumbents
                             Skate Bikes
                             Scooters

	Free Wheelers
	Tandems
	Exercisers
Basis of analysis:	ATB Terrain
	Beach Cruiser
	City Bikes
	Mountain Bikes
Basis of analysis:	20 inch Wheel
	Free Style
	Cruisers
	BMX
	Racing

When you subclassify a subject, you can shift the basis of analysis. The important thing to remember is that on each level of analysis the basis of analysis must be consistent. The subject of bridges can serve as an example. Suppose that you chose as your subject **fixed bridges.** This subject was selected from the analysis of bridges on the basis of type. If you were to further analyze this subject, you would most likely shift your basis of analysis and subclassify on the basis of construction principle:

Subject:	fixed bridges
Basis of analysis:	construction principle
	single beam
	suspension
	arch
	truss
	cantilever
	Bailey

If you decided to write a detailed analysis of the subject of fixed bridges constructed according to the **arch principle,** for example, you would continue to subclassify—but probably next on the basis of construction materials:

Subject:	fixed arch bridges
Basis of analysis:	construction materials
	cement
	steel

Dividing a Singular Subject

Singular subjects require analysis by division. In order to make a logical division, you must divide on only one basis at a time. Once again the subject of bridges will serve as an example. Suppose you chose for your subject **moveable bridges.** There are five types of movable bridges:

Subject: movable bridges
Basis of analysis: types
  transporter
  pontoon
  vertical lift
  swinging drawbridge
  Bascule

A civil engineering student living in an area of waterways with many drawbridges might find it interesting to investigate the single subject of the Bascule bridge. He would analyze this subject by division on the basis of component parts:

Subject: the Bascule bridge
Basis of analysis: component parts
  bridge leaf
  pit
  trunnion pin
  motor
  driving gear
  bridge drive rack
  counter weight

Division of a subject usually involves an analysis of the component parts, but it can also involve an analysis in time or an analysis of the steps or stages of a subject. An analysis of any one of the systems of a car is an example.

Subject: the fuel system of car
Basis of division: stages in the combustion cycle
  intake
  compression
  power
  exhaust

A further division of each of these stages would involve the parts of the car concerned with each of the stages.

STEP 11 Recognizing Problems in Analysis

You should avoid three errors that will produce a confusing or illogical analysis.

Cross Ranking

If you classify or divide on more than one basis at a time, you are actually shifting the basis of analysis. This problem is called cross ranking. Here are two examples.

Subject: modeling
children
Fisher-Price toys
television commercials

To eliminate cross ranking, the writer selects only one basis of analysis. For example, if the writer wanted to write a paper discussing the effectiveness of selling toy products, using children as models to advertise toy products, the writer would classify the subject by discussing specific products such as the following: Real Baby dolls, Fisher-Price trucks, and Lego building blocks.

Overlapping

Your classifications or divisions on any one level of analysis must be mutually exclusive This means that one entry cannot be subclassified or subdivided under any one of the other entries. Two examples of overlapping follow:

> **Subject:**   Buick automobiles
> Century
> Regal
> Le Sabre
> Electra
> Luxury

Overlapping occurs in this analysis because Electra is a subdivision of Luxury.

> **Subject:**   Large city daily newspapers
> Washington Post
> Chicago Tribune
> New York Times
> Sports
> Miami Herald

Overlapping occurs in this analysis because sports is a section of a newspaper and is thus a subdivision.

Incompleteness

Your analysis of a subject should be as complete as possible for the limited subject you select. The number of subclassifications and subdivisions you have depends upon the length of your paper and the number of details you wish to include. Suppose you were consulting a consumer's guide for a complete analysis of compact cars manufactured by American companies. The analysis would be incomplete if it looked like this:

> **Subject:**   American-made compact cars
> General Motors
> Chrysler Corporation

The Ford Motor Company is obviously missing. Similarly, you would not have a complete analysis of specialized dictionaries if the guide's analysis looked like the following.

Subject: Specialized dictionaries
Literary
Religious
Business
Medical

The analysis is incomplete because two important categories of dictionaries are not included: scientific and legal dictionaries.

Exercise 7-1 Identifying the Basis for Classification (Analysis)

In each of the following groups. underline the item that is inconsistent with the others. Then identify the basis for classification (analysis) that has been used for the other terms in the group.

Example:

baseball   Basis of analysis: sports that require striking equipment
hockey
polo
tumbling
tennis

1. natural history museum   Basis of analysis: _____
   art museum
   medical museum
   science and industry museum
   metropolitan museum

2. *Time*   Basis of analysis: _News   magazines_
   Newsweek
   U.S. News and World Report
   Psychology Today

3. set construction   Basis of analysis: _____
   history of the theater
   lighting
   set design

4. choir   Basis of analysis: _____
   symphonic orchestra
   brass band
   jazz ensemble

5. cotton   Basis of analysis: _natural materials_
   linen
   silk
   rayon

6. nudniks   Basis of analysis: _societys misfits_
   nerds
   gossips
   catatonic schizophrenics

7. percussion
    brass
    woodwinds
    glockenspiel

    Basis of analysis: _____

8. Porsche
    Corvette
    Jaguar

    Basis of analysis: ___Sports Cars___

9. cape cod
    colonial
    victorian
    duplex
    art deco

    Basis of analysis: _____

10. compassionate
    high IQ
    empathetic
    contented

    Basis of analysis: ___Characteristics___

Exercise 7-2 Identifying Analysis Problems

In each of the following groups, name the following major analysis problem(s). Some groups may have one, two, or all of the problems (*cross ranking, overlapping, incomplete analysis*).

1. **Clubs**
   honorary societies
   student government association
   Tau Beta sorority
   Pi Delta Epsilon (journalism)

   Problem: _____

2. **Academic Administration**
   Dean of Fine Arts
   Dean of Student Affairs
   Dean of Science and Technology
   Dean of Students

   Problem: _____

3. **Students**
   -- women students
   engineering students
   honor students
   married students

   Problem: _____

4. **Academic Majors**
   engineering students
   liberal arts students
   medical students
   architecture students

   Problem: _____

5. **Degree Programs**
   business administration
   electrical engineering
   journalism
   police science
   robotics

   Problem: _____

Exercise 7-3 Working Classification and Division

Select one subject from the list below. Subclassify the subject into at least three classes.

Example:
Subject: Pollution
    air
    land   Basis of analysis: element polluted
    water

Then select one of the classes, divide it into subclasses, and name the basis of analysis.

Subject
Example:

Subject: Water Pollution
    garbage
    sewage   Basis of analysis: types of pollutants
    chemical
    thermal

Subject choices:
    1. Systems of government
    2. Bands
    3. Methods of exercising
    4. Snack foods
    5. Wars

Subject- Bands   Basis of analysis: Popular bands

    - The spice girls

    - Roxette

    - Midnight oil

    - the cranberries

The Basis for Classification and the Thesis Statement

You already know that the thesis statement must contain (1) the limited subject, (2) the major inference, and (3) the minor inferences. Your work in Exercises 7-1 and 7-2 should help you to see that the minor inferences should not be cross ranked or overlapped. Each minor inference should be important enough so that interesting and adequate supporting details can be supplied to support it.

One point concerning the thesis statement that has not yet been discussed is the necessity for stating the minor inferences in terms that are grammatically parallel. Following is an example of a thesis statement that is awkward because it is not grammatically parallel.

A high school band entering state competition is judged on concert performance, how well they march, and dress inspection.

The minor inferences *concert performances* and *dress inspection* are parallel because they are both noun phrases (nouns modified by adjectives), but the minor inference *how well they march* is a clause. Cast in grammatically parallel terms, the thesis would read:

A high school band entering state competition is judged on concert performance, marching ability, and dress inspection.

Thus, when you construct your thesis, you should pair nouns with nouns, infinitive phrases with infinitive phrases, noun phrases with noun phrases, dependent clauses with dependent clauses, independent clauses with independent clauses.

The last point you need to remember is that in a well-constructed thesis statement the basis of classification is clear. If it is clear, it will indicate the pattern of development and will help the reader to follow your exposition.

The bases of classification are

types of any subject
characteristics of a subject
parts of a system, institution mechanism, operation, or object
parts of a problem
parts of a solution
parts of an argument
divisions in time

Exercise 7-4 Criticizing Thesis Statements

Following are thesis statements written by freshman composition students in preparation for their first analysis theme. They chose subjects from personal experience. Criticize each of the thesis statements by identifying (1) the limited subject, (2) the major inference, (3) the minor inferences, (4) the basis of analysis. If the thesis is faulty, indicate the problem you find in it. If the thesis is satisfactory, write **s** in the space following **Thesis problem**. Thesis problems are listed below.

Thesis problems

A. Limited subject not readily apparent
B. Subject not limited enough
C. Unsuitable major inference
D. Unacceptable minor inferences
   1. Cross ranking or overlapping of minor inferences
   2. Dead-end minor inferences (too little or no factual information needed)
   3. Minor inferences not grammatically parallel
   4. No minor inferences
E. Illogical thesis

Example:
Thesis: The United States armed forces must be on alert and ready to act on any confrontation that may arise because no one knows where or when a war will start.

Limited subject: The subject "armed forces" is not limited enough.
Major inference: There is no single major inference. The major inferences listed are "must be on alert and ready to act on any confrontation."
Minor inferences: The minor inferences stated are "because no one knows where or when a war will start." These are ambiguous.
Basis of analysis: Since there are no suitable minor inferences, there is no basis of analysis.
Thesis problem: A, C, D

1. **Subject:** Boats
   There are three decisions that the model boater is faced with when deciding to build a model. They are the design of the boat, the materials required to construct the boat, and the type of engine needed to power the boat.

Limited subject: model boats

Major inference: C   There are 3 decisions

Minor inference: design of boat, materials required, type of engine

Basis of analysis:

Thesis problem(s):

2. **Subject:** NASA
   The NASA astronaut rescue team, developed to handle emergencies with the space shuttle personnel, understands the need for the team, the personal requirements, and the intense training.

   Limited subject: _The team_ _not gramatically parallel_

   Major inference:

   Minor inferences:

   Basis of analysis:

   Thesis problem(s):

3. **Subject:** Alcoholics
   Children of alcoholics experience severe developmental problems during their formative years, their personality isn't good either, and an increased tendency to become alcoholics themselves.

   Limited subject: _Children of alcoholics_

   Major inference:

   Minor inferences: _overlap - to broad_

   Basis of analysis:

   Thesis problem(s):

4. **Subject:** Hobbies
   Car model building, an indoor hobby that is adopted by people who are proficient with their hands, is divided into three major versions.

   Limited subject: _Model Cars_

Major inference: *unsuitable*

Minor inferences: *are none*

Basis of analysis: *there is none*

Thesis problem(s):

5. **Subject:** United States
    In retaliation for the numerous hijacking attempts on American citizens, the United States bombed Libya.

Limited subject: — *statement of fact*

Major inference:

Minor inferences:

Basis of analysis:

Thesis problem(s):

6. **Subject:** Scholarships
    Each spring colleges throughout the United States award scholarships to outstanding high school students such as honor students, athletes, minorities, and children of distinguished alumni.

Limited subject:

Major inference:

Minor inferences: *Too many minor*

Basis of analysis:

Thesis problem(s).

7. **Subject:** Little Leagues
    Little Leagues should be abolished because they discriminate against the child who is not a natural athlete, they allow parental prejudice to interfere with the selection of

players during a game, and they do not set examples of good sportsmanship.

Limited subject:

Major inference:

Minor inferences:

Basis of analysis:

Thesis problem(s):

8. **Subject:** Child abuse
   Several causes of child abuse include the inability of young parents to cope with monetary problems, the permissive attitude of the parents, and the submissiveness of the child.

Limited subject:

Major inference:

Minor inferences:

Basis of analysis:

Thesis problem(s):

9. **Subject:** Politics
   The United States should develop relations with South American countries by allocating funds for only the friendly Democratic governments, by opening up avenues of dialog with the governments, and by sending teams of medical and technological experts to those countries that are underdeveloped.

Limited subject:

Major inference:

Minor inferences:

Basis of analysis:

Thesis problem(s):

Exercise 7-5 Criticizing Introductory Paragraph Statements

Read the following introductory paragraphs to analysis themes. Decide which lead-ins are effective. If the lead-in is inappropriate or ineffective, discuss the reasons. Of those lead-ins that are inappropriate or ineffective, select one and rewrite the introductory paragraph.

1. **Subject:** Movies
   Movies are enjoyed by most people, and there are all types of movies for all types of people. There are cartoons for children, science fiction and adventure for teenagers, and love stories and adult comedies for young adults. The movies that are most popular today are those movies which involve teenagers and their problems. Three such movies are The Breakfast Club, Sixteen Candles, and Pretty in Pink.
   Rewrite of lead-in, if necessary:

2. **Subject:** The World's Fair
   Traditionally the World's Fair was the only place that one could experience the culture of many countries. In one full day a visitor could enjoy Chinese art, French cuisine, and the new technology from such countries as Australia. In the past most families would travel miles to visit the World's Fair, held once a year, since there was no other like it. Today, however, it is possible to enjoy such an experience every day of the year, for located in Orlando, Florida, is Epcot. There one can enjoy the sights, sounds, and food of countries such as Germany, Canada, and Italy. However, the four countries in Epcot that are unique are Morocco, Mexico, China, and Japan.
   Rewrite of lead-in, if necessary:

3. **Subject:** Television commercials
   Lately television commercials have begun to use humor to attract the viewer's attention. But commercials that use humor are not always successful, and there are several reasons for that: they may offend a specific group of viewers, they may prove to be distasteful, and the humor may not always be evident.
   Rewrite the lead-in, if necessary:

4. **Subject:** Buying cars
   With so many new cars on the market, one must shop around at several dealers to find just the right car with all of the right options. However, since this task might be difficult for some people, it might be wise instead for the buyer to consider purchasing a motorcycle. Some advantages of buying a motorcycle are less expenditure for gasoline, easier

maneuvering in heavy traffic, and a smaller initial cost.
Rewrite of lead-in, if necessary.

5. **Subject:** Radio controlled boats
    Radio controlled boats have become a well-known hobby throughout the United States. The technology that is incorporated into these models make them similar to the real boats that compete in races on the country's waterways. The three decisions that the model boater is faced with when trying to build a model are the design of the boat, the materials required to construct the boat, and the engine required to power the boat.
    Rewrite of lead-in, if necessary.

Exercise 7-6 Writing Thesis Statements

Following are four subjects. The minor inferences are given. First supply a major inference. Then using the information listed, write a thesis statement which contains a narrowed subject, the major inference, and the minor inferences.

Example:

Subject: Television commercials
Major inference: Attract viewer's attention in three ways
Minor inferences:
    I.   Reporting straight information
    II. Enlisting testimonials
    III. Incorporating humor

Thesis statement: Television commercials for breakfast cereals attract the viewer's attention by one of the following three ways: reporting straight information, enlisting testimonials, and incorporating humor.

1. **Subject:** Traditional weddings
    Major inference: *Are celebrated in three popular locations.*

    Minor inferences:
      I.   Public villas or estates
      II. Private gardens
      III. Restaurant gardens

    Thesis Statement: *Traditional weddings are no longer limited to church's, and are now celebrated in three popular locations which include: public villas, private gardens and restaurant gardens*

2. Subject: Household pets
   Major inference:

    Minor inferences:
      I.   Determining the purpose of a pet
      II. Choosing a compatible pet
      III. Training the pet

Thesis statement:

3. **Subject:** Cruise
   Major inference:

   Minor inferences:
      I.   Tournaments and games
     II. Lectures and classes
    III. Special events

   Thesis statement:

4. Subject: Traveling
   Major inference:

   Minor inferences:
      I.   Plan a budget for the trip
     II. Decide the amount of time needed for travel
    III. Select the vacation spot.

   Thesis statement:

Exercise 7-7 Writing the Introductory Paragraph

Write an introductory paragraph for one of the thesis statements which you have just written from Exercise 7-6. Before doing so, complete the corresponding exercise below the model paragraph. For example, an appropriate introductory paragraph for a thesis statement on television commercials is as follows:

SEEING IS BELIEVING

Over the last century companies wishing to advertise and promote their products have relied on a multitude of mediums to convey their messages. In the early 1900's the press, the radio, and street billboards all provided adequate, if somewhat limited, exposure. It was not until after World War II, with the advent of television and its subsequent popularity, that advertisers finally encountered the ideal means for disseminating their messages. With its tremendous growth in popularity, television quickly became the favorite medium of communication for advertising. Soon companies began to increase their advertising budgets, vying for a better position in their respective markets. Despite the overwhelming number of television commercials on the air, most of them attract the viewer's attention in three ways: reporting straight information, enlisting testimonials, and incorporating humor.

Newton Berwig

Now complete the following exercise.

Title:

General Subject:

Specific Subject:

Thesis Statement:

On a separate sheet of paper, write an introductory paragraph concluding it with the thesis statement.

Exercise 7-8 Examining Analysis Charts and Introductory Paragraphs

On the following pages you will see analysis charts made by freshman composition students. In each case the student elected to write on a subject he already knew a great deal about—his job, his hobby, or a special interest. Study these analysis charts to see to what extent the student had to classify and divide to get a subject that would be manageable in a theme of five hundred to eight hundred words.

Opposite each chart is a worksheet on which you can make a critique of the student's introductory paragraph. The critique sheet on *Aquariums* is filled in as an example of a completed critique. Notice that the sentences in each introductory paragraph are numbered for easy identification. You can answer the questions on the critique sheet by placing the number of the correct sentence(s) in the blank.

Example: Introductory Paragraph

(1) Man's fascination with the sea is steeped in recorded history. (2) The ancient Romans, for instance, built huge ponds, sometimes directly connected to the sea, which they stocked with rare and valued specimens. (3) On the other hand, the Chinese bred ornamental fishes, such as goldfish suitable for keeping in small containers. (4) However, it was not until 1853, in Regent's Park, London, that the first glass-sided aquarium made its appearance. (5) Since then the collection of marine creatures has developed into an interesting hobby for the young and old. (6) However, setting up a home aquarium takes planning, for the owner must select a suitable type of tank, determine the kinds of fish that will be included, and choose the accessories that will go into the tank.

General subject: Aquariums
Narrowed subject: Home aquariums
Specific subject: Setting up the home aquarium
Lead-in sentences: Sentences 1-5
Thesis statement: Sentence 6
   Major inference: Takes planning
   Minor inferences: Select a suitable type of tank. Determine the kinds of fish that will be included. Choose the accessories that will go into the tank.

Note that the minor inferences are stated in grammatically parallel terms.

The basis of analysis indicates classification.

If the thesis statement were converted into the framework for the paper, it would look like this:

THESIS STATEMENT: Sentence 6
   I. Select a suitable type of tank
   II. Determine the kinds of fish that will be included
   III. Choose the accessories that will go into the tank

Exercise A

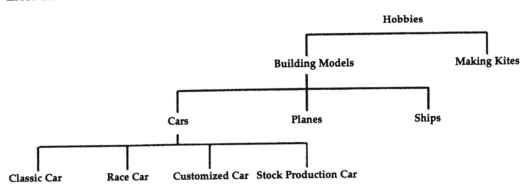

Introductory Paragraph

(1) A large number of people resort to hobbies to get a refreshing break from the hustle and bustle of today's fast paced lifestyle. (2) Although building models is more popular with young males, it is a hobby that is enjoyed by many people from both sexes and different age groups. (3) It is certain that a model car is one of the most popular choices made by enthusiasts. (4) Furthermore, building a model car is very enjoyable and rewarding. (5) Nevertheless, a difficult choice one has to make is to decide whether to build a classic car, or race car, a customized car, or a stock production car.

General subject:

Narrowed subject:

Specific subject:

Lead-in sentences:

Thesis statement:

Major inference:

Minor inferences:

Basis of analysis:

Convert the thesis into the framework for the paper:

Thesis statement:
   I.

   II.

   III.

   IV.

Exercise B

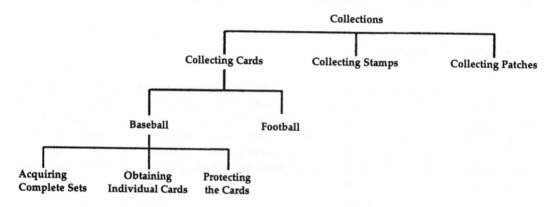

Introductory Paragraph

(1) Many people in the United States enjoy the hobby of collecting baseball cards. (2) Baseball card collecting has been around for many years, and the cards can be passed down from one generation to another. (3) In addition, the cards can become worth much money if they are collected over a period of years and taken care of well. (4) However, the three major considerations for card collectors are the acquiring of complete sets, obtaining individual cards, and protecting the cards to keep their value.—Joseph J. Hone

General subject:

Narrowed subject:

Specific subject:

Lead-in sentences:

Thesis statement:

   Major inference:

   Minor inferences:

Basis of analysis:

Convert the thesis into the framework of the paper:

Thesis statement:
  I.

  II.

  III.

Exercise C

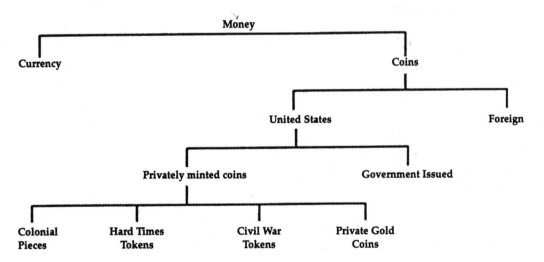

Introductory Paragraph

Most of us take the change in our pockets for granted; and we assume that we have always had the penny, the nickel, the dime, the quarter, the half dollar, and the silver dollar.

However, money was not really important to the American colonist since he bartered with others for goods he did not produce. Although the first coin struck for use in the American colonies was in 1652, it was the Coinage Act of 1792 that established the national mint and the first system of money in the United States, setting the dollar as the basic unit of this system. The new system established both gold and silver coins, known as government-issued coins; however, to a collector the most interesting coins are the ones that were privately minted and circulated by private companies, private citizens, assayers, bankers, and special interest groups. Four of the most interesting types of privately minted coins are the Colonial pieces, Hard Times Tokens, Civil War Tokens, and gold coins.

General subject:

Narrowed subject:

Specific subject:

Lead-in sentences:

Thesis statement:

Major inference:

Minor inferences:

Exercise 7-9 Making an Analysis Chart

Select one subject from the list below and make an analysis chart. Work the chart down by classifying and dividing until you get a limited subject with several categories that you think could be developed in a five hundred to eight hundred word theme.

Subject:

1. Fishing
2. Music
3. Comic book heroes
4. Education
5. Politicians
6. Art
7. Boats
8. Friends
9. Professors
10. Aspects of a character
11. Movies
12. Crime
13. Musical instruments
14. Jewelry
15. Religions
16. Foods —
17. Part-time jobs
18. Commercials
19. Hobbies
20. Comic Strip characters

General Subject:

ANALYSIS CHART

Exercise 7-10 Writing a Thesis Statement from the Analysis Chart

Taking your minor inferences from the bottom of your analysis chart, write a thesis statement in which the classifications or divisions are evident.

Thesis statement:

Model: By Classification and Division

In the following example, the writer classifies the antics of the comic strip character Cathy.

CATHY: THE MIRRORED IMAGE

Thesis Statement: Most women can relate to the comic strip character Cathy because of her humorous views on exercise, on fashions, and on relationships.

I. The never-ending saga of exercising
   A. Weekly visits to the health club
      1. Physically challenging
      2. Mentally challenging
   B. Locker room experiences
      1. Creates feelings of insecurity
      2. Prompts stop at fast food restaurant
   C. Investments in exercise machines and products
      1. The Stairmaster
      2. Thigh reducing cream

II. The role fashions play
   A. Shopping for the perfect swimsuit
      1. Weight gain problem
      2. Fitting room dilemma
   B. Avoiding the aggressive saleswoman
   C. Shopping for evening wear
      1. Trying on numerous dresses
      2. Becoming exhausted and depressed
      3. Purchasing similar type dress

III. The most frustrating experiences with relationships
   A. Relationships with dates
      1. Blind dates
         a. Sometimes fakes illness
         b. Waits until bill is paid
      2. Exceptions to "losers"
         a. Spends hours waiting for calls
         b. Checks telephone receiver frequently
   B. Relationship with mother
      1. Receives frequent telephone calls
      2. Gets unwanted advice
      3. Ends conversations in a debate

Concluding Statement: While real life experiences may not always be pleasant, Cathy faces hers with an amusing view that most career women can appreciate and can allow themselves to laugh at their own idiosyncrasies and foibles.

CATHY: A MIRRORED IMAGE

Comic strip characters are able to translate the realistic aspects of daily life into whimsical expressions on paper. Families easily relate to "For Better or For Worse" or "The Family Circus" while pet owners identify with "Garfield" or "Marmaduke." However, it was not until cartoonist Cathy Guisewite introduced "Cathy" that career woman saw a mirrored image of themselves. Most women can relate to the comic strip character Cathy because of her humorous views on exercise, on fashions, and on relationships.

Exercise seems to be a never-ending saga in Cathy's life. Her weekly visits to the health club are more mentally challenging for her than they are physically. For example, in her aerobics class, she always goes to the back of the room in order to avoid embarrassment because she lacks coordination. Either she tangles herself in the equipment or in her own feet. When class is over, she joins the rest of the girls in the locker room. Drenched in sweat, she ponders why most of the girls look like they just had a fashion makeover but she does not. With a sigh, she heads home, but not without first stopping at a local fast food restaurant. Later she experiences overwhelming guilt after eating the sundae or the fat-laden food. As a result, Cathy has a history of investing in the latest exercise machines and products that promise weight loss results overnight. Two of her recent purchases include a Stairmaster and a fat-reducing thigh cream. After walking hundreds of flights of stairs and getting nowhere, she abandons the Stairmaster and convinces herself that she will benefit more from the Stairmaster if she uses it instead as a coat rack. Still, she never gives up her quest for a slim body.

In addition to exercise, fashion plays a major role in Cathy's life. Like most women, shopping for the perfect swimsuit proves to be a very frustrating experience. Time after time she convinces herself that the extra five pounds she has gained is not really a gain at all, but the manufacturer's reduction of size in the new swimsuit styles. As if this humiliation is not enough, she discovers that the fitting room mirrors are not on the inside of the room, but on the outside. There she must endure the stares of the salesclerk who tries to convince her that it is "women who renew the earth with color and style" but who gossips with the other clerks about Cathy's lack of style. In order to avoid the aggressive saleswoman waiting for her and to ignore the muffled laughter of the other shoppers, she decides to get dressed and purchase what she calls the "$250.00 four-foot piece of electric pink fabric" advertised as a swimsuit. As she exits the store, she considers returning the suit if it does not fit or buying a huge beach umbrella.

Evening wear is another highlight of Cathy's shopping escapades. Whenever she has a date or must attend a special event, she runs to the mall, hoping to find that unique evening gown that will make her stand out in a crowd and attract the handsome bachelors. After trying on numerous dresses, she decides the styles are getting longer and tighter, not that she is shorter than the ideal woman and wider. Exhausted and depressed, she leaves the store after purchasing a simple black dress, similar to the one she had purchased the year before. At home, she hangs the dress up in her closet along with the ten other black dresses she had purchased from years past. Nevertheless, in Cathy's eyes, black is truly a girl's best friend.

Of all of the womanly issues that Cathy reflects on, her experiences with relationships are definitely the most frustrating. Like most women, the dating game is a nightmare, especially when it comes to a blind date. Some of Cathy's blind dates have included a married man, an alcoholic, and an egotistical football player. When on a blind date, in order to avoid further torture, she always fakes an illness, such as a headache, but only after her date pays the dinner check. Although she considers most of her dates "losers," there are a few exceptions. Whenever Cathy foresees a perspective boyfriend on a date, she tends to have high expectations. After the date is over, she returns home and eagerly anticipates his call. Hour after hour, she anxiously waits by the phone, only to receive calls from her mother, who not only wants to check on how successful the evening was, but also wishes to give advice. The phone call always ends in a debate between the two. Meanwhile, Cathy continues to check the receiver every half-hour to make sure that it is not off the hook. This behavior turns into a vicious cycle that finally ends with an angry phone call from Cathy to her date, only five hours after he had taken her home. Because of her neurotic behavior, in the five years that Cathy has been dating, she has had only one boyfriend, Irving. At first, she fantasizes that he was the one that she wanted to marry, to be the father of her children. Unfortunately, he did not feel the same way. She began to dread the oncome of the seasons for football, baseball, hockey, or any other sport because he would spend all day and night in front of the television. When she discussed commitment with him, he made up excuse after excuse. She finally realized that the only "man" that had a place in her heart was her dog Electra. With that realization, she kicked her boyfriend out and let her dog in. The reader knows that Cathy's relationships will continue to play a major roll as they do with many other women.

Like Cathy most career girls are faced with similar decisions: what to wear, what to purchase, how to achieve that elusive size 4 model figure, how to find a meaningful relationship that may lead to a lifelong commitment. While real life experiences may not always be pleasant, Cathy faces hers with an amusing view that most career women can appreciate and can allow themselves to laugh at their own idiosyncrasies and foibles.

Karen Foglio

Stage 8 | The Outline

1. **Recognizing Types of Outlines**
2. **Learning the Mechanics of Outlining**

In working through Stage 7, you have seen that it is a long way from a random list of ideas on a subject to an orderly presentation of those ideas to your reader. But you have also seen that once you have put your inferences into a thesis statement and formed a brief outline by pulling down the minor inferences to form headings for the major categories of your paper, you have really roughed out the whole theme. In Stage 8 you will be working with the formal outline, which is a systematic arrangement of all your inferences and proof details showing the complete analysis of your subject. Many freshmen consider outlines an artificial exercise which has little or no relation to the actual themes they write. But you know from your work with classification and division in Stage 7 that outlining is actually a natural process which comes about as a result of your attempt to show the relationships between your main ideas and your proof details. All you need to learn now are the technicalities of formal outline writing.

Consider the first stage in building construction, the architect's blueprint. The blueprint from which the builder will work shows the basic outline of the entire building; in addition, the blueprint illustrates the division of space, the location of doors and windows, and diagrams and locations of all the systems—heating, cooling, wiring, and plumbing. The blueprint can be changed up until the time of construction; after that, changes are cumbersome and costly. The outline for a piece of expository writing is similar to the blueprint for a building: the outline is the design for a structure of ideas; the blueprint, for a physical structure.

In addition to the fact that the outline is a necessity for effective organization, it will also save valuable time in the writing process itself. The outline will assist you in the following operations:

1. *The outline helps you to decide on the method of presentation.* Having decided upon your purpose, your major and minor inferences through analysis of your subject, you will have to decide which order of presentation is most suitable; order of importance, chronological order, spatial order, or causal order.

153

2. *The outline assists you in judging adequacy of content.* When you arrange your proof details under the category to which they belong, you can see at a glance whether you have sufficient support for each inference.

3. *The outline assists you in judging proportion in your paper.* While there is no standard rule about the number of proof details under each inference, the outline will tell you at a glance if any category is out of proportion. For instance, if you have only two proof details under one category, perhaps what you considered a major category was not one at all, or you have not considered other possible proof details for the inference.

4. *The outline assists you in judging the logic of your paper.* By looking at an outline, you can tell at a glance whether each supporting detail "adds up" to support the category under which it is classified. If there are any classification problems, such as cross ranking or overlapping, the problem will be evident immediately.

STEP 1   Recognizing Types of Outlines

There are two types of outlines: the *sentence outline* and the *topic outline.* The sentence outline is often used by the beginning writer because it helps to formulate and organize ideas in complete thought patterns. The topic outline, commonly used by the more experienced writer, consists of brief phrases or single words which note the key idea of each sentence. Both types of outlines use the same mechanics for showing the order and the relative importance of the major categories of discussion and their supporting details.

Here are two outlines written by a student in preparation for his analysis on his hobby: street bikes.

Model: By Classification and Division

In the following example, a student who was interested in motorcycles wanted to explain to the novice rider that the selection of a motorcycle can be easy. The writer considers his audience first. Since the writer is addressing his essay to readers that already have some knowledge of motorcycles, he begins by classifying motorcycles by engine size. Then, he organizes his details in either a sentence or topic outline and uses a more informal style and tone for his audience.

Sentence Outline

STREET BIKES

THESIS STATEMENT: However, a novice rider will find that the selection of a street motorcycle is quite easy because motorcycles are divided into three classes by engine size: lightweight, middleweight, and heavy weight.

I. The light weight class is the best choice.
   A. These motorcycles have a lighter construction.
      1. Top speeds are limited.
      2. Handling is excellent.
   B. Maintenance is very inexpensive.
   C. The motorcycles are inexpensive.

II. The next choice is the middleweight class.
   A. Their construction gives two advantages.
      1. They are a good choice for town riding.
      2. The new design and improvements enhance handling.
         a. The new designs include smaller sixteen-inch front wheels.
         b. Improvements came with the lightweight aluminum frame.
      3. Speeds are over 135 miles an hour.
   B. There are simple scheduled maintenance checks required.
      1. Tune ups and valve adjustments are necessary.
      2. Chain tightening, oil changes, and cable adjustments are all necessary.
   C. These motorcycles cost below $3,500.

III. The most powerful are the heavyweights.
   A. These are considerably larger than the middleweights.
      1. Since the engines are larger, the motorcycles require a radiator.
      2. Frames withstand more torque.
      3. These motorcycles have more horsepower.
         a. They have 100 to 150 horsepower.
         b. They have speeds of 160 miles an hour.
   B. These motorcycles are difficult to handle.
      1. The extra weight makes the touring bicycles difficult to handle.
      2. As the rider turns a corner, he can be thrown.
   C. Comfort varies for these motorcycles.
      1. The rider stays in an upright position.
      2. The rider remains in a crouched position.
   D. The cost of buying and keeping these motorcycles is expensive.
      1. The initial cost can be as high as 515,000.
      2. Maintenance is more expensive.
   E. Motorcycles are not kept in stock.

CONCLUDING STATEMENT: In conclusion, the buyer should take into consideration all of the pros and cons of each of the three main classes of street motorcycles so that he can choose a motorcycle that fits his budget and riding experience.

Topic Outline

STREET BIKES

THESIS STATEMENT: However, a novice rider will find that the selection of a street motorcycle is quite easy because motorcycles are divided into three classes by engine size: lightweight, middleweight, and heavyweight.

I. The lightweight class
    A. Lighter construction
        1. Limited top speeds
        2. Excellent handling
    B. Inexpensive maintenance
    C. Inexpensive prices

II. The middleweight class
    A. Two advantages for their construction
        1. Good choice for town riding
        2. Enhanced handling through design and improvements
            a. Smaller sixteen-inch front wheels
            b. Lightweight aluminum frame
        3. Faster speeds: over 135 miles an hour
    B. Simple required maintenance checks
        1. Tune ups and valve adjustments
        2. Chain tightening, oil changes, and cable adjustments

III. The heavyweights
    A. Considerably larger than the middleweights
        1. Require a radiator
        2. Withstand more torque
        3. Have more horsepower
            a. Have 100 to 150 horsepower
            b. Have speeds of 160 miles an hour
    B. Difficult to handle
        1. Difficult because of extra weight
        2. Ease of being thrown while turning a corner
    C. Variation of comfort for the rider
        1. When riding in an upright position
        2. When riding in a crouched position
    D. Cost of buying and maintaining these motorcycles
        1. High initial cost: as much as $15,000.00
        2. Expensive maintenance costs
    E. Difficult to find in stock

CONCLUDING STATEMENT: In conclusion, the buyer should take into consideration all of the pros and cons of each of the three classes of street motorcycles so that he can choose a motorcycle that fits his budget and riding experience.

STEP 2 Learning the Mechanics of Outlining

The outline is headed by the title, opens with the thesis statement, and ends with a concluding sentence. Each minor inference or classification category that appears in the thesis appears in the same order in the body of the outline under a Roman numeral. For example, look at the classification chart for "Street Bikes." The student went from the general subject "Motorcycles" to a narrowed subject, and then to a specific subject.

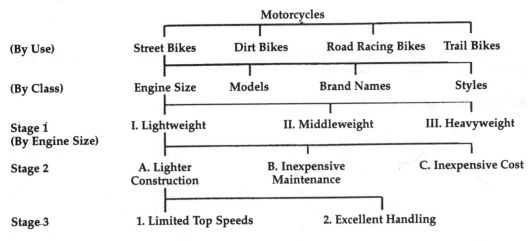

For example, the student arranged the minor inferences "Lightweight," "Middleweight," and " Heavyweight" as the Roman numerals, I, II, and III. If the writer were to complete the classification chart, all of the proof details would appear as the various stages in the outline. Notice that Stage 2 is represented by the capital letters (A, B, C), and Stage 3 is represented by Arabic numbers (1, 2, 3, 4, and so on).

The example you have seen for "Motorcycles" represents four stages of classification and division. Although a three stage outline is usually adequate for a five hundred to eight hundred word paper, a writer could use a four, five, or six stage outline for longer papers with a great deal of detailed information. The pattern for a six stage outline would look like the following.

The Six Stage Outline

TITLE

THESIS STATEMENT

I.

A.
B.
    1.
    2.
        a.
        b.
        c.
            (1)
            (2)
                (a)
                (b)

II. continue . . .

CONCLUDING STATEMENT: Regardless of how many stages you have for your outline, there are certain basic rules to follow:

Rules for Outlining

1. Center the title above the outline in capital letters.

2. Then write the thesis statement. The thesis statement carries no numeral because it controls the entire paper and is not a subdivision in itself.

3. Be sure that the order of the minor inference or classification category for each Roman numeral follows the order presented in the thesis statement.

4. Be consistent in form. If you have a sentence outline, write all entries as full sentences. If you have a topic outline, write all entries in topic form. Do not mix forms.

5. Write the entries in parallel grammatical form. For example, in a topic outline, make all Roman numeral entries nouns, noun phrases, or gerund phrases. Similarly, keep the entries on the next level of classification parallel.

6. Make sure that there are two or more entries on every level of classification. That is, every A must have a B, every 1 must have a 2. The logical reason for this is that nothing can be broken into fewer than two parts.

7. Place a period after every numeral and every letter of the outline except those in parentheses.

8. Capitalize the first word of each entry.

9. Use no end punctuation in a topic outline.

10. Single space the entries within a Roman number category, and double space between Roman numerals.

11. Keep corresponding numerals and letters in vertical columns.

12. Place Capital A under the first letter of the first word entry in Roman number I. Similarly, all other numbers and letters follow this pattern. (Note model outlines.)

Discussion: If you compare the sentence outline with the completed theme, you will see that the student has expanded each of his basic sentence entries, varying the sentence structure and elaborating on details.

STREET BIKES

Choosing a motorcycle can be a perplexing experience, especially for the first time rider. First, the rider must decide whether he wants a street, a dirt, a road racing, or a trail motorcycle. With all of the different sizes, models, and brand names, and styles, one just does not know where to begin. However, a novice rider will find that the selection of a street motorcycle is quite easy because motorcycles are divided into three classes by engine size: lightweight, middleweight, and heavyweight.

The lightweight class of motorcycles is probably the best choice for small, light riders, someone under 100 pounds, and novices. These bikes usually range from 125 to 350 cubic centimeters (cc). Motorcycles in this class, which may weigh only 300 pounds, usually have small, light frames and one or two cylinder engines. Two stroke motors are very common in this class of motorcycles, and the styles of the smaller motorcycles generally are the same as the larger ones, only a scaled down version. Smaller motorcycles, as a rule, are not very fast. Top speeds are up to 120 miles an hour, and quarter-mile time will run under the thirteen second mark. Although these motorcycles are not fast, they have excellent handling characteristics. Their smaller frames and tire sizes make close cornering and faster turns easier. Maintenance on small models is very basic, usually just oil changes and a tightening of the chain whenever it comes loose. However, on the two-stroke models, the piston rings must be changed after certain intervals. The lightweight models are inexpensive, ranging from 1,000 to 2,500 dollars. This price makes them very popular, especially to the younger rider.

From the small lightweight motorcycles, the rider's next choice is the middleweight class, from 400 to 700 cc's. Middleweight motorcycles are a good choice for in-town riding. They are light, have good power, and usually handle very well. Most of the design changes on motorcycles appear in the lightweight class because of their popularity. Some of the newer designs in this class include aluminum or lightweight alloy frames and smaller front wheels. In the past few years, the small sixteen-inch wheels have shown improved handling immensely. Most improvements and design changes in this class have come from motorcycle racing. Because the two-stroke motorcycles are returning to popularity, especially in the 500 cc size, these models are almost exact copies of the factory road racing motorcycles. In addition, speed and handling make the middleweight bikes popular. Some of these motorcycles are hitting quarter-mile times of a high of 11 seconds and top speeds of over 135 miles an hour. Motorcycles in the upper end of this weight class will even outrun some of the heavyweight ones. Because these motorcycles have lightweight frames and good power, they have excellent handling characteristics; and, with an experienced rider, they can be exciting to ride. Furthermore, keeping one of these motorcycles running is generally easy if the scheduled maintenance checks, such as tune ups and valve adjustments, are followed. Owner maintenance, like chain tightening, oil changes, and cable adjustments, should also be done. The middleweight family of motorcycles range in price from about 2,500 to 3,500 dollars, depending on the make and model. The cost makes this class very popular because the rider can buy a relatively fast motorcycle with excellent handling characteristics without having to spend much money.

The biggest and most powerful of the motorcycle classes are the heavyweights. There are two types, sport and touring. These range from 750 cc's and up, with some over 1,300 cc's. Motorcycles in the heavyweight class are constructed considerably larger than the middleweight ones. Their engines are much larger and require more cooling to keep them from overheating; consequently, most of the heavyweights have radiators or are oil cooled. Also, the frames on these models are constructed to withstand the large amounts of torque that these engines generate. The motorcycles in this class produce tremendous amounts of horsepower, compared to the average economy car that weighs over 1,800 pounds and has approximately 20 to 100 horsepower; whereas, one of these motorcycles weighing between 50 and 650 pounds will have from 100 to 150 horsepower. With that type of horsepower, these motorcycles can cruise well past the 140 mile per hour mark as far as 160 miles per hour and burn through the quarter-mile in the ten-second range. However, this type of performance can only be expected of the sport models. The touring or cross county motorcycles are much heavier and not as fast. They also do not handle as well as the sport heavyweights. They tend to cruise through corners at an even pace while the sport motorcycles, ridden at a higher speed than the touring models, can be thrown into turns by the rider. Nevertheless, heavyweight models, whether sport or touring, are not for the novice rider. In the hands of the novice, the additional horsepower can be dangerous, for it can cause a rear tire to burn off or force the rider to bring the front tire up into the air. In addition, because of the extra weight, the larger touring motorcycles can be very difficult to handle. However, although they are more difficult to control, they are very comfortable for the rider on long journeys because their seats are larger, and the rider can sit in an upright position. On the other hand, the sport motorcycles are designed for speed and handling, and the rider sits in a crouched position, putting stress on his wrists and lower back. But the purchaser may have additional concerns.

The cost of buying and maintaining a heavyweight motorcycle can be expensive. A major consideration is the price of a sports model, which costs from $3,500 to $15,000 for some of the exotic Italian or German motorcycles. The touring ones usually range from $7,000 for a basic model to $10,000 for one with all accessories. A second concern is the cost of parts and maintenance. For example, one tire can cost $125 compared to $75 for the lightweight and middleweight models. Also, with all of the power that these motorcycles deliver, parts tend to wear out faster than those on the lighter models, and novice riders and those with a limited income should take these facts into consideration before purchasing a heavyweight motorcycle. Furthermore, because of the high initial cost of the motorcycle, not many of them are kept in stock, and a buyer may have to wait from three to six months to purchase a model of his choice.

In conclusion, the buyer should take into consideration all of the pros and cons of each of the three main classes of street motorcycles so that he can choose a motorcycle that fits his budget and riding experience.

Stephen Grasso

Exercise 8-1 Identifying Outline Problems

Following are two outlines. The first was written by a student as a topic outline, the second as a sentence outline. Using the principles you have learned about a subject limitation and classification and division of Stage 7, and rules of outline in Stage 8, criticize these two outlines. Then rewrite them, eliminating, relocating, and adding entries as the need arises.

Outline A: Topic

BRITAIN'S NATIONAL HEALTH SERVICE—SOME DRAWBACKS

Thesis Statement: Although Great Britain has free medical care available to everyone, their nationalized health plan has some drawbacks: shortage of government funds, inadequate opportunity for physician specialization, lack of incentive, and hospital admission delays.

   I. Shortage of government funds
      A. The financing is overwhelmingly governmental
         1. Must compete with education funds
         2. With transport funds
         3. With defense funds
      B. Britain devotes a smaller portion of its GNP to health care

  II. Inadequate opportunity for physician specialization
      A. Large scale exodus of medical men out of Britain
         1. Net outflow of 400 per year
         2. One out of three medical school graduates leave
      B. British hospitals are staffed by immigrant doctors
         1. Immigrant doctors from India, Pakistan and other nonwhite Commonwealth countries
         2. Account for more than 40 percent of medical staffs in British hospitals
         3. Trained only temporarily in Great Britain

 III. Lack of incentive
      A. System encourages general practitioners to provide the minimum service
      B. System encourages general practitioners to refer any serious or complicated cases to specialists

 IV. Hospital admission delays
      A. More than 500,000 seek hospital admission at present
      B. Average delay for tonsil removal is twenty-two weeks

Concluding Statement: In reviewing some of the drawbacks of the British system, the United States should think twice before adopting a medical system that is operated almost exclusively by the central government and financed almost entirely out of general tax revenues.

Outline B: Sentence

HOW TO SELECT A VACATION

Thesis Statement: In planning a vacation, one must consider the problems of choice, where to go, how much to spend, and how to get there.

I. There are many spots to choose from in planning a vacation.
   A. There are resorts such as Miami Beach and Las Vegas and tranquil spots such as the Virgin Islands.
   B. There are many big cities which are often visited along with dude ranches.
   C. Instead of staying in one place, you can travel from spot to spot.
      1. From Miami Beach you can visit the Islands.
      2. From Mexico City you can travel to Acapulco.
      3. The resorts of Maine are only a short hop away from Canada.
   D. After you decide where you want to go, obtain a map of the nearby cities of interest.

II. The second problem is that of cost.
   A. The average vacation for two runs about $200 to $300 a week.
      1. A week's camping in a state or national park starts at about $25.
      2. You must also add round trip transportation and other extras.
   B. You can buy a package vacation before you go.
      1. It includes rooms and meals.
      2. You will know in advance how much you will have to spend.

III. Transportation is the third problem in planning a vacation.
   A. Besides driving you can travel by rail, plane, or ship.
   B. A cruise offers a carefree vacation.
      1. Everything is provided.
      2. The ship is your hotel.
   C. Cost varies with the cabin you choose.
      1. The tips are not included in the ship's price.
      2. When paying the tips it is best to give a lump sum at the end.

IV. Consequently it is essential that you plan in advance.
   A. Plan your trip from three to six months in advance.
   B. Package deals are only available certain times of the year.

Exercise 8-2 Filling in the Outline

In the outline form below, you are given the thesis statement and the minor inferences. Using the list of proof details on the following page, fill in the outline. At the bottom of the outline, list the detractors by number.

AN INSTRUCTOR'S MANUAL OF STUDENTS

Thesis statement: Any teacher can identify the unprepared students in a class by the techniques they use to conceal their lack of preparation, and these students can be classified as the excuse experts, the class bluffers, and the students who organize group efforts to harass the instructor.

I. The excuse expert comes in three types: the no-show, the textbook terror, and the one who is without an assignment.

   A.

      1.

         a.

         b.

         c.

         d.

      2.

         a.

         b.

         c.

   B.

      1.

      2.

      3.

      4.

C.

    1.

    2.

    3.

    4.

    5.

    6.

II. The class bluffers also come in two varieties, the verbal and the nonverbal.

    A.

        1.

            a.

            b.

            c.

        2.

            a.

            b.

            c.

    B.

        1.

        2.

        3.

        4.

III. Perhaps the most inventive are the students who participate in group efforts to harass the instructor.

    A.

    B.

        1.

        2.

        3.

    C.

    D.

Concluding statement: Therefore, it is easy for any instructor to spot the unprepared students.
Detractors:

    A. _____

    B. _____

    C. _____

List of Details

1. The nonverbal bluffer is very inventive with gestures.
2. He rustles the pages of his spiral notebook audibly and shakes it to "locate" the homework he said he was up until 2:00 A.M. doing.
3. There are at least four basic excuses.
4. "I really felt that I could accomplish more work at home "
5. I had (a tournament), (a game), (a job interview), (a cross country training flight), (bronchitis), (a jury duty)
6. The no show relies on various excuses.
7. "I left my paper at home."
8. The textbook terror who is determined never to purchase a book, or, if he has bought one, never to bring it to class, has his set of excuses.
9. Some students are creative with excuses.
10. "I left the book in my boyfriend's car, and the car was stolen at the mall."
11. "I can't possibly afford a textbook this month because I am still behind one car payment."

12. "I left my paper at home because I knew that you would have trouble reading it since the printer needed an ink cartridge."
13. "I went to visit my cousin whose ship was in dry dock, and the next morning I woke up and found myself at sea."
14. This bluffer takes superfluous notes to convince the teacher that what is being said is really important to him as well as to the instructor.
15. "My (roommate), (mother), (maid) cleaned my room and accidentally threw the paper away along with all of my notes.
16. He seldom looks up while taking notes; the teacher will assume he is legitimately busy and call on another student.
17. "I had (to go to a wedding), (to take my father to the airport), (to drive my sister to work), (to babysit with my little brother)."
18. "I never read textbooks anyway."
19. The puppy chewed my notebook, and I couldn't read the directions for the assignment.
20. Another kind of bluffer looks excessively bright eyed and attentive so that the instructor will call on someone who is obviously withdrawn, sleeping, or hostile.
21. The student walks into class with a box of kleenex, a box of throat lozenges and whispers to the teacher, "I have a sore throat, and I can't answer any questions in class today because I am singing in a concert tonight."
22. "You didn't say that the assignment was due today."
23. While I was brushing my teeth, I jerked my neck, and I had to go to the emergency room.
24. I had to return home because I forgot my soccer shoes.
25. The verbal bluffers can be identified as the volunteer and the distractor.
26. He always asks a question about a current event or about a subject on which he knows that the teacher is hooked, thus avoiding the issue of being questioned.
27. The distractor will do anything to get the teacher off the subject.
28. He always volunteers quickly for the questions he does know the answers to.
29. He volunteers basic information early in the class so the instructor thinks he is prepared and will look for others to call on.
30. He always asks extraneous questions which makes him look eager for extra information on the subject.
31. The volunteer is chiefly concerned to hide the fact that he isn't prepared.
32. A dedicated non-conformist, he challenges the teacher on every point, thus intimidating the instructor so that he won't be called on.
33. In language classes, he volunteers to translate the first three lines of the assignment—the only ones he has completed.
34. The students organize late teams and operate them in relays so that each day several come in tardy at staggered moments, thus creating problems for the instructor.
35. In the technique known as brainwashing, the students collectively try to convince the teacher that she never gave the assignment.
36. He puts his head down on the desk, pretending he has a headache.
37. The tardy types upset the lecture.

38. The leaders organize mass resistance to handing in homework in order to bring forth lectures on responsibility and the meaning of education.
39. The late teams also cause attendance-taking problems.
40. The evader makes the answer to a question so general that in questioning him more closely, the teacher supplies the answer.
41. The latecomers make it possible for students to insist they didn't get papers handed back at one time or another.
42. The hesitator waits until a bright or enthusiastic student answers the question, then quickly adds, "That's just what I was going to say."
43. The harassment experts organize coughing and yawning extravaganzas which will bring about time-consuming lectures on maturity.
44. I thought that we wouldn't need a textbook this term. I don't use them in my other classes.
45. Then there are those students who for one reason or another do not have their assignments.
46. I needed a vacation.

Exercise 8-3 Writing the Outline

Listed below are forty facts about David Wark (D. W.) Griffith, whose film productions became models for directors all over the world and whose cinematic achievements signified the beginning of the American motion picture as an art form. First, classify the details. Then write a thesis statement. Complete the outline by arranging the sentences in minor inferences and subdivisions. Since only the letter *A* is given under each Roman numeral, you will have to supply the other letters according to the number of supporting details that relate to each minor inference. At the bottom of outline, list the detractors (irrelevant statements) by number.

1. D. W. Griffith never intended to make movies.
2. Billy Bitzer was Griffith's cameraman.
3. In five years, between 1908 and 1913, he directed over 400 films.
4. Not only was Griffith innovative with the camera, but he also was innovative with his actors.
5. Before Griffith, the only acceptable film shot was the full shot, including the full figures of the story's characters as well as the background scenery.
6. By moving the camera's dolly on a track, Griffith was able to film galloping horses, racing wagons, and rushing trains.
7. D. W. Griffith discovered the effectiveness of the close-up.
8. Griffith developed a full series of shooting perspectives.
9. Editing allowed Griffith to switch the story from one time to another.
10. Griffith's greatest film was *The Birth of a Nation,* still controversial today.
11. He became his own casting director and selected actors to play specific roles according to their physical characteristics.
12. Griffith began the Biograph stock company.
13. Griffith's actors were always directed to underact.
14. Billy Bitzer used gauze on the camera lens to soften the facial features of the actresses, especially Mary Pickford.
15. Through the use of cross cutting, Griffith was able to create suspense.
16. Griffith was the first director to focus the camera on an article, such as a letter, a bedpost, a flag, or a mirror, a technique that is common today.
17. He was the first director who rehearsed the actors before filming them.
18. Another innovation was increased length; he went from the one reel film to the two reel one. *The Birth of a Nation* was twelve reels.
19. Griffith's films were among the most expensive to make.
20. Griffith's name was not known until 1912 because directors and actors received no screen credits.
21. Griffith used flash backs, cut backs, and close ups.
22. Griffith turned the camera into an observer of human nature.
23. *The Birth of a Nation* was presented for the first time on March 3, 1915, at the Liberty Theater in New York City.

24. As a director he was not the first person to use the long, medium, and close-up shot.
25. By using the pan shot, a horizontal sweep from left to right, Griffith was able to follow the action of the actor.
26 Editing a film became a standard tool for Griffith.
27. Charles Dickens, the English novelist, also switched the passage of time in his novels.
28. Until Griffith, most directors followed the character from place to place in chronological order; they did not cross cut.
29. Before Griffith, actors and actresses were directed to use exaggerated gestures and dramatic poses.
30. Cross cutting is an editing technique that brings together scenes that have been separated in space and time by switching the scenes back and forth.
31. Griffith introduced the flashback.
32. Griffith was the first to use creative lighting effects.
33. He was the first director to film a scene at night.
34. *The Birth of a Nation* cost $100,000 to make, but it grossed $18,000,000 in a few years.
35. He uses a combination of shadows and beams of light to sustain the mood of a scene.
36. Although Griffith did not discover all of the filming innovations, he was the first director to use the discoveries for dramatic purposes.
37. In some films, Griffith used a whiteout as visible transition from one scene to another rather than a blackout.
38. He was the first to use the close up as an integral part of the film to develop either a character or the plot.
39. Through the use of cross cutting, Griffith was able to create suspense.
40. Early actors thought that rehearsing a scene was a waste of time.

D. W. GRIFFITH

Thesis Statement:

I.

   A.

II.

   A.

III.

    A.

IV.

    A.

Concluding Statement:

Detractors (list only the numbers)

Writing Suggestion: The Analysis Theme

A. Choose a subject from the following list of suggestions. Limit the subject to a level that gives you a topic that can be handled in a multi-paragraph theme of about five hundred to eight hundred words. Construct a formal outline with at least three levels of classification

B. Write your analysis theme from the outline including transitional devices. Suggested subject: traditions, customers at a checkout counter, academic degrees, politicians, job opportunities, disasters, bicycles, robots, races, parades, holidays. **Or:** From the picture below, select a subject that is suggested by one of the subjects in the picture. For example, you might classify children, tourists, birds, or European public squares.

Planning the Classification and Division Paper

Before beginning to write your Classification and Division paper, write a classification chart. Then use the following worksheets to complete the planning of the paper.

Photograph 8.1. (Photo by Stephen Grasso)

Exercise 8-4 Writing a Thesis Statement from the Analysis Chart

Taking your minor inferences from the bottom of your analysis chart, write a thesis statement in which the classifications or divisions are evident.

Thesis:

Limited subject:

Major inference:

Minor inferences:

Exercise 8-5 Making a List of Proof Details

Now make a list of proof details that support your minor inferences.

Exercise 8-6 Classifying the Details

Examine your list and group the entries that have something in common. Then consider:

1. Do you have more classifications than appear in your thesis?
2. If so, would you like to add a class or category to the thesis in the form of another minor inference?
3. If you add another category to the thesis, can you still manage the paper in five hundred to eight hundred words?
4. If you think you have too many categories in your thesis to begin with, decide which one(s) you can omit and still write an interesting paper.

Reminder: When you estimate word count, assume that you are writing full sentences around your list of proof details. The average typewritten page of double-spaced text runs about 225 to 250 words.

Now case the framework for your paper.

TITLE:

Thesis (revised if necessary):

I.

II.

III.

(etc.)

Exercise 8-7 Classifying Details Under Minor Inferences

Now you have a thesis and a framework for a theme. Place the proof details under the minor inferences they will support. Be sure that you have *at least* four substantial proof details for each minor inference.

Thesis:

Minor inference   I.

Proof details   A.

                     B.

                     C.

                     D.

Minor inference   II.

Proof details   A.

                     B.

                     C.

                     D.

Minor inference   III.

Proof details   A.

                     B.

                     C.

                     D.

Reminder: This outline provides for the required three minor inferences. If you have additional minor inferences, include them as IV, V, and so on.

Exercise 8-8 Writing the Introductory Paragraph with Lead-In and Thesis

Write the introductory paragraph.

Exercise 8-9 Using the Critique Sheet to Analyze the Preparation

Select a student from your class to criticize your proposed paper. Tear out Exercises 8-13 and 8-14 and attach to this sheet. You can also use this sheet to criticize your own proposed paper. When you get the papers back (or when you catch your own problems), you can then make any revisions necessary.

Author:

Critic:

Thesis:

1. What is the limited subject?

2. What is the major inference?

3. What are the minor inferences?

   a   Are the minor inferences grammatically parallel?

   b. Can the writer support this thesis within the word limit of the assignment?

   c. If not, can you suggest further limitation?

   d   How many developmental paragraphs are these likely to be?

   e. Are there any thesis problems? (Check page 133 for the kinds of thesis problems and list any you find.)

Lead-in:

1. Is it appropriate for the subject?

2. Does it create enough interest to make you want to read the paper?

3. If not, can you suggest revision?

Proof details:

1. Are there at least four proof details to support each minor inference?

2. Does each proof detail specifically relate to the minor inference?

3. If not, list the proof details which are irrelevant (Example: IID, IIIA, and so on.)

OUTLINE RATING SHEET

	Yes	No
Title		
Appears above the thesis statement	✓	
Indicates contents of paper	✓	
Thesis Statement		
Is the limited subject apparent?	✓	
Is the major inference clear?	✓	
Are the minor inferences clear?	✓	
Are the minor inferences mutually exclusive (do they justify a separate category)?	✓	
Is the basis of analysis clear?	✓	
Body		
Do the minor inferences appear as entries following the Roman numerals?	✓	
Does each supporting proof detail (A, B, C) directly relate to the inference under which it is classified?	✓	
Are there adequate proof details to support each minor inference?	✓	
Is each minor inference developed in proportion to the others?	✓	
Concluding Statement		
Does the statement summarize the paper without introducing additional material?	✓	
Mechanics		
Is the outline form consistent (all topic entries or all sentence entries)?	✓	
Are the entries on each level of classification grammatically parallel?	✓	
Does every A have a B? Does every 1 have a 2?	✓	
Have you followed capitalization, punctuation, and spacing rules for the outline?	✓	

OUTLINE RATING SHEET

	Yes	No
Title		
Appears above the thesis statement		
Indicates contents of paper		
Thesis Statement		
Is the limited subject apparent?		
Is the major inference clear?		
Are the minor inferences clear?		
Are the minor inferences mutually exclusive (do they justify a separate category)?		
Is the basis of analysis clear?		
Body		
Do the minor inferences appear as entries following the Roman numerals?		
Does each supporting proof detail (A, B, C) directly relate to the inference under which it is classified?		
Are there adequate proof details to support each minor inference?		
Is each minor inference developed in proportion to the others?		
Concluding Statement		
Does the statement summarize the paper without introducing additional material?		
Mechanics		
Is the outline form consistent (all topic entries or all sentence entries)?		
Are the entries on each level of classification grammatically parallel?		
Does every A have a B? Does every 1 have a 2?		
Have you followed capitalization, punctuation, and spacing rules for the outline?		

ANALYSIS RATING SHEET

	Poor	Average	Good	Excellent

Outline

_____ Correct form

_____ Complete

Title

_____ Indicates contents of paper

Introduction
Lead-in statement

_____ Interests the reader

_____ Shows relevance to subject

Thesis statement

_____ Limited subject apparent

_____ Major inference clear

_____ Minor inferences clear

_____ Minor inferences mutually
exclusive

Body
Content

_____ Topic sentence with controlling
inference introduces each paragraph

_____ Number of proof details

_____ Quality of proof details

_____ Relevance of proof details

Organization

_____ Pattern of organization evident

_____ Effectiveness of transition

_____ Appropriate language level

| | Poor | Average | Good | Excellent |

_____ Specific word choice

_____ Clear phrasing

_____ Sentence variety

_____ Individuality of expression

Concluding Statement

_____ Summarizes main points of paper

_____ Uses appropriate transition

Mechanics
Manuscript form

_____ Title in capitals

_____ Pagination

_____ Margins

_____ Legibility and neatness

_____ Spelling

_____ Sentence structure

_____ Grammar

_____ Punctuation

_____ Capitalization

_____ Expression of numbers

ANALYSIS RATING SHEET

	Poor	Average	Good	Excellent

Outline

_____ Correct form

_____ Complete

Title

_____ Indicates contents of paper

Introduction
Lead-in statement

_____ Interests the reader

_____ Shows relevance to subject

Thesis statement

_____ Limited subject apparent

_____ Major inference clear

_____ Minor inferences clear

_____ Minor inferences mutually exclusive

Body
Content

_____ Topic sentence with controlling inference introduces each paragraph

_____ Number of proof details

_____ Quality of proof details

_____ Relevance of proof details

Organization

_____ Pattern of organization evident

_____ Effectiveness of transition

_____ Appropriate language level

	Poor	Average	Good	Excellent

_____ Specific word choice

_____ Clear phrasing

_____ Sentence variety

_____ Individuality of expression

Concluding Statement

_____ Summarizes main points of paper

_____ Uses appropriate transition

Mechanics
Manuscript form

_____ Title in capitals

_____ Pagination

_____ Margins

_____ Legibility and neatness

_____ Spelling

_____ Sentence structure

_____ Grammar

_____ Punctuation

_____ Capitalization

_____ Expression of numbers

Stage 9

Definition

1. Learning to Write the Formal Definition
2. Recognizing Errors in Formal Definition
3. Writing Extended Definitions
4. Writing the Extended Definition Paper
5. Recognizing Errors in the Extended Definition
6. Writing the Extended Definition Introductory Paragraph

Your entire purpose in working from Stages 1 through 7 has been to communicate as specifically and as logically as possible. You accomplished your first purpose, to write specifically, by making your proof details concrete. You made your presentation logical by carefully analyzing and classifying your inferences and proof details. You know how to answer the question, "What do you mean by. . . ?" because you know how to supply proof details for your inferences.

Now you will find that you often need another method of precise communication that answers the question, "What do you mean by. . . ?" This method is called *formal definition*. Assume that you are in a group that is having a discussion of equal rights. You might hear any number of terms, such as *radical, conservative, affirmative action plan, sexism, male chauvinism, gray power,* etc. Any number of times during such a discussion, one or another of the speakers may be called upon to explain what he means. He would be asked to "define his terms."

Suppose you were having a discussion about the occult with some people who were fascinated with the subject and with others who were skeptical about it. You might hear such terms as *ESP, aura, seance, levitation, regression, graphology,* and *astrology.* Suppose now that you are a person who is interested in astrology but not very well informed about it. Someone in the group asks you just what astrology is all about. In an attempt to explain, you might reply: "Well, astrology is when you tell things about a person's life by reading the stars."

Examine this statement. Would the other people in the discussion group understand now what astrology really is? Does your definition give an exact explanation? Does it tell them whether astrology is an animal, a vegetable, a mineral, a science, or a parlor game? Does it tell what kinds of things can be told about a person's life or how they can be told? Look at your definition again: "Astrology is when you tell things about a person's life by reading the stars."

The first problem with your definition is that the word *when* does not indicate the class of objects or ideas or processes to which astrology belongs. *When* indicates time. You wouldn't be any better off if you said, "Astrology is where you tell things about a person's life by reading the stars," because *where* indicates location, not a class of things.

The second problem with your definition is the word *things*. *What kind of things* does astrology tell about a person's life?

The third problem with the definition lies in the phrase *by reading the stars. How* does an astrologer read the stars? Someone in the group might recall having seen a picture of a storybook astrologer wearing a pointed hat encircled with figures of the sun, the moon, and the stars; that person might ask you if "reading the stars" is the only way an astrologer works.

Now you need some expertise. You need to know how to write the most exact and useful kind of definition, the **formal definition**.

STEP 1   Learning to Write the Formal Definition

Writing the formal definition involves two operations. First, you, must place the **term** in the **class** to which it belongs. Because you are using classification, the formal definition is also sometimes referred to as a **logical definition.** Second, you must show how the term differs from all other members of the particular class into which you have placed it. This is called the **differentia** because you are differentiating your term from other members of its class. A formal or logical definition, then, has three parts: the term, the class, and the differentia.

Think for a moment about what class astrology belongs to. You will find that it is not an exact science and that it therefore must be classified as a pseudoscience. A pseudoscience is a practice or an art for which there is conjecture but no scientific proof. Other pseudosciences would be palm reading, seances, and tarot card reading. Now you can see why you need the third part of a logical definition—the differentia. You must explain how astrology differs from the other pseudosciences.

STEP 2   Recognizing Errors in Formal Definition

Before you can write a good formal definition, you will need to be able to recognize certain common definition errors:

Circular Definition

Do not repeat the term or a derivative of the term in the differentia.

Example: A radical is a person having radical views.
Correction: A radical is a person who favors fundamental or extreme change, specifically of the social structure.

Nonparallel Grammatical Form

The grammatical structure must be maintained in the sentence pattern of a formal definition. The sentence pattern is:

Subject (noun) + linking verb + subject complement (noun)

Incorrect: Cramming is when a student attempts to learn most of the contents of a course in a day or two.

Discussion: This definition is incorrect because there is no subject complement. The when clause functions as an adverb; it is not the noun or noun phrase needed to indicate the class to which cramming belongs.

Correction: Cramming (noun) is a method of study (noun phrase) in which a student prepares for an examination in a hurried, intensive way for the purpose of learning the contents of a course in a short time.

Improper Classification

A. The class is over inclusive (too broad).

TERM		CLASS	DIFFERENTIA
Incorrect:			
A pig	(is)	an animal	characterized by a long, broad snout; a thick, fat body; cloven hoofs; sexual immaturity; and a weight under 120 pounds.

Discussion: The class *animal* is over inclusive because there are many classifications of types of animals.

Correction:

TERM		CLASS	DIFFERENTIA
A pig	(is)	a young swine	characterized by a long, broad snout; a thick, fat body; cloven hoofs; sexual immaturity; and a weight under 120 pounds.

You may now want to consult several dictionaries and perhaps an encyclopedia or two. Drawing from several general reference sources, you can explain the differentia in the way that would be most clear for your reader Here is the way your one-sentence formal definition for astrology will look:

TERM		CLASS	DIFFERENTIA
Astrology	(is)	a pseudoscience	which claims to foretell the future of human affairs and earthly

events by the study of the relative positions and hence the influences of the sun, the moon, and the stars.

If you wanted to define palmistry, the class would remain the same, but the differentia would have to change:

TERM		CLASS	DIFFERENTIA
Palmistry	(is)	a pseudoscience	in which the palmist reads a person's character or aptitudes, his past and possible future, from the general shape of his hand and fingers and the lines, mounts, and marks of the palm.

Now look at the formal definitions for some other words which many people use without much precision

A neurotic	(is)	an emotionally disturbed person	characterized by excessive use of energy for unproductive purposes to control anxiety, compulsions, or phobias.
Soul	(is)	a slang expression native to the Black culture	which indicates that a person is in harmony with himself and that he expresses in an uninhibited way such intensities of life as joy sorrow, hardship, and brotherhood.
A hot rod	(is)	an automobile	rebuilt or remodeled with a highly improved engine and body design for increased speed and acceleration.

Incorrect:

A draftsman's compass	(is)	an instrument	consisting of two pointed legs connected at one end by a pivot used for drawing arcs or circles and taking measurements.

Discussion: The class instrument is overinclusive because an infinite number of mechanisms are instruments.

> **Correction:**
> A draftsman's compass is a mechanical drawing instrument consisting of. . . .

B. The class is over restrictive (too narrow).

TERM	CLASS	DIFFERENTIA

Incorrect:

TERM	CLASS	DIFFERENTIA
A pig	(is)	a domesticated swine etc.

Discussion: The class *domesticated swine* is overrestricted because it excludes wild pigs.

Improper Differentia

A. The differentia is overinclusive (too broad).

TERM	CLASS	DIFFERENTIA

Incorrect:

TERM	CLASS	DIFFERENTIA
A poet	(is)	a creative writer	who has great imaginative and expressive gifts and who possesses a great sensitivity to language.

Discussion: This differentia includes every kind of creative writer.

B. The differentia is overrestrictive (too narrow).

TERM	CLASS	DIFFERENTIA

Incorrect:

TERM	CLASS	DIFFERENTIA
A poet	(is)	a creative writer	who writes rhymed, rhythmical lines.

Discussion: The differentia is overrestrictive because it excludes poets who write in blank verse, which is not rhymed, or in free verse, which is neither rhymed nor necessarily rhythmical.

> **Correction:**
> | A poet | (is) | a creative writer | who composes verse. |
> |------|-------|-------------|----|

Highly Technical Language

TERM		CLASS	DIFFERENTIA
Dysgraphia	(is)	a transduction disorder	resulting from a disturbance in the visual motor integration of a child.

Discussion: The instructor of children with learning disabilities would be able to understand this definition, but a general audience learning about particular disorders in the learning process probably would not.

Correction:

Dysgraphia	(is)	a learning disorder	in which the child sees or knows what he wants to write but cannot make his motor system carry out his idea; hence, he cannot write correctly.

Exercise 9-1 Writing a Formal Definition

Select three of the following words and write a formal definition for each. Check your definitions against Step 2 to make sure that you have not committed any of the errors in formal definition. Try first to write the definition from your own understanding of the word. Then, check your definitions against those in two different dictionaries.

TERM	CLASS	DIFFERENTIA
1. Disability		
2. Black list		
3. fiend		
4. gothic literature		
5. Docudrama		
6. Chutzpa		
7. dolly		

FORMAL DEFINITION RATING SHEET

Term _____	Poor	Average	Good	Excellent
Completeness (term, class, differentia)				

Faults:

_____ Circular

_____ Class too broad

_____ Class too narrow

_____ Class not grammatically parallel

_____ Differentia too broad

_____ Differentia too narrow

_____ Language too technical

Term _____	Poor	Average	Good	Excellent
Completeness (term, class, differentia)				

Faults:

_____ Circular

_____ Class too broad

_____ Class too narrow

_____ Class not grammatically parallel

_____ Differentia too broad

_____ Differentia too narrow

_____ Language too technical

Term _____	Poor	Average	Good	Excellent
Completeness (term, class, differentia)				

Faults:

_____ Circular

_____ Class too broad

_____ Class too narrow

_____ Class not grammatically parallel

_____ Differentia too broad

_____ Differentia too narrow

_____ Language too technical

STEP 3 Writing Extended Definitions

From scholarly written books to the back panels of cereal boxes, readers can learn more about a single word than they imagined. Usually a word's definition is associated with a standard dictionary; and for most people, this definition, known as the "formal, logical definition," is adequate. However, there are times when the history of the word makes the meaning clearer to the reader. At other times, it is necessary to use another method to explain the meaning of the word. When the definition goes beyond the formal, logical definition and we use other methods to explain the term, we say that we extend the definition; and we call this method *extended definition*. There are ten other ways to define a word. However, when we want to begin to define a word, we do so by defining it with the formal definition.

The Formal, Logical Definition

The formal definition is composed of three parts: The *term* itself; the *class* to which the term belongs; and the *differentia*, which tells how this term differs from all other words in the same class.

Example:

> *A myth is a legendary story about gods, legendary heroes,* or
> (term)　　　　　　(class)　　　　　　　　　　(differentia)
> *superhuman beings which usually concerns the creation of the natural world and its inhabitants.*

Definition by Etymology

The life of a word began with a "parent word," known as its etymology. This type of definition traces the earliest history of the word to find its derivation. In some cases, the "parent word" can be traced to a very early era, showing the evolution of the spelling of the word as it moved from the spoken language to the written one. Sometimes the meaning of the word changed, such as the term *ambition* which in Roman times was restricted to politicians and meant "to go around," obviously to make political speeches. In the dictionary, etymology is enclosed in brackets, and it is often necessary to check the "Legend" in the front of the dictionary for an explanation of the symbols.

> **Examples:**
> *Husband* is derived from the late Old English term *husbunda; hus*, meaning "house," and *bunda*, meaning "owner." The word referred to any man who owned his own home and a few acres of land.
> *Precocious* came from the Latin *prae*, meaning "before," and *coquere*, meaning "to cook," which combined to form *praecoquere*, meaning "to cook beforehand."

Definition by Coined Words or Common Usage

As words evolved some entered the English language with nearly the same meaning as the original one. In other cases, the meaning changed. For example, the "parent word" (etymology) for a broker was the French *brokiere,* which meant "one who opened a cask of wine." Later, because the *brokiere* also became a wine salesman, the meaning changed, and the word entered the English language during the fourteenth century when it then meant "any agent who negotiates contracts for a fee or a commission." Thus, the *origin* is the entrance of the word into common usage in the English language.

Examples:

The term *birth control* was coined by Margaret Sanger, a public health nurse in New York City in 1914.

The term *macadam* originated from the name of John Loudon McAdam, the British engineer who was the first to recognize that a pavement of crushed rock packed into thin layers and bound with asphalt, cement, or tar could support the weight of the traffic.

In the late 1980's the term *grazing* was coined to mean eating tidbits or small delicacies as a substitute for a meal.

Definition by Contrast

At times the meaning of the word becomes clearer to the reader if the writer contrasts it with another word.

Examples:

The fable, unlike the myth, is usually devised to convey some useful lesson and often uses animals as the central characters.

In Spain an *hombre de bigote* symbolized a man who was forceful and who, though firm in his convictions, had spirit; in contrast, today a bigot is somewhat intolerant because he has unchangeable views.

Definition by Description

Another method of extending the formal definition is by a description of the term.

Examples:

The rialto in New York is the area between Fortieth and Fiftieth Streets with its numerous shops and theaters.

A macadam road surface is built up with large rocks as a foundation and covered with small stones that are held together with slag or gravel and bound by cement or tar.

Definition by Synonym

Synonyms are words in the same language which have the same or nearly the same meaning as the term being defined. Many times there will be several synonyms listed for a particular term, but often no two synonyms will have the exact meaning since English is a very forceful language comprised of words having many different shades of meaning. Because of these variations in meaning, it is important to use an exact equivalent of the term being defined.

Examples:
Birth control is also referred to as "family planning" or "planned parenthood."
Reporters such as Robert Woodward and Carl Bernstein who wrote *All the President's Men* while they were reporters for *The Washington Post* preferred to be known as investigative reporters, not muck-rakers.

Definition by Negation

This definition tells the reader what the term is not.

Examples:
A 'moving picture" is not a motion picture. An economic depression is not a recession.

Definition by Using a Quotation of a _____

In some instances another writer's original explanation of the meaning of a word may be useful as well as, perhaps, more colorful. The quotation itself is generally one of the other methods, such as an example, a synonym, or a description. Thus, the definition is said to be a "Quotation of a Description" or a "Quotation of an Example." A writer should select only those quotations that are unusual.

Examples:
H. L. Mencken refers to the colloquial expression *okay* as the "most shining and successful Americanism ever invented."
American journalist Ambrose Bierce described slang as "the speech of him who robs the literary garbage cans on their way to the dump."
English professor Mary Ellen Grasso claims that mirrored or dark sun glasses are "walls that keep the wearer in and the viewer out."

Definition by Process or Growth

This type of definition traces the changes or growth of the word, its meaning and usage, as it came through to modern day.

Examples:
A curfew during the Middle Ages required French peasants to extinguish their fires at a set hour each evening; later the Norman French adopted the word *curfew* as *curfu*, meaning the hour that citizens were to return to their homes; while today *curfew* is a signal for children to go home.

Before the early 1900's, the term *muckraker* had been used only for politicians who "raked up mud" to use against their opponents. Then President Teddy Roosevelt in a speech at the Gridiron Club in 1906 applied the term to the reformers who exposed corruption in business, in politics, and in society.

Definition by Comparison

In this method, the term is compared to another that is, perhaps, more familiar to the reader. At times, the comparison is a loose one that is implied and not stated because the word *like* is not used.

> **Examples:**
> Some people believe that asphalt is tar.
> The Pathe newsreels during the early 1930's and 1940's which appeared as one of the of the "short subjects" in movie theaters were like the short current events now broadcasted on the television networks during the early evening and the late night news programs.

Definition by Example

This method explains a term by giving a specific instance of it.

> **Examples:**
> In earlier times the bridegroom was literally the "bride's groom" because during the marriage feast, which sometimes lasted for several days, he acted as a table waiter to his bride, serving her food and drink.
> One example of a custom is the use of the X at the end of a letter to symbolize kisses, evolving from the medieval legal practice when the sign of St. Andrew, a cross, was required after each signature on important documents to show good faith and mental competence. The sign was kissed to guarantee loyal performance of one's obligation to his client.

STEP 4 Writing the Extended Definition Paper

The length of an extended definition paper depends on the writer's purpose and the reader's needs. A single paragraph may be adequate; on the other hand, the writer may need an entire chapter to explain a particular term. Sometimes an entire book is actually an extended definition of a series of extended definitions.

When you write an extended definition, you have many options. As a brief example of options, ask your classmates what they know about the apparently simple subject of asphalt—since people ride on it every day; and since they hear the term used frequently in the building trades, they ought to be familiar with it. One student may try to describe it in terms of color, texture, or consistency. Another may know where is comes from; still another may tell you where it is used and under what circumstances. One student might try to give a synonym, and another might explain how it differed from other surfacing materials. If you were to assemble all of their comments and do a bit of research yourself, you would find that you could write a good extended definition.

Exercise 9-2 Identifying Methods

After reading the Extended Definition of "Asphalt," fill in the blanks by identifying the method of definition which each sentence represents. At times a sentence may be a combination of methods. Notice that the writer has added a lead-in statement and a thesis which is a generalization about asphalt. His extended definition begins with the formal definition. Notice also that he has used his quotation appropriately in the concluding paragraph. The definitions are numbered so that you can complete Exercise 9-2.

METHODS

1. Formal, logical definition
2. Synonym
3. Description
4. Example
5. Comparison
6. Contrast
7. Negation
8. Coined word or Common usage
9. Etymology or "parent word"
10. Process
11. Quotation

ASPHALT

During the Depression era of the 1930's the Works Progress Administration (WPA) authorized a project for covering the brick paving in American towns and cities with asphalt. Through this project many thousands of people were given work, and millions were introduced to a new and smoother kind of motoring. While many people think of the word *asphalt* as only a road surfacing material, it is much more.

One of the best products in the United States, (1) asphalt is a mineral substance, a dark solid that is somewhat plastic or cementlike, found in natural beds or obtained as a residue in petroleum refining. (2) Before asphalt solidifies, it has a strong odor. (3) The word itself comes from the Middle English *aspaltoun*, which comes from Late Latin *asphaltus*. (4) These in turn came from the Greek *asphaltos*, meaning "binding agent used by stone masons." (5) Asphalt is not tar, although many people sometimes call it that. (6) While asphalt is like tar in its appearance, in that it is a dark, oily, viscous appearance, it is composed of bitumens. (7) Bitumens are obtained from native deposits or as a by a product of petroleum. (8) In contrast tar is composed of hydrocarbons, produced by the destructive distillation of organic substances such as wool, coal, or peat, rather than petroleum. (9) Neither is it only a bituminous surfacing material, sometimes called "black top," used in paving roads, roofing and waterproofing.

In fact, asphalt is much more. (10) It is used to line reservoirs, waste storage ponds, and irrigation canals as well as lining underground pipelines against corrosion. (11) In addition, asphalt is used as an ingredient in varnishes, inks, and paints. (12) Although many people use the word *asphalt* for *macadam*, the words are not interchangeable, for a macadam road is a pavement which consists of crushed rock packed into thin layers with asphalt as the binding agent. (13) Neither is asphalt the same as cement. (14) Cement differs from asphalt in that it is an adhesive consisting of powdered, calcined rock, and clay materials. (15) Asphalt as a road surfacing material came into common use during the 1920's when cars began to dominate the roads and there was a nationwide campaign for building better ones. (16) Asphalt was chosen as a surfacing material because it is relatively stable, and it is not greatly affected by extremes of heat and cold. (17) Also, it "gives" and is less likely to buckle or crack in areas that are subject to the stress of abrupt changes in weather or extremes of weather of one type or another. (18) There is no doubt that asphalt is here to stay. According to the County Highway Commission, "asphalt is a prime material for surfacing roads because it is relatively stable, it is not greatly affected by extremes of heat and cold, and it is easily obtainable." Thus, from road surfaces to roof shingles, varnishes to inks, asphalt may well be one of the best used products in America.

Directions: Identify each of the sentences by writing the method of the extended definition after each number.

1.   10.

2.   11.

3.   12.

4.   13.

5.   14.

6.   15.

7.   16.

8.   17.

9.   18.

STEP 5 Recognizing Errors in the Extended Definition

While the ten methods of extending a formal definition are helpful, they present certain problems if they stand alone as the only definition or if they are used in place of the formal definition. Here are examples of what would happen if you were to use the following types of definition alone:

1. **Example:** An example of a stream of consciousness novel is James Joyce's *Ulysses*.
   Discussion: While examples are excellent ways of illustrating a term, they don't help much if you don't know what the term means in the first place and if you aren't familiar with the example given—in this case, the book. Thus, *stream of consciousness novel* would have to be defined first.

2. **Description:** A discotheque has psychedelic lighting and decorations and very loud music.
   Discussion: The term *discotheque* must be placed in a class of dancing establishments before it can he described in further detail.

3. **Comparison:** A hypocrite is like a pretender.
   Discussion: If you don't have a precise formal definition of **hypocrite,** your reader is not ready to see in what ways he is like a pretender.

4. **Synonym:** A hypochondriac is a malingerer.
   Discussion: No two words in the English language mean exactly the same thing. For instance, a hypochondriac and a malingerer are alike in that both sometimes use illness to escape work or unpleasant duties. But the difference is that the hypochondriac truly believes he is ill, whereas the malingerer only pretends to be ill. Therefore, unless you were to give a formal definition of **hypochondriac** first, the comparison would be incomplete and inexact.

STEP 6 Writing the Extended Definition Introductory Paragraph

The Extended Definition paper, like any other, begins with a lead-in that serves two purposes. First, the lead-in should be interesting enough to attract a reader and to hold his attention; second, it should relate to the subject and lead the reader into the thesis. The thesis should allow the reader to anticipate what supporting details will be used. Notice that in the examples that follow there is a key term in each thesis that signals an extended definition. The key term may be *word, term, expression,* or *phrase.*

Examples:

FEMINISM

There are *Americanism, liberalism,* and *momism*—all coined during the twentieth century. While none of these words was forceful enough to divide Americans, another word coined during the same century has. The term is *feminism;* and since its entrance into the Women's Rights Movement and the English language, it has undergone many abuses.

UNIDENTIFIED FLYING SAUCERS

Ezekiel claimed he saw "the flying wheel," and twentieth century man reported "flying saucers," so named because or their unusual shape. However, the words *unidentified flying object* may be a better term since these UFO's often appear in the other forms.

HOODWINK

During the Civil War the term *hoodwink* was used to mean "blindfold," such as in the *Daily Democrat* newspaper article of July 18, 1863, which reported that "two confederate officers were hoodwinked . . . and conducted to a safe point." However, the term is now used with a much different concept.

Note: In the above example, an obsolete meaning of a word can also be used as the lead-in.

CHILD ABUSE

During the 1870's an organization for the prevention of Cruelty to Animals became interested in the case of a nine-year-old girl from a New York tenement. This case prompted the agency to include in its protection statements, "abuse to children as well as to animals." Yet, today, more than one hundred years later, the subject of child abuse is still being debated as the term takes on additional meanings.

Note: At times, one of the methods of the extended definition is used for the lead-in, such as a coined word or common usage.

The Order of Extended Definition

The order in which you use the types of sentences as proof details to extend your formal definition depends upon their appropriateness to your subject and your own preference. If there is an etymology for a word, it is often helpful to use that first because it reveals the history of the word and the changes it has undergone. It is sometimes useful to give the synonym next because a reader may be more familiar with the synonym than he is with the term itself. If, however, the synonym is more obscure than the original term, it is best not to use it. Description as a method of extending a definition can include size, weight, color, specific details, and composition. The Coined Word or Common Usage is a good method to include, for it explains the actual source, cause, or circumstances connected with the beginning of the word and its entrance into common usage in the English language. Students sometimes confuse etymology and the coined word or common usage; however, etymology refers strictly to the derivation of the word while the other method explains where the object or idea comes from. Process or growth explains the stages from etymology to present object, material, or idea and traces the changes in meaning that the term has undergone. Negation is used when it is useful to explain what the word is not in order to avoid confusion among several terms. Comparison and contrast often follow negation naturally in an extended definition, for the reader can see the term compared to something it is like and then see how it differs from something with which it has been compared. Finally, examples are always helpful because they show specifically how the word is used.

STEP 7 Writing the Extended Definition Theme

You have seen how the formal definition can be extended to a short theme by using some or all of the ten methods of extended definition as proof details. Some subjects, however, lend themselves to longer papers. The paragraphs divide naturally into the kinds of information to be given— perhaps etymology, process and growth, then description, then examples. The student paper which follows, written on the subject of *mob*, is a good example of how a particular term lends itself to extended definition in multiparagraph form. Notice how the student's introductory paragraph consists of the lead- in statement and the thesis. Notice also that the body of the paper begins with the formal definition. Except for those sentences in the introductory paragraph and the topic sentence, the definitions are numbered so that you can complete Exercise 9-3.

MOB

Muckraker, shyster, quack—these words associated with people give an unfavorable image while words such as *compassionate, kind*, and *considerate* give a favorable impression. Some words, like *manners*, are elegant and are linked with elegant people. Other words are vulgar and obscene and are, therefore, associated with vulgar, low-class people. *Mob* is such a word, and the history of the word shows that it has undergone several changes.

(1) A mob is a crowd that is large and disorderly. (2) According to *The American Heritage Dictionary*, "a mob is a society of bodies voluntarily bereaving themselves of reason." (3) The word derived from the Latin *mobile*, meaning "the excitable or fickle crowd," during the medieval period. (4) It was not until the eighteenth century that the British began shortening words in the English language. (5) Among these they developed a new vulgarism, *mob* (Funk 63). (6) This practice of clipping off the ends of words annoyed essayist Joseph Addison, who exclaimed arrogantly, "It is perhaps this Humor of speaking no more than we needs must which has so miserably curtailed some of our words" (63).

The word passed several stages as its meaning changed. (7) In 1691, the uncultured or illiterate members of the lower class were referred to as a *mob*. (8) However, just three years earlier, in 1688, in Australia, the word had no such disorderly implication. (9) It simply meant "a crowd." (10) In later years and in different English-speaking countries, the word *mob* came to mean an organized gang of hoodlums or a crime syndicate. (11) More specifically, it meant a gang of pick pockets working in collusion (OED 559). (12) Eventually, a descriptive term evolved from the word: *swell mob*, which meant a class of pick pockets who dressed stylishly to carry on their occupation

(Onions 1266). (13) A strange obsolete meaning of the word *mob* was "a strumpet," used in 1697. (14) Then in 1712 the word had an altogether different meaning, which may be associated with the meaning in 1697. (15) It simply meant a "neglige attire," a loose garment worn by women during informal occasions (OED 559). (16) However, today this meaning is also obsolete.

(17) Even though *mob* is the usual term when describing an orderless crowd, there are other expressions that mean the same thing. (18) For instance, a rabble is a worthless, purposeless, or despicable crowd. (19) On the other hand, a rough crowd suggests a horde, and a throng implies that the crowd is in constant movement, and (20) a word borrowed from the French, *canaille*, means "the lowest class" (Onions 1266). (21) However, a mob may be rich and influential when dealing with the government, which, of course, depends on the populace or masses, even if they are ignorant or poor, for the practice of their laws. (22) A mob may have a desperate or effective purpose. (23) Usually, a crowd is drawn out of curiosity, but some strong, dominating excitement is needed to create a mob.

(24) Several authors used the term in their writing. (25) Among them is Daniel DeFoe, who, in the book *The True Born Englishman*, used the term mob in derogatory terms. (26) He wrote:

> From this ambitious ill-born mob began, that vain ill-natured thing, an Englishman. (170:12)

On the contrary, Charles Dickens suggested in his novel *The Fat Boy*:

> 'It's always best on these occasions to do what the mob do.' 'But suppose there are two mobs?' suggested Mr. Snodgrass.
> 'Shout with the largest,' replied Mr. Pickwick.' (178:31)

(27) In 1849 Macaulay's *History of English, Volume I* contained a passage that referred to the army as a mob (*Oxford American* 816). (28) Today, while the army may no longer be referred to as a mob, there are other examples of mobs. (29) Concert goers become mobs when they crowd an auditorium to hear their favorite performer. (30) Unruly union-backed factory workers are sometimes referred to as mobs, and even women who crowd department stores during bargain day sales can be considered a mob.

(31) Although the written word *mob* refers to a crowd, it is still an entertaining word because it leaves the description of the crowd to a person's imagination (32). It also lets the reader see people in terms that describe them.

Joe Swails

BIBLIOGRAPHY

DeFoe, Daniel. "Mob." in *The Oxford Dictionary of Quotations*. 2nd ed., London: Oxford UP, 1969.

Dickens, Charles. "Mob." in *The Oxford Dictionary of Quotations*. London: Oxford UP, 1959.

Funk, Wilfred, Litt. D. "Mob." *Word Origins and Their Romantic Stories*. New York: Funk, 1950.

" Mob." *The American Heritage Dictionary*. Ed. William Morris. Boston: Houghton, 1976.

" Mob." *Funk & Wagnall's Standard Handbook of Synonyms, Antonyms, and Prepositions*. New York: Funk, 1947.

"Mob." *The Oxford American Dictionary*. New York: Oxford UP, 1980.

"Mob." *The Oxford Dictionary of English Etymology*. Ed. C.T. Onions. London: Oxford UP, 1939.

"Mob." *The Oxford English Dictionary*. 16 Vols. London: Oxford UP, 1933. Vol 6.

Onions, C. T. "Mob." *The Oxford Universal Dictionary*. Oxford: Clarendon, 1933.

Exercise 9-3 Identifying Methods of Extended Definition

Each sentence in the body of the theme on " Mob" is numbered. Fill in the blanks by identifying the method of extended definition which each sentence represents. Keep in mind that each sentence may illustrate more than one method of extending the definition.

METHODS

Formal Definition

1. Etymology
2. Synonym
3. Description
4. Coined word or common usage
5. Process or growth

6. Negation
7. Comparison
8. Contrast
9. Example
10. Quotation

DEFINITIONS

1. _____

2. _____

3. _____

4. _____

5. _____

6. _____

7. _____

8. _____

9. _____

10. _____

11. _____

12. _____

13. _____

14. _____

15. _____

16. _____

17. _____

18. _____

19. _____

20. _____

21. _____

22. _____

23. _____

24. _____

25. _____

26. _____

27. _____

28. _____

29. _____

30. _____

31. _____

32. _____

Writing Suggestion: The Extended Definition

1. Write a paragraph or a short multiparagraph theme of extended definition. Define any word you choose, but if you have no special word in mind, you might try one of the following: nutrition, bigot, muckraker, lagniappe, dope, philanthropy, prejudice, custom, veteran, buccaneer, fire.

Or: Examine the photographs below. Many images may come to you. Choose a term that comes to mind and use it for your extended definition.

Photograph 9.1. (Photo by Stephen Grasso)

Photograph 9.2. (Photo by Stephen Grasso)

2. Consult at least three dictionaries before writing your extended definition. One should be the *Oxford English Dictionary*. Another should be an unabridged dictionary such as *Webster's Third New International Dictionary*. This would also be a good opportunity to consult a specialized dictionary—there are many of these on a variety of subjects. They are listed in the card catalog of the library under "Dictionaries" by subject. For example, if you choose to define a slang term, you could consult *The Dictionary of American Slang*, ed. Harold Wentworth and Stuart Berg Flexner *A Dictionary of Slang and Unconventional English*, ed. Eric Partridge *Dictionary of American Underworld Slang*, ed. Hyman E. Golding; or the *Dictionary, of Contemporary Usage*, ed. Bergan Evans and Cornelia Evans.

3. Begin your paper with a lead-in statement. If you write only a paragraph, the formal definition will follow the topic sentence; if you write a theme, the formal definition will follow the thesis.

4. Extend your formal definition by using as many of the methods listed below as possible. The order in which you use the methods is up to you and will be determined by appropriateness to the term you are defining.

METHODS

Formal Definition

1. Etymology
2. Synonym
3. Description
4. Coined word or common usage
5. Process or growth
6. Negation
7. Comparison
8. Contrast
9. Example
10. Quotation

5. Your research may include but not be limited to the following: the history of the word, the ways the word is used. other words derived from the term. Use examples and illustrations to explain the definitions

Extended Definition Rating Sheet

Formal Sentence Definition

	Poor	Average	Good	Excellent
Completeness (term, class, differentia)				

Faults:

_____ Circularity
_____ Class too broad
_____ Class too narrow
_____ Class not grammatically parallel
_____ Differentia too broad
_____ Differentia too narrow
_____ Language too technical

EXTENDED DEFINITION

_____ 1. Etymology
      Comment:

_____ 2. Synonym
      Comment:

_____ 3. Description
      Comment:

_____ 4. Coined word
      Comment:

_____ 5. Process or growth
      Comment:

_____ 6. Negation
      Comment:

_____ 7. Comparison
      Comment:

_____ 8. Contrast
      Comment

_____ 9. Example
      Comment

_____ 10. Quotation
      Comment

Process Analysis

1. Directional Process Analysis
2. Informational Process Analysis
3. Learning the Organization for the Process Theme
4. Examining Student Models of Process Themes

Process analysis is a method of explaining how something is made, how it is used, how it is operated, how it is organized, or how it developed. There are two kinds of process analyses, directional or informational.

STEP 1   Directional Process Analysis

A directional process analysis is the "how to do it" kind of process analysis. Everywhere you look, you see this kind of analysis, which is actually a set of directions written in the imperative (command) mood. Consider directions for mounting a smoke detector, for example:

Check with the local fire department about code requirements.

Find a location as close to the center of the ceiling as possible.

Do not select a location near forced air heating or air conditioning ducts.

If the ceiling is sloped, gabled, or high peaked, mount the detector between four and six inches from the highest point in the ceiling.

When mounting the smoke alarm near the center of the ceiling is not practical, find a location on the ceiling four inches from where the ceiling and the wall join.

STEP 2   Informational Process Analysis

While directions instruct a person in the actual performance of a process, the informational description informs the reader about a particular process for the purpose of increasing his general knowledge. There are three basic types of informational process. The first is the historical, which describes how an idea, an event, or an institution came about. In this category you might see such subjects as "How the Pony Express Developed," "How a Bill Becomes Effective Through a State's Legislature," "How a Marketing Campaign Is Planned," and "How Sound Came into the Production of Movie Making."

The second type of informational process describes a scientific, mechanical, or natural process. In this category you might learn about such subjects as "How the Depletion of the Ozone Level Affects Environment," "How a Battery Ignition System Works," and "How Detergent Discharges Affect Natural Waterways."

The third type of informational process is that which describes a logical or organizational process. In this category you would see such subjects as "How a Crime Is Investigated," "How a Sales Campaign is Planned," and "How a Bill Becomes a Law."

Explaining a process clearly and concisely is one of the most difficult forms of analysis. You may recall the times that you have had to follow directions or to assemble a product only to find that certain steps were omitted or obscurely described, causing you untold frustration, loss of time, or even making it impossible for you to complete the process at all. Perhaps you have asked directions to a particular place and have found people so inept at giving directions that you had to stop several times for instructions. You would be equally frustrated in reading an informational process if the writer failed to include all the relevant steps in explaining the sequence of events that led to an historical event; a scientific, mechanical or natural process; or a logical or organizational process.

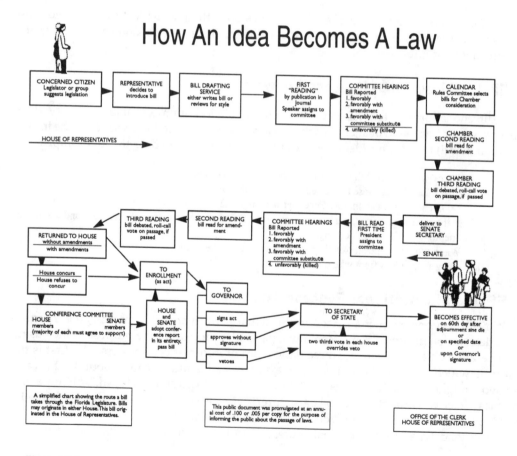

Figure 10.1

Exercise 10-1 Classifying Steps for Process Analysis

Read the simplified chart showing the route a bill takes through the Florida legislature. Then complete the following exercise.

1. How many major steps are there? _____

2. What are they? _____

    _____

    _____

3. Write two different thesis statements:

    DIRECTIONAL: _____

    _____

    _____

    INFORMATIONAL: _____

    _____

    _____

STEP 3 Learning the Organization for the Process Theme

Title

Write a precise, descriptive title that indicates whether the process will be directional or informational.
Example:

> **Directional:**
>   HOW TO SELECT A CAMPSITE
>   HOW TO REPOT AN AFRICAN VIOLET
> **Informational:**
>   LIFTING LATENT FINGERPRINTS
>   DONNING AND OPERATING A SCBA UNIT

Outline

Write an outline. The information given below under BODY will show you the kinds of entries which must appear in the process analysis outline in addition to the thesis statement.

Introductory Paragraph

1. **The Lead-In Statement.** As with other types of themes, the introductory paragraph begins with a lead-in statement, which consists of two parts.
   a. It should contain one or several sentences that explain why you are writing this particular analysis.
   b. It should contain a formal definition which includes, if possible, who performs the process, where it is performed, when it is performed, and why it is performed. An example of the lead-in statement for the directional process analysis "How to Repot an African Violet" follows:

   > As a general rule, most plant lovers find raising African violets a difficult hobby—either they are intimidated by its fragile appearance, or they lack the knowledge to care for the plant. One of the procedures that seems to cause the novices trouble is repotting. There are two areas that seem to create the most problems. First, the novices do not seem to know what to put in the pot to prepare it properly, and second, they are afraid the plant will be damaged in repotting. These problems can be solved by learning how to repot correctly. To repot an African violet, follow these five steps. First, assemble the materials; second prepare the soil; third, prepare the wick pot; fourth, remove the root bound plant; and, fifth, repot the plant.
   >
   > Marcia Frantz

   c. An example of the lead-in statement for an informational process analysis "Donning and Operating a SCBA Unit" follows:

   > It is a fundamental rule in many fire departments that Self Contained Breathing Apparatus (SCBA) be worn while entering a contaminated atmosphere. Failure to wear SCBA could incapacitate firefight-

ers, which could lead to the failure to perform the rescue. The proper donning of this breathing apparatus allows firefighters to enter a contaminated area which could be oxygen deficient, have elevated tem-
peratures and smoke conditions, or be filled with toxic gas. Such equipment includes the air cylinder,
harness, regulator, low pressure breathing hose, and the face piece. There are three steps to putting on
an operating breathing apparatus; first, identifying the parts; second, understanding the use of each part;
and third, putting on the unit.

Joseph Gannon

2. **The Thesis Statement.** In most types of writing, the thesis statement contains the major
    inference and the minor inferences that indicate the categories of discussion. In the
    process analysis, however, the thesis statement lists the main steps of the process. There
    are two considerations for writing the thesis for a process analysis.

General Example: **(informational process)**	(process)_____ includes _____ main steps: first, _____ing the _____; second, _____ing the _____; third, _____ing the _____; and, finally,_____ing the _____.
Specific example:	Repotting an African violet involves five steps: assembling the materials, preparing the soil, preparing the wick pot, removing the root bound plant, and repotting the plant.
General example: **(Directional Process)**	To (process), follow these five steps; first, _____ the _____; second, _____the _____third; _____the _____; fourth, the _____; and fifth, _____ the _____.
Specific example:	To repot an African violet, follow these five steps; first, assemble the materials; second, prepare the soil; third, prepare the wick pots; fourth, remove the root bound plant; and fifth, repot the plant.

If the process cannot be reduced to five main steps, or fewer, do not list all of the steps
Instead, state the total number of steps, mentioning only the first and final step.

General example:	(process) involved ___ main steps, beginning with ____and ending with _____.
Specific example:	In the process of preparing a balance sheet, an accountant follows nine steps, beginning

with obtaining balances from the general ledger of the asset liability and capital accounts and ending with determining if the total assets equal the total liabilities and proprietorship.

Body

1. If the process is one which requires specific equipment and materials, then Roman numeral I will be headed "Equipment and materials." Provide a precise list of all tools, equipment, supplies, and apparatus.

    Vague example: The dive rescue specialist needs five pieces of equipment.

    Specific example: The dive rescue specialist needs an air cylinder, a harness or backpack, a regulator, a low pressure breathing hose, and a face piece.

2. Discuss the individual steps in the order they are listed in the thesis statement. Define the first step in a formal definition or state the purpose of the step if understanding the purpose is necessary to the reader.

    Example of stated purpose not necessary: Each major part of the Self Contained Breathing Apparatus Unit must be identified prior to donning the equipment.

    Example of stated purpose necessary: The diver should check the gauge at the top of the cylinder to determine the air pressure within the cylinder. The cylinder pressure should read 2,250 pounds per square inch. This is done to assure the diver that the tank is full.

3. Define or explain any term which might possibly confuse or puzzle the reader.

    Example: The process of making a blister package consists of placing an object in a blister (plastic bubble), covering it with a card, and sealing both cards together by applying heat and pressure.

4. Define an abbreviation the first time it is used.

    Example: The pilot then determines the TC (true course) of the line; and using the proper procedure, he finds the MH (magnetic heading) of the line.

5. Indicate any special conditions, requirements, preparations, and precautions.

    Example of a special precaution: It is important that the fingerprint tape is pulled up carefully and slowly. If this is done correctly, the tape will not stick to anything but the fingerprint card

    Example of special condition: The medical assistant must also consider the importance of selecting the proper site for injection, the site should be as far as possible from major nerves and vessels and capable of holding a large volume of the injected fluid.

6. Indicate directional process by using imperative mood. Imperative mood gives a command with the subject *you* implied. This means that you will not write "you should" or "you must" for directional process.

    Incorrect example: In planning a cross country flight, first you need to locate the course line and draw it on the chart.

    Correct example using imperative mood: In planning a cross country flight, locate the course line and draw it on the chart.

7. Indicate informational process by using indicative mood The subject *you* is not used.

    Incorrect example: In planning a cross country flight, first you need to locate the course line and draw it on the chart.

    Correct example using indicative mood: In planning a cross country flight, the pilot must locate the course line and draw it on the chart.

    The following guide explains the voices and moods to be used in process analysis.

Imperative Mood

Imperative mood, with the subject *you* implied, is used for giving directions.

Example: The first step in blister packaging is to start the sealer. Take the cord in hand, plug it into a 110 volt outlet, and wait approximately fifteen to twenty minutes for the unit to warm up. While waiting for the unit to warm up, load the blisters with the objects. Then clear off an area around the sealer end place a product in each blister.

Indicative Mood

Indicative mood, active or passive voice, is used for giving information. However, use active voice whenever possible because it makes your writing more direct.

Example of active voice: The first step in blister packaging is to start the sealer. The operator takes the cord in his hand and plugs it into a 110 volt outlet. He waits approximately fifteen to twenty minutes for the unit to warm up. During this time the operator loads the blisters with the objects. He then clears off an area around the sealer and places a product in each blister.

Example of passive voice: The first step in blister packaging is to start the sealer. The cord is taken in the operator's hand and is plugged into a 110 volt outlet. Fifteen to twenty minutes is needed for the unit to warm up. During this time, the blisters are loaded with the objects. An area around the sealer is then cleared off and a product is placed in each blister.

Conclusion

One or more of the following can be covered in the conclusion. Some of the points may already have been covered in the introduction.

1. **Discuss the advantages of the process:**

   Example: Data processing during registration saves both time and money for the college and the students.

2. **Discuss the disadvantages of the process (if any).**

   Example: The only disadvantage to administering an intramuscular injection is that all muscular sites available are very close to major nerves and vessels.

3. **Discuss the effectiveness of the process.**

   Example: Blister packaging best protects the products from the elements, provides an eyecatching display, and protects the merchants from the high incidence of pilferage today.

4. **Evaluate the results of the process.**

   Example: Candles made by rubber molds can be given as personalized gifts, or they can be sold to friends and specialty shops at a profit.

5. **Discuss the importance of the process.**

   Example: Preparing a balance sheet is important because it will accurately reflect the financial condition of a business on a specified date.

6. **Discuss how the process is related to other processes or to other work that is being done or reported on.**

   Example: Blister packaging is related to many other modern packaging processes such as skin packaging and shrink packaging.

STEP 4   Examining Student Models of Process Themes

Following are two themes with their outlines. The first, "How to Repot an African Violet," is written to give directions. The second, "Lifting Latent Fingerprints," is written to provide information. Both themes were written from personal experience.

Directional Process Analysis: Outline

HOW TO REPOT AN AFRICAN VIOLET

Thesis Statement: To repot an African violet, follow these five steps: first, assemble the materials; second, prepare the soil; third, prepare the wick pot; fourth, remove the rootbound plant; and fifth, repot the plant.

I.   Assemble the materials.
   A.   Set aside the rootbound violet.
   B.   Assemble the items for planting.
      1.   Have on hand a wick pot and saucer.
      2.   Make sure that the potting soil is sterile.
      3.   Wash the stones.
      4.   Get the Perlite.
      5.   Get and crush some charcoal.
II.   Prepare the soil correctly.
   A.   Measure the items.
      1.   Use two parts of soil.
      2.   Use two parts of peat moss.
      3.   Use one part of Perlite.
III.   Prepare the wick pot.
      1.   Insert the wick.
      2.   Spread the wick's ends.
   B.   Place the pot in the center of the saucer.
   C.   Add the soil preparation.
      1.   Place in one-fourth inch of stones.
      2.   Put in one-half inch of crushed charcoal.
      3.   Put in one to two inches of the soil mixture.
IV.   Remove the rootbound plant.
   A.   Hold the plant correctly.
   B.   Loosen the plant.
   C.   Ease the plant from the pot.
V.   Repot the plant.
   A.   Position the plant carefully.
      1.   Place the plant in the pot.
      2.   Center the plant.
   B.   Place the prepared soil mixture in the pot.
      1.   Firm the soil.
      2.   Irrigate the soil.

3. Drain the soil.
4. Resoak the soil.

Concluding Statement: The plant lover will understand that following these instructions is not as difficult as it seemed. Done correctly, this process will prevent the plant from being damaged.

HOW TO REPOT AN AFRICAN VIOLET

As a general rule, most plant lovers find raising African violets a difficult hobby—either they are intimidated by its fragile appearance, or they lack the knowledge to take proper care of the plant. One of the procedures that seems to cause the novice trouble is repotting. There are two areas that seem to create the most problems: first, the novice does not seem to know what to put in the pot to prepare it properly, and, second, the person is afraid the plant will be damaged in repotting. These problems can be solved by learning how to repot correctly. To repot an African violet, follow these five steps: first, assemble the materials; second, prepare the soil; third, prepare the wick pot; fourth, remove the rootbound plant; and fifth, repot the plant.

First, assemble the materials necessary to repot the African violet. The various materials needed are one rootbound African violet, a wick pot with a saucer, potting soil, sterile rocks, crushed charcoal, Perlite, water, scissors, and a spoon. The wick pot can be made out of clay or plastic with a hole in the center of the bottom. The wick is spun glass or any organic material approximately four inches long. The potting soil mixes come already sterilized, and some soil is especially formulated for African violets. The Perlite is granulated styrofoam, which is used to hold moisture and keep the soil light and porous. The potting soil, crushed charcoal, sterile stones, and Perlite can be purchased at any nursery. Once the materials are assembled on the table, go on to the next step.

In the second step, prepare the soil by putting one part Perlite, two parts peat moss, and two parts potting soil in a pile on the table; then mix the ingredients until they are well blended. After the soil is prepared, proceed to the third step, preparing the wick pot.

To set up the wick pot for planting, insert the wick through the hole in the bottom of the pot, and leave two inches inside and two inches outside the pot. Spread both ends of the wick so that they will absorb water evenly and place the pot in a saucer. Cover the wick inside the pot with a one half inch layer of sterile stones, a one-fourth inch layer of crushed charcoal, and a one to two inch layer of potting mixture depending on the size of the pot. Now you are ready for the fourth step, removing the rootbound plant.

To remove the rootbound plant from its container, slip a hand under the rosette of leaves with a palm against the soil surface. Hold the plant's crown between the fingers; then turn the pot upside down and tap it sharply against the table edge. Try to ease the plant from its container. The root ball and the soil should end up in the palm of the hand, and the plant leaves should be against the back of the hand. If it is not free, slide a knife around the inside edge of the pot until the plant is loose. Now the plant is ready for repotting.

The last step is repotting the plant into the new pot. Center the plant on the mound of potting mixture. If the plant sits too low in the pot, lift it out and add more soil; if the plant is too high, lift it out and take away some soil. After the plant is positioned correctly in the center of the pot, fill in and around the root ball with additional mixture. Rap the bottom of the pot sharply on the table to settle soil, and firm the soil with a spoon or the fingers and thumbs. Fill the container with soil to within one half inch of the pot's rim; this allows space for the water when you top water your plant. Thoroughly soak the newly-potted plant with water at room temperature and let it drain. Resoak the soil to get rid of any air bubbles that may still be in the mixture. Place the plant aside in a place with indirect lighting, and keep it barely moist for the next few weeks. Now the repotting is finished.

In conclusion, the pride and sense of accomplishment that the plant lover feels when enjoying the beautiful African violet will far outweigh the effort put into raising the plant. Also, the plant lover will understand that following these instructions is not as difficult as it seemed. Done correctly, this process will make sure the plant will not be damaged.

Marcia Frantz

Informational Process Analysis: Outline

LIFTING LATENT FINGERPRINTS

Thesis Statement: The lifting of latent fingerprints includes six main steps: beginning with assembling the materials and ending with placing the fingerprint tape on the card.

I. Gathering the necessary materials
    A. A flashlight
    B. Dusting powder
    C. Fiber-glass bristle brush
    D. Items to lift the print
        1. Fingerprint tape
        2. Fingerprint card
II. Locating the print
    A. From a smooth surface
    B. With a flashlight
III. Dusting the print
    A. Using the bristle brush
    B. Placing the brush in the powder
    C. Dusting the print
IV. Taping the print
    A. Pressing the tape on the print
    B. Checking for defects
        1. Air bubbles
        2. Wrinkles

V. Removing the tape
    A. Removing in opposite direction as placed
    B. Pulling up slowly and carefully
VI. Preserving the print
    A. Placing the print on a card
        1. On a three-by-five card
        2. On either side
        3. In the same manner as applied
    B. Positioning the tape and pressing it down

Concluding Statement: Most people do not realize that this type of fingerprint can easily be lifted and transferred; however, patience and skill is needed.

LIFTING LATENT FINGERPRINTS

There are two kinds of fingerprints, latent and inked. Inked fingerprints occur when ink is applied to the fingers and the fingers are then pressed onto paper. These fingerprints are usually obtained during the arrest process and are kept on file for future reference. Latent fingerprints are hidden fingerprints that are found on various items with smooth surfaces. As the name implies, latent fingerprints are not readily visible. The lifting of latent fingerprints includes six main steps, beginning with assembling the materials and ending with placing the fingerprint tape on the card.

Before any latent fingerprint can be lifted, there are certain materials that must be obtained. The materials needed in this process include a flashlight, dusting powder, a fiberglass-bristled brush, fingerprint tape, and a fingerprint card. Once these items have been gathered, locating the latent print can begin.

Latent fingerprints can only be lifted from smooth surfaces; therefore, the fingerprint expert can only look on those surfaces for prints. Using a flashlight is the easiest method to locate such prints. The beam of the flashlight, held at an angle across the surface, will show the oil ridges by the finger. This is the place where the dusting powder will be applied.

The first step in dusting a fingerprint is to place the fiberglass-bristled brush in the powder, which is usually black. A very small amount of powder is placed on the brush, for too much powder will cause the print to be unreadable. The next step is to place the powdered brush lightly on the surface over the print and briskly twirl the brush between the thumb and first two fingers: the lighter the touch is, the better the results are. The print can always be dusted again if sufficient powder was not applied the first time. As soon as the print can be seen, it is time to apply the fingerprint tape over the surface of the print.

Fingerprint tape is a clear cellophane tape, similar to household cellophane tape; but it is two inches wide instead of half an inch wide. The tape is pulled off from the spool, usually four to five inches at a time. One edge of the tape is pressed onto the surface about one inch before the fingerprints begin. The tape is then slowly and carefully pressed onto the surface across the print at least one inch past the trailing edge of the visible fingerprint. The tape is then checked for any air bubbles or wrinkles. If they are found, they are pressed out before the tape is lifted from the surface. Once this has been checked, it is time for the tape to be removed from the surface.

The fingerprint tape is removed in the opposite direction from which it was placed on the surface. The last end that was put down is the first end that is lifted up. It is important that the tape is pulled up slowly and carefully. If this is done correctly, the tape will not stick to anything but the fingerprint card.

In the last step, the tape must be placed on a card. The fingerprint card is a three by five-inch card that is shiny on one side and dull on the other. The tape is placed on either side of the card in the same manner that it was applied to the smooth surface. The edge of the tape is placed on one edge of the card and slowly pressed down until the entire piece of tape is pressed onto the card. As soon as this step has been completed, the latent fingerprint has been preserved indefinitely.

The process of lifting latent fingerprints is not difficult. Most people do not realize that this type of fingerprint can easily be lifted and transferred; however, patience and skill are needed. There is no second chance when dealing with latent fingerprints.

Joe Swails

PROCESS ANALYSIS RATING SHEET

	Poor	Average	Good	Excellent

OUTLINE

_____ Correct Form

_____ Complete

TITLE

_____ Indicates directional or
process analysis

INTRODUCTION

_____ Interest statement

_____ Explains why process is being
described

_____ Gives formal definition of
process

_____ Thesis statement

_____ If no more than five main steps,
lists steps

_____ If more than five main steps, mentions
number of steps and lists only first
and last.

BODY

_____ Lists materials and equipment needed

_____ Discusses main steps in order as listed in thesis

_____ Defines or explains unfamiliar terms

_____ Defines abbreviations first time used

_____ Uses indicative mood

	Poor	Average	Good	Excellent

CONCLUSION

_____ Discusses advantages of process

_____ Discusses disadvantages (if any)

_____ Discusses effectiveness of process

_____ Evaluates results of process

_____ Discusses importance of process

_____ Mentions how process is related to other similar processes

PROCESS ANALYSIS RATING SHEET

	Poor	Average	Good	Excellent

OUTLINE

_____ Correct Form

_____ Complete

TITLE

_____ Indicates directional or
process analysis

INTRODUCTION

_____ Interest statement

_____ Explains why process is being
described

_____ Gives formal definition of
process

_____ Thesis statement

_____ If no more than five main steps,
lists steps

_____ If more than five main steps, mentions
number of steps and lists only first
and last.

BODY

_____ Lists materials and equipment needed

_____ Discusses main steps in order as listed in thesis

_____ Defines or explains unfamiliar terms

_____ Defines abbreviations first time used

_____ Uses indicative mood

	Poor	Average	Good	Excellent

CONCLUSION

_____ Discusses advantages of process

_____ Discusses disadvantages (if any)

_____ Discusses effectiveness of process

_____ Evaluates results of process

_____ Discusses importance of process

_____ Mentions how process is related to other
similar processes

Writing Suggestion: The Process Analysis Theme

A. Select one of the topics listed below. Following the guideline in Step 3, write first the outline and then the process theme.

General Topics
> Planning a hiking trip, trip to a foreign country, political campaign, etc. Selecting a used car, a college or university, an apartment. Planning a career.

For the business person
> Balancing a checkbook
> Programming a computer
> Starting a business

For the do-it-yourselfer type
> Soldering an electrical connection
> Tuning a motor
> Refinishing furniture
> Painting a house
> Restoring an antique
> Building a _____

For the hobbyist
> Building models (cars. trains, airplanes. ships)
> Making stained glass panels
> Collecting (cars, badges. stamps, coins, shells)

For the medical assistant
> Preparing a porcelain filling
> Taking X-rays
> Administering CPR
> Assisting the doctor in the _____ procedure

For the pet lover
> Training an animal
> Showing an animal

For the political scientist
> Campaigning for a political candidate
> Taking a survey

For the sleuth
> Apprehending a suspect
> Tracing a missing person

For the outdoorsman
> Pitching a tent
> Selecting a campsite
> Hunting with a bow and arrow
> Fishing for _____
> Scuba diving

B. The photographs on this page and the next illustrate two different processes in photography: taking pictures and mounting them. Write a process analysis about any one of the various stages of photography.

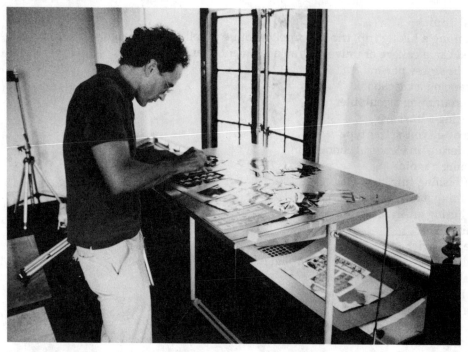

Photograph 10.2. Photographer John Perino mounts photographs for placement in a portfolio. (Photo by Stephen Grasso)

Photograph 10.3 (Photograph by Stephen Grasso)

Stage
11 | Comparison and Contrast

1. Using Comparison and Contrast for Evaluation
2. Comparing and Contrasting for General Knowledge
3. Using Analogy as Loose Comparison
4 Writing the Thesis for the Comparison/Contrast Theme
5. Structuring the Outline for the Comparison/Contrast Theme
6. Examining Student Models of Comparison/Contrast Theme

When you discover the similarities between two or more objects, ideas, institutions, or people, you are analyzing by comparison. When you discover the differences, you are analyzing by contrast. As with any kind of analysis, when you compare and contrast a set of subject, you are increasing your store of knowledge.

STEP I Using Comparison and Contrast for Evaluation

Comparison and contrast is most commonly used for practical purposes of evaluation. Analysis by comparison and contrast helps you to make decisions about what products to buy, what decisions to make, and what actions to take. Suppose, for example, that your family was planning to buy a motor home for a summer tour of the United States. You volunteered to help them select one. One of the first details that you need to know about making a logical analysis by comparison and contrast is that all of the items or subjects under consideration must be in a comparable class. If your family was on a limited budget, you certainly would not start comparison shopping by considering a Bluebird or a Prevost with a Jayco. The Bluebird sells for $300,000 and Prevost sells for about $150,000 while the Jayco costs about $35,000. Instead you would probably compare the Jayco with the Honey and the Coachman since they are all in a comparable price range. Once you have established the likenesses, your main concern would involve the contrasts. Thus, you would be likely to select such points of difference, as standard features, the use of space, the size, the availability of parts, the number of service centers available across the country, and the initial price compared to the features. A comparison and contrast analysis, then, involves a set of subjects (two or more) and a number of points of comparison or contrast. Most people, no matter what their interests or their occupations, often find it necessary to make comparison/contrast analyses in order to gain additional knowledge.

STEP 2 Comparing and Contrasting for General Knowledge

In addition to evaluation as a very practical reason for comparison and contrast analysis, comparison and contrast can greatly increase your store of knowledge in two ways:

1. You may compare and contrast two subjects, both of which you know something about and both of which are of interest to you. Analyzing the two subjects on selected points of comparison or contrast, or both, you reveal basic principles or ideas which can broaden your knowledge and inform your reader. Many people, for instance, think of communes as a recent development in America; they do not realize that communes are very much a part of America's history. The Shakers, for example, had a segregated religious commune near Albany, New York, as early as 1776. Then by 1826, the Shaker religion with its commune spread westward to eighteen states. On the other hand, the Brook Farm commune, an experimental farm at Roxbury, Massachusetts, from 1841 to 1847, was not segregated, and it encouraged group members to become manual laborers in an attempt to make the commune self sufficient. Over a century later, the commune concept arose again in the 1960's with B. F. Skinner's Walden II experiment at Twin Oaks, Virginia. A writer interested in the development of communes could profitably compare and/or contrast a combination of these. The points of comparison/contrast that would give a revealing picture would be basic ideology, initial money pledged, method of work distribution, cultural and religious activities, marriage and child rearing practices, and relationship to the community at large.

2. You may compare and contrast two subjects, one of which is known and one of which is relatively unknown, in order to make the unknown subject more understandable. Suppose, for example, that while reading an article about England, you learned that Scotland Yard was a branch of England's Criminal Investigation Department (CID). Your government professor mentioned that the CID is parallel in many ways to our FBI; but that, in fact, the CID is the most well-known and highly respected investigation department in the world. Here is a case where you could learn a great deal about an unknown in terms of the known. An extremely informative paper would result from a comparison/contrast analysis of the FBI and the CID on the following points: established purpose, services offered to other agencies, departments within each organization, types of investigations conducted, personnel structure, and personnel selection methods.

Regardless of the set of subjects you use in comparison and contrast analysis, the *class* in which you place those subjects is determined by your particular interest. Suppose that within a city limit there were two or three five acre tracts of undeveloped land for sale. If you were the city planner in charge of recreation and preservation, your special interest would lead you to classify these parcels of land as park and recreation areas. In this case your points of comparison and contrast in recommending a purchase to the city commissioners would be the cost to the city, the location in relation to public transportation and density areas, the natural resources already present, the cost of developing the land, and the tax rates. On the other hand, if you were a housing developer, your interest would lead you to classify these parcels of land as high density profit parcels. In selecting one parcel of land to recommend for purchase by your corporation, your points of comparison and contrast would be zoning possibilities; initial cost; proximity to schools, churches, and stores; and the cost of developing the land.

Exercise 11-1 Classifying Sets of Subjects

Put two of the following sets of subjects in a particular class, and then give a few points of comparison or contrast for each set.

Example:

Set: Acrylic paints and oil paints
Class: Artist's materials

Points of comparison:
    A Both are effective media
    B. Both have wide color range possible

Points of contrast:
    C. Drying time differs
    D. Texture achieved differs

Sets of subjects

1. Set: Single parent family vs. the traditional family
   Class:

   Points of comparison:

   Points of contrast:

2. Set: Community colleges vs. four-year universities
   Class:

   Points of comparison:

   Points of contrast:

3. Set: Living in an off-campus apartment vs. living in a college dormitory
   Class:

   Points of comparison:

   Points of contrast:

4. Set: A film vs. the novel
   Class:

   Points of comparison:

   Points of contrast

241

Exercise 11-2 Choosing Sets for Comparison/Contrast According to Interest

A. Choose two sets of subjects of interest to you. Be sure each set of subjects is in the same class. (Whales and sharks won't work because one is a mammal and one is not.)
B. Then state at least three points on which you would compare or contrast your subjects. You may wish to use only comparison or only contrast here.

Example:

Set: Studio Standard by Panasonic vs. Hitachi
Class: VCR's

Points of comparison:
   A. Cost
   B. Size
   C. Cabinet finish

Points of contrast:
   D. Availability of the number of pre-set channels
   E. Quality of tone
   F. Availability of programming

1. Set:

   Class:

   Points of comparison:

   Points of contrast:

2. Set:

   Class:

   Points of comparison:

   Points of contrast:

STEP 3 Using Analogy as Loose Comparison

Up to this point you have seen that subjects suitable for comparison/contrast analysis were in the same general class and were of equal importance. However, another kind of comparison involves subjects that are not of the same general class or importance. This is a loose comparison known as *analogy*. Analogies are not strict or exact comparisons; but in using them, the writer attempts to make his reader see the similarities between two subjects in a striking, thought-provoking, or unusual way.

One of the most common analogies currently used is the comparison of a computer to a human brain. Obviously, one is a natural object and one a man-made object; they are, however, loosely comparable in that both are capable of planning, computing, and producing results. A general science teacher might resort to analogy in order to enlighten his class about the structure of the human eye by comparing it to a camera. He would explain that the similarities lie in their reactions to light, their methods of receiving images, their methods of focusing light image, and their methods of limiting light reception.

This kind of analogy is often used for teaching purposes. Another form of analogy, the **figure of speech,** is often used for illustrative and artistic purposes. In these figures of speech, called similes and metaphors, a person or an object or even an abstraction is likened to something outside of its own class. The writer thus attempts to sharpen the reader's understanding of a complex idea, to increase his sensory perception, or to make him see a new image.

A **simile** indicates comparison by use of the words **like** or **as.** For example, the poet Langston Hughes would say, "A dream dries up like a raisin in the sun." The user of a simile that is a cliche would say, "He shot out of there like a bullet."

In a **metaphor** the comparison is implied. The expression "The ship plowed the sea" implies that the ocean is a vast field and that the ship will cut through it as a tractor does the earth. Adjectives can also form metaphors; for example, one hears such expressions as "a bittersweet experience," " the camera's eye," "an A-frame building," "the baby is a little imp," "passing the acid test," and "the head of the household."

Sophisticated writers often extend analogies to a paragraph or more; poets, obviously, use the device extensively. However, because analogy is primarily imaginatively illustrative rather than strictly logical, you will be concerned in your next paper with strict comparison and contrast. In other words, you will be choosing a set of two subjects and three or more points of comparison, contrast, or comparison/contrast for the purpose of making an evaluation or increasing your general knowledge.

STEP 4 Writing the Thesis for the Comparison/Contrast Theme

Subjects can be treated either by comparison or by contrast alone, or by a combination of both comparison and contrast. Your choice depends upon the point you are trying to make and the scope of your paper. The thesis must clearly indicate which method you are using. You will recall that the thesis for the analysis paper states the limited subject, the major inference, and the minor inferences which indicate the categories of development. The thesis statement for the definition paper is a generalization about the word to be defined. The thesis statement for the process paper introduces the process and mentions the major steps to indicate the categories of development.

Comparison and contrast is a complex type of analysis because it involves not just one, but a set of two or more subjects which are then compared, contrasted, or compared and contrasted on at least two, and usually more points. The thesis statement, then, must be carefully set up so that the reader knows exactly what to expect. Here are some examples of thesis statements for comparison/contrast analysis:

1. **Method:** Comparison
   Subject: Lifestyles
   Thesis Statement: The lifestyles of the baby-boom generation is similar to that of their parents in their move to the suburbs, in their selection of careers, and in their weekend activities.
   (The writer uses three points of comparison.)
2. **Method:** Contrast
   Subject: Physical Fitness Machines
   Thesis Statement: Soloflex and the Dax Fitness Machine differ in respect to size, special features, and available accessories.
   (The writer chose three points to contrast.)
3. **Method:** Contrast
   Subject: Automobiles
   Thesis Statement: At the time that the American public first became aware of an oil shortage, Toyota sold more automobiles than did General Motors by providing the public with an automobile that was fuel efficient, with a smaller vehicle, and with a better quality product that needed fewer repairs. (The writer discusses three points of contrast.)
4. **Method:** Comparison/Contrast
   Subject: Mountain Bikes
   Thesis Statement: For the beginning bicycle rider, it is possible to purchase a good entry-level bike for under $350, which compares favorably with the more expensive ones in the construction of the frame, the types of rims, the gear and brake components, and the seat-posts and saddles, but it will differ in performance and durability. (The writer chose four points of comparison and two points of contrast.)
5. Suppose you choose a subject which, for your particular purposes, you want to treat exclusively by comparison, and yet you want to anticipate your readers' awareness that there is, after all, a basic difference between your set of subjects. You can handle the thesis statement like these:
   Method: Basically comparison
   Subject: Outlines
   Thesis Statement: Writing an outline for a theme is slightly different from writing one for a speech, but the process is similar in that the writer works with the beginning stage, the organizational stage, and the final stage. (The writer may mention some contrasts but will work on similarities primarily.)
   Method: Basically comparison
   Subject: Leisure activities of two countries
   Thesis Statement: Although Red China and the United States differ in their political philosophies, their selection of leisure activities for school children are similar at summer

camps, at school, and at public gymnasiums. (The writer mentions the difference and then moves to the similarities.)

6. Similarly, if you have a subject which you want to treat exclusively by contrast yet there are obvious similarities between the sets involved, then you can handle the thesis accordingly:

   a. **Method:** Basically contrast

   Subject: Bunker gear

   Thesis Statement: Although there has always been some type of protective clothing for firefighters, bunker gear for today's firefighter differs from that of the fireman of the past in respect to the fabrics used, the gear's resistance to fire, and its overall body protection. (The writer acknowledges that firefighters have always had protective clothing, but the writer will focus on the differences of the gear worn today.)

   b. **Method:** Basically contrast

   Subject: Automotive manufacturers

   Thesis Statement: According to his autobiography, Lee Iacocca was president for both the Ford and Chrysler companies; but when he left Ford Motor Company to become president of Chrysler, he found profound differences in Chrysler personnel organization, in provision for policy formation, and in financial structure. (The writer may mention a few similarities, but the main purpose is in explaining the contrasts.

STEP 5 Structuring the Outline for the Comparison/Contrast Theme

In the kinds of themes you have written up to this point, you have seen that there is really only one way to write an outline and that the major points of your discussion, indicated by Roman numerals, are dictated by the order of points made in your thesis statement. However, because in the comparison/contrast theme you are dealing with a set of two or more subjects and any number of points of comparison and contrast, you have two options for organizing the outline.

The Block Method of Outlining

The first method is called the *block method* because you present your first subject and then discuss in order each point of comparison and/or contrast you plan to make. Next, you present your second subject and discuss in turn the corresponding points of comparison and/or contrast. This is a simple method of organization; and it is effective if you have a readily understood set of subjects, and the points of comparison and contrast are relatively few and uncomplicated. This method would not be too effective, however, if you had many points of comparison and contrast that contained statistics, complicated details, or technical information. By the time your reader reached the second "block" of your paper, which discussed your second subject in the set, he would be inclined to forget much of the information that had been presented about your first subject in the first block.

Here is an example of an outline for a comparison/contrast analysis developed in block form:

> **Method:** Comparison and contrast
> **Type of Outline:** Block
> **Title:** Vacations: By Air or Sea?
> **Thesis Statement:** Air travel and sea travel are similar in that they achieve the ultimate objective of the tourist; but they vary with respect to cost, duration, itineraries, and special features.
>
> I.   Air travel
>   A. Costs
>   B. Duration
>   C. Itineraries
>   D. Special features
>
> II. Sea travel
>   A. Costs
>   B. Duration
>   C. itineraries
>   D. Special features

The Alternating Block Method of Outlining

The **alternating block method** of outlining involves setting up the major categories by points of comparison and/or contrast rather than by the subjects to be compared and contrasted. This method is usually preferred when there are a number of points to be compared and contrasted or when detailed information is included under the points to be compared and contrasted.

Here is an example of an alternating block outline form:

> **Method:** Contrast
> **Type of Outline:** Alternating Block
> **Title:** Air Cooled and Water Cooled Engines
> **Thesis Statement:** When purchasing a car, people should be aware of the differences between air cooled and water cooled engines before they make a decision. Although these two types of engines are both four cycle internal combustion motors, they differ with respect to parts, maintenance, and performance.

I.   Parts
    A. Air cooled engines
    B. Water cooled engines

II. Maintenance
    A. Air cooled engines
    B. Water cooled engines

III. Performance
    A. Air cooled engines
    B. Water cooled engines

Block and Alternating Block Outlines: Same Subject

Now you can look at a block outline and an alternating block outline on the same subject Notice that in the block form the subjects are the entries for the Roman numerals; the points of comparison and contrast are the capital letters.

On the other hand, in the alternating block outline, the points of comparison are the entries for the Roman numerals, and the two subjects of the set are then entered alternately as capital letters A and B.

In the following block outline about the Seminoles and Cherokees, there are only two major paragraphs, one which discusses the Seminoles and then one which discusses the Cherokees.

In the alternating block outline, there are four major paragraphs in the paper; each paragraph discusses in detail the differences between the two tribes one point at a time.

Notice that whether the block or the alternating block form of outline is used, the thesis and the concluding statements remain the same.

SEMINOLE AND CHEROKEE INDIANS

Thesis statement: Although the Seminole and Cherokee Indians live on reservations, their life styles differ with respect to tribal customs, financial earnings, living quarters, and feelings toward white men.

BLOCK
- I. SEMINOLE
  - A. *Tribal customs*
  - B. *Financial earnings*
  - C. *Living quarters*
  - D. *Feelings toward white men*
- II. CHEROKEE
  - A. *Tribal customs*
  - B. *Financial earnings*
  - C. *Living quarters*
  - D. *Feelings toward white men*

ALTERNATING BLOCK
- I. *Tribal customs*
  - A. SEMINOLE
  - B. CHEROKEE
- II. *Financial earnings*
  - A. SEMINOLE
  - B. CHEROKEE
- III. *Living quarters*
  - A. SEMINOLE
  - B. CHEROKEE
- IV. *Feelings toward white men*
  - A. SEMINOLE
  - B. CHEROKEE

Concluding statement: Although the Seminoles and the Cherokees are considered the same by most Americans, they do differ in many respects.

Exercise 11-3   Converting from Block to Alternating Block Outline

Convert the block outline to alternating block form.

SITE-BUILT HOMES VS. MOBILE HOMES

Thesis statement: People who are moving to a new area or who are preparing to retire most often make a decision whether to buy a site-built home or to purchase a mobile home. The prospective buyer should consider carefully the differences in initial building costs, grounds maintenance, building upkeep, and safety factors.

BLOCK   ALTERNATING BLOCK

I.   Site-built homes

    A.   Initial building cost

    B.   Grounds maintenance

    C.   Building upkeep

    D.   Safety factors

II. Mobile homes

    A.   Initial building cost

    B.   Grounds maintenance

    C.   Building upkeep

    D.   Safety factors

Concluding statement: Unless the buyer weighs these factors, he may make a hasty decision that he will regret in the future.

STEP 6 Examining Student Models of Comparison/Contrast Themes

Following is an outline in alternating block form written by a student who selected as her subject the differences in two revolutions.

Method: Comparison
Type of Outline: Alternating Block

TWO REVOLUTIONS

Thesis statement: The similarities in the American and Russian revolutions involve the methods used in gaining the support of the majority, the tactics used, the kinds of outside help obtained, and the final outcome of these revolutions.

I. Methods used in gaining support of majority
  A. Americans
    1. Emphasized dislike of rule by foreign monarch
    2. Protested taxation without representation
    3. Offered Continental Congress solution
  B. Bolsheviks
    1. Organized against oppressive rule by Czar Nicholas II
    2. Rallied against starvation among the peasants
    3. Proposed solution of soviets
II. Tactics in war
  A. Americans
    1. Planned underground
    2. Demoralized enemy
    3. Used surprise attack (Battle of Trenton)
  B. Bolsheviks
    1. Planned underground
    2. Demoralized enemy
    3. Used surprise attack (St. Petersburg uprising)
III. Outside help obtained
  A. Americans
    1. Used French arms
    2. Used French military aides
    3. Used French navy
    4. Took advantage of France's war with England
  B. Bolsheviks
    1. Used German revolutionary literature
    2. Used German arms
    3. Used German funds
    4. Took advantage of Germany's hostility with Czarist Russia
IV. Final outcome
  A. Americans
    1. Political changes

    a. Defined central government's powers
    b. Created interstate commerce
    c. Extended territory by Northwest Ordinance
  B. Bolsheviks
    1. Political changes
      a   Overthrow by Czar
      b. Government by Lenin
    2. Economic and social changes
      a. Peasants gained farmland
      b. Workers gained control of factories
      c. Workers controlled local soviets

Concluding statement: Though Americans look at the Communist movement as an evil of today's world, they must remember that the ultimate purpose of the American and the Russian revolutionaries was the same—to obtain a better standard of living and a better way of life for the people of their respective nations.

TWO REVOLUTIONS

Although the ideological differences between America and Russia are constantly stressed, a study of the revolutions of both nations reveals some remarkable similarities. The likenesses in these two revolutions involve the methods used in gaining the support of the majority, the tactics used, the kinds of outside help obtained, and the final outcome of the revolutions.

In gaining the support of the people, both the American and Bolshevik revolutionaries took advantage of the people's hatred toward their rulers. The American colonists disliked being ruled by a monarch in another land. Their major complaint was that they were being taxed but had no voice in local affairs. As a result, the Continental Congress offered the angry colonists a solution—a republic in which every citizen had a voice in national affairs. Similarly, in Russia the working classes were discontent with the oppressive rule of Czar Nicholas II. The peasants were starving while the Czar and his family dined extravagantly and indulged in countless luxuries. Consequently, the Bolsheviks also offered a solution—a classless society in which all men would be treated as equals.

Once the two revolutionary groups accepted the ideological solutions, they employed similar tactics in their revolutions. Both American and Russian leaders went underground to plan the war against the oppressors. Both revolutionary groups used methods to demoralize the enemy in attempts to slow him down. The Americans constantly harassed the already weary British troops with war cries and stealthy night raids on british camps. The Bolsheviks used propaganda to demoralize the enemy. Such slogans as "Peace, bread, and land" made the weary Czarist soldiers more anxious to leave their posts. Both revolutionary groups used the element of tactical surprise to defeat the foe. This is exemplified by the Americans in the Battle of Trenton and by the Russians in the uprising in St. Petersburg.

In addition to using similar tactics, both revolutionary groups sought the help of foreign countries. The American Revolution was supported by French arms, French military aides, and the French navy. Because the French were at war with England at the time, they felt that any loss for the English was a French gain. In a similar manner, German funds, arms, and revolutionary literature helped the Bolshevik cause. Germany was fighting a war with Russia, and any collapse of the Russian political structure would very possibly end this war.

In the outcome both the American and the Russian revolutionaries won important political and social changes. In America the people for the first time had a voice in the nation's affairs. In the summer of 1787, a new government was framed when representatives met in Independence Hall. At this convention, the powers of the central government were clearly defined and the states were given specific powers and control over their own government. During this period the Constitution of the United States was formed. In addition to political gains, economic changes led to international trading for the United States. Rather than import goods from Europe, Americans were urged to buy products manufactured at home. In addition, the Northwest Ordinance of 1787 created a new territory for expansion. In Russia the peasants began to have control of their country. Once the Czar was overthrown and the new Russian government headed by Lenin was formed, the peasants were given control of the farmland for a short period of time. Meanwhile, economic and social changes brought about the control of the factories by the workers. In addition to controlling the factories, the workers played an important role in the local soviets.

Though Americans tend to look at the Communist movement as an evil of today's world, they should remember, however, that the ultimate purpose of both the American and the Bolshevik revolutionaries was the same—to obtain a better standard of living and a better way of life for the people of their respective nations.

Following is an outline, also in alternating block form, on the similarities between two countries, Bolivia and India. After listening to a guest lecturer, a visiting educator from India, an international student suggested similarities between the two countries. You will notice that the paragraphing for this paper differs from others in the text. A major point may be subdivided into more than one paragraph. Still the same principle applies for a paragraph: each paragraph must have a topic sentence.

BOLIVIA AND INDIA

Thesis statement: Although Bolivia and India have many differences, they are similar in their forms of government, their system of education, their distribution of people, and the diversity of languages spoken.

I   Forms of government
    A. In Bolivia
        1. Has a democratic government
            a. Constituted in 1925
            b. Formed by parliament, supreme court, and a president
        2. Conducts popular voting
        3. Centralizes government in LaPaz
    B. In India

      1. Is a Federal Republic
        a. Constituted in 1950
        b. Formed by parliament, cabinet, president, and prime minister
      2. Holds popular elections
      3. Centralizes government in New Delhi

II. Systems of education
  A. In Bolivia
      1. Legislation required attendance
        a. For those age seven to fourteen
        b. For those under twenty-one who are illiterate
      2. Free education
      3. The university system
        a. Those that are public
        b. Those that are private
  B. In India
      1. Mandated attendance
        a. For those age six to fourteen
        b. For the adult illiterate
      2. Free education
      3. The university system

III. Distribution of people
  A. In Bolivia
      1. In large urban areas
      2. In specific regions
      3. In rural areas
        a. On farms
        b. In mining camps
  B. In India
      1. In large urban areas
      2. In rural areas

IV. Diversity of languages spoken
  A. In Bolivia
      1. Language spoken in the highlands
      2. Other predominate languages
      3. Official language
  B. In India
      1. Number of diverse languages spoken
      2. Official language
      3. "Associate language"
      4. Reorganization for language unity

Concluding statement: In the case of Bolivia and India, the countries that colonized them, Spain and England, determined their similarities.

BOLIVIA AND INDIA

Many cultures have much in common, especially when they are in close proximity. Such is the case between the European countries, Spain and Portugal and Yugoslavia, France, and northern Italy. As a result, it is believed by many that similar cultures have to be in adjacent areas, but this opinion is not always true. In fact, in recent years countries that have similar cultures and that once were colonies are alike in another way. They have won their freedom. Such is the case of India, that got its freedom from England, and of Bolivia, that got its freedom from Spain. Yet, even though these countries were thousands of miles away, their way of life remained constant; and in some instances are similar to one another. Although it is apparent that Bolivia and India have many differences, they are similar in their forms of government, their systems of education, their distribution of people, and the diversity of the languages spoken.

One of the legacies that remained from the countries that conquered and colonized both Bolivia and India was their system of governments. In fact, their form of governments is very similar. For instance, Bolivia has a democratic government. In 1825 it was constituted as the "Democratic Republic of Bolivia." Furthermore, the government is formed by the legislature, the Chamber of Deputies and the Senate; the president, who is head of the government and chief of state; and the Supreme Court. Moreover, the president, as well as the members of the legislature, is elected by popular vote. In addition, the government is centralized in La Paz, the capital.

Likewise, India is a democratic country. The country's government, constituted in 1950, is a Federal Republic that has a parliament-cabinet type of government, similar to that of Bolivia, which is presided over by the prime minister who is appointed by the president. There are two legislative bodies: the lower house, the House of the People; and the upper house, the Council of States. Members of both houses are elected by the adult voters, with the exception of 12 of the 250 members of the Council of States, who are appointed by the president because of special achievements in arts, letters, science, and other fields. On the other hand, the president, who is only a ceremonial head of state, is elected by the legislature for a five-year term. The prime minister, however, is the leader of the political party that has the most seats in parliament. Like that of Bolivia, the government is centralized in the capital New Delhi. However, there are many similarities than just Bolivia's and India's forms of government, for they have similar educational systems.

Because the percentage of illiteracy is still very high, both countries have enacted legislation to strengthen their education systems. For example, in Bolivia there are two centralized and distinct public school systems. There is one for rural children and one for all others. The educational system in Bolivia requires that all children between the ages of seven and fourteen attend school. Those under twenty-one years of age who are illiterate are also supposed to attend school. However, this law is not enforced in the rural areas because Bolivia has few teachers and schools and because many school-age children are needed at home. Still 80 percent of the present children attend primary school for at least two years, and 35 percent of the high-school-age students attend high school. Bolivia has eight public universities, financed through taxes. Education is free for all of those students who qualify through an entrance examination. There are also private institutions that charge monthly tuition, the equivalent of ten dollars in American money.

The Indian constitution has a similar required educational program. All children between the ages of six and fourteen receive free education, and like Bolivia, India does not have enough schools or teachers; and throughout the country schools are very crowded. About 62 percent of those between the ages of six and eleven and 22 percent of those between twelve and fourteen are enrolled in school. Yet, India has the same problems as does Bolivia. Children from poor families must go to work instead of school. Nevertheless, India continues to support programs for the illiterate adult; as a result, a rising literacy rate has resulted. Nearly all of the schools are public; only five percent are privately owned. Since India's independence, the number of universities and colleges has more than doubled. These universities are very inexpensive, charging, in some instances, only one and a half dollars (in American money) each month. As in Bolivia, an entrance examination is required in India for admittance to a university. Despite existing problems, both countries continue to develop education programs to reduce illiteracy.

Although the population of India is much larger than that of Bolivia, the distribution of people in the different areas is similar. Their populations are not equally distributed throughout either country, but there are three classes: the wealthy, the middle, and the poor In both countries there is a higher percentage of people living in the rural areas. For instance, in Bolivia two out of every three live in the highlands and only about 27 percent of the population live in large urban areas; two-thirds of the population live in or near the cities on the western plateau and the other third live near Cochabama, along the slopes of the Cordillera Real. The lowland regions, which cover seven tenths of Bolivia, are sparsely populated. However, the rural areas, which also have the greatest concentration of poor, are the most populated. Although two-thirds of the Bolivians are farmers, only about two percent of the land is cultivated because the farmers, mostly Indians, will not leave their ancestral homes and cultivate the richer farm lands in eastern Bolivia. Since mining is Bolivia's most important industry, two out of every one hundred workers are miners. Unfortunately, these Bolivians who live on farms or in mining camps still have few comforts of life, if any.

Likewise, India has the greater percentage of its population in the rural areas. The urban areas have only 20 percent. The caste system is still quite evident in the rural areas; however, in the cities there are three distinct classes, the upper class, the middle, and the poor, with 65 percent of those belonging to the poor class. The rural population accounts for 15 percent craftsman and 85 percent farmers. There are 20 percent of the population living in urban areas and 80 percent in the rural areas. However, more than one-third of those who live in the city have migrated from villages. The highly populated regions are the Gangetu Plain in the north and the coastal strips along the side of the southern peninsula, but areas that have low density are the jungles, the mountains (the Himalayas), and the Thar Desert. Because many villagers leave the overcrowded rural areas to look for work in the cities, the population of India's cities has more than doubled. It is evident that both countries have similar population distribution.

Because of the great diversity of ethnic groups that form each of the countries, more than one language is spoken even though there are official languages. Half of the people in Bolivia are Indians and speak in their own dialect, and there are four language groups. Aymaran is spoken in the highlands, Quechuan and Guaranis in the lowlands and in the major cities, and a native dialect among those primate forest groups living in parts of the lowlands that are not accessible. However, the official language is Spanish; and although some of the Indians speak Spanish, they prefer to speak only the Indian dialect. However, Spanish is widely spoken in the urban areas by both the Indians and the mestizos (mixed Indian and European), for it is the accepted language of politics, education, and business.

In the same way, India's people speak more than one language. Although there are about 140 languages, or major dialects, there are four language groups in India. However, Hindi is the official language. English, a secondary language, is the common language among most educated Indians. Like Bolivia, those who speak the official or secondary language usually have the best jobs in government, science, and industry. Still some of India's best literature is written in a language other than Hindi or English. The constitution does recognize fifteen languages, including English; for if English were eliminated, the country would be cut off from the world. Usually Indians who speak a similar language live in the same state, for it was in 1956 that the government reorganized the states according to the language group spoken. Once more the similarities between Bolivia and India are evident.

Sometimes countries that are thousands of miles away from each other may be more similar than those countries that are adjacent. Obviously distance may not always account for differences in political systems, in educational policies, in the distribution of their populations, or in the number of languages spoken. In the case of Bolivia and India, the countries that colonized them, Spain and England, determined their similarities.

Writing Suggestion: The Comparison/Contrast Theme

1. The following is a list of suggested subjects for comparison, contrast, or comparison/contrast theme. If you prefer, choose a subject from your own area of interest.

   Marriage customs
   Part-time jobs
   Presidents
   Governments
   Holidays
   Careers
   Editorials
   Countries
   Artists
   Music

Or: Study the photograph on page 247. Select a set of subjects suggested by the photograph and write a comparison/contrast paper.

2. After you have selected your set of subjects, decide upon at least three points of com-

parison, contrast, or comparison and contrast.

3. Develop your thesis according to the guidelines in Step 5. Make sure that the thesis clearly indicates whether you are using comparison, contrast or both

4. Construct your outline and indicate type of outline—block or alternating block.

5. If your outline indicates that your theme might exceed the word limitation suggested by your instructor, then consider eliminating one or more of the points of comparison and/or contrast.

6. Use appropriate transitional devices in your theme: *similarly, likewise, similar to, just as, in a like manner,* for comparison; and *in contrast, however, but, nevertheless, on the other hand, still, unlike, different from, opposite to, on the contrary,* to indicate contrast.

Photograph 11.1 (Photo by Stephen Grasso)

COMPARISON/CONTRAST RATING SHEET

	Poor	Average	Good	Excellent

OUTLINE

_____ Indicates block or alternating block

_____ Indicates comparison, contrast or C/C

_____ Complete

_____ Correct form

INTRODUCTORY PARAGRAPH
Lead-in

_____ Interests reader

_____ Shows relevance to subject

Thesis statement

_____ Subject sets apparent

_____ Points of comparison/contrast clear

BODY
Content

_____ Topic sentence with points of comparison/
contrast introduces each sentence

_____ Number of support statements

_____ Quality of support statements

_____ Relevance of support statements

Organization

_____ Pattern of organization evident

_____ Effectiveness of transition

	Poor	Average	Good	Excellent

Style

_____ Appropriate language level

_____ Specific word choice

_____ Clear phrasing

_____ Sentence variety

_____ Individuality of expression

CONCLUDING PARAGRAPH
Manuscript Form

_____ Title in capitals

_____ Text double-spaced

_____ Pagination

_____ Margins

_____ Legibility and neatness

_____ Spelling

_____ Sentence structure

_____ Grammar

_____ Punctuation

_____ Capitalization

_____ Expression of numbers

COMPARISON/CONTRAST RATING SHEET

	Poor	Average	Good	Excellent

OUTLINE

_____ Indicates block or alternating block

_____ Indicates comparison, contrast or C/C

_____ Complete

_____ Correct form

INTRODUCTORY PARAGRAPH
Lead-in

	Poor	Average	Good	Excellent

_____ Interests reader

_____ Shows relevance to subject

Thesis statement

_____ Subject sets apparent

_____ Points of comparison/contrast clear

BODY
Content

	Poor	Average	Good	Excellent

_____ Topic sentence with points of comparison/
contrast introduces each sentence

_____ Number of support statements

_____ Quality of support statements

_____ Relevance of support statements

Organization

_____ Pattern of organization evident

_____ Effectiveness of transition

	Poor	Average	Good	Excellent

Style

_____ Appropriate language level

_____ Specific word choice

_____ Clear phrasing

_____ Sentence variety

_____ Individuality of expression

CONCLUDING PARAGRAPH

Manuscript Form

_____ Title in capitals

_____ Text double-spaced

_____ Pagination

_____ Margins

_____ Legibility and neatness

_____ Spelling

_____ Sentence structure

_____ Grammar

_____ Punctuation

_____ Capitalization

_____ Expression of numbers

Stage

12

Cause and Effect

1. Reasoning from Causes to Effects
2. Reasoning from Effects to Causes
3. Writing the Thesis Statement for Analysis by Cause and Effect
4. Recognizing Pitfalls in Causal Analysis
5. Recognizing Cause and Effect Analysis in Research

"Why can't I save any money?" "Why do I always get my papers in late and lose a letter grade?" "Why do students drop out of school?" "Why are students in medical school deciding to switch careers?" "Why does every car I buy cost me so much in repairs?" Don't you hear yourself and other people ask at least some of these questions from time to time?

While these are questions, they are also statements of effects; and they are important questions because the results affect the quality of your life. If you could analyze the causes that bring about these effects, you could eliminate some of the problems which make your life confusing, uncomfortable, or otherwise not as satisfactory as you would like it to be.

In the realm of public experience as well as personal experience, there are hundreds of questions that concern causes and effects. These questions, too, directly and indirectly affect people's lives. "What are the long term consequences for firefighters who ingest fumes of methacrylic acid?" "What are the effects to office personnel as computers have revolutionized office efficiency?" "What is the real cost of credit to purchase a car?" "Why is there not a total management program for the Great Lakes?" "Have robots displaced factory workers?" "Why are medical malpractice suits on the increase?" "Why are children with AIDS barred from attending classes with their classmates?"

In order to answer any of these questions, you need a systematic and logical method to investigate the causes that produce these effects. This method is analysis by cause and effect. Your starting place, of course, is with the subject itself, but there are two reasoning approaches to analysis by cause and effect.

STEP I Reasoning from Causes to Effects

A. You can start with a set of observable circumstances, and with sufficient data you can arrive at a conclusion which is stated in the form of a possible or predictable effect. The subject of child abuse is a case in point. A great deal of research has been conducted recently on the types of child abuse, the kinds of adults who do the abusing, and the kinds of children who are abused. The reason for this research, of course, is that the problem of child abuse is becoming an increasingly serious one in the United States. Here is a given set of circumstances:

> Johnny is three years old.
> He is a middle child.
> The boy is highly active.
> His parents are under thirty years of age.
> His mother suffers from feelings of rejection.
> Johnny's father was overdisciplined and was severely beaten by his own parents when he was a child.
> Johnny's mother has difficulty coping with her everyday household duties and with the management of three children who are under four years of age.

A possible effect of this set of circumstances is that Johnny might be an abused child Researchers on the subject would predict that Johnny is a possible candidate for child abuse because there are so many factors in his life that correlate with those of abused children.

B. You can start with a set of circumstances (causes) and draw a verifiable conclusion (effect). A set of circumstances about an elementary school child who stutters illustrates this approach to analysis by cause and effect. Since it is estimated that over 1.5 million of our elementary school children stutter, much research is concerned with this problem. Here is the given set of circumstances concerning David, age eight.

> David has certain physiological problems.
> He has abnormal movements of two muscles in the middle ear.
> He also has badly misaligned teeth.
> He has an unusually high and narrow hard palate.
> David has some psychological problems.
> He has been upset since the birth of his baby brothers.
> His other brothers and sisters speak for him.
> His parents place great emphasis on David's speech patterns and constantly correct him.
> His parents are involved with many projects and do not demonstrate a great deal of affection for David.
> A verifiable effect is that David is a stutterer.

STEP 2 Reasoning from Effects to Causes

"Why" questions begin with the effect. The natural question when discussing effects is, "What caused this?" In this kind of causal analysis, you can begin with an observable conclusion (effect) and work back to the cause or the causes.

Assume that an elementary school counselor received the following report from David's teacher:

> David, age eight, has become a behavior problem in his second grade classroom. He is uncooperative in most activities, he disrupts the class, he has occasional temper tantrums, he displays convulsive physical movements, and he refuses to communicate verbally.

If the counselor is to help David, she must first find all of the causes that might be contributing to his behavior problem; hopefully, she may find the basic or primary cause that leads to these observable effects. The counselor must ask questions of those persons who are in a position to observe David. Thus, she asks questions of David's teacher, his doctor, the school psychologist who has already seen him, and his parents. Here is the list the counselor compiles which helps to lead her to the cause of David's problems:

From David's teacher

> David is uncooperative in class activities.
> He has never mastered basic phonetic skills.
> He wants constant attention while others are speaking.
> During reading sessions, he must be isolated from class so that the other children will not be disturbed by his disruptive behavior.
> He refuses to communicate orally; when he does try to do so, he stutters.
> The other children laugh at him.
> In place of speaking, he uses convulsive movements such as blinking his eyes, contorting his face, and jerking his hands and legs.
> However, he will partake in singing or enacting a role in a playlet; when he does so, he does not stutter.

From the school psychologist:

> Game playing with David indicates that he is an anxious child.
> David displays some hostilities that are inappropriate to the situation.
> David will enact little "roles" with a normal speech pattern.
> David stutters in normal conversation.

From David's doctor

> David has teeth that are misaligned and badly spaced.
> He has a hard palate that is unusually high and narrow.
> He has an abnormal movement of two muscles in the middle ear.

From David's parents:

> The birth of his baby brother made him jealous.
> His mother says that his father often severely reprimands him.
> His mother says that other children supply words for him when he stutters.

> Both his parents correct his speech when he talks.
> His father says that David's mother dominates the boy.

The school counselor, after consultation with David's teacher, school psychologist, family doctor, and parents, comes to the conclusion that this child's stuttering originates from a combination of physiological and emotional circumstances and that the stuttering consequently causes a chain of behavioral effects. Having determined why David is a stutterer and what the effects of the problem are, the counselor can now recommend action to be taken by David's classroom teacher, by his parents, and by the school speech therapist to whom she will refer the child.

In summation, then, there are two methods of reasoning using cause and effects:

> **Induction:** When you begin with a set of observable data which lead into a predictable or verifiable conclusion (effect), you are using *inductive* reasoning.
>
> **Deduction:** When you begin with an observable conclusion (effect) and lead away from that conclusion by supplying a set of pertinent contributory proof details, you are using *deductive* reasoning.
>
> **Deduction and Induction Working Together:** Notice that David's teacher sent the counselor a report which was stated in the form of a series of conclusions about David's behavior in class. The counselor then began to collect from other sources, facts, and observations about David. Working inductively from this set of facts, the counselor drew the deduction that David's problems grew primarily from the fact that he is a stutterer.

STEP 3   Writing the Thesis Statement for Analysis by Cause and Effect

Suppose that David's counselor was presenting her findings in a formal case study of David. The opening of her report would consist of a thesis statement as follows:

> Consultation with David S.'s teacher, school psychologist, family doctor, and parents reveals that his stuttering is caused by a combination of physiological and emotional circumstances and that the stuttering is primarily responsible for his behavioral problems in the classroom.

The thesis statement for analysis by cause and effect is similar to the thesis statement for analysis by classification and division because it has a major inference and minor inferences.

> **Major inference:** Stuttering is primarily responsible for David's behavioral problems in the classroom.
>
> **Minor inferences:** The stuttering is caused by physiological and emotional circumstances.

Exercise 12-1   Working from Causes to Effects

From your own experience or observation, give a list of circumstances (causes) that lead up to a verifiable conclusion (effect).

Exercise 12-2   Working from Effect to Cause

From your own experience or observation, state an effect and list the possible circumstances (causes) that could be responsible for that effect.

STEP 4   Recognizing Pitfalls in Causal Analysis

You have studied analysis by classification and division, by process, by definition, and by comparison and contrast. But analysis by cause and effect is perhaps the most difficult because of the several pitfalls to a logical and thorough analysis. You will need to familiarize yourself with these problems in cause and effect reasoning.

1. **Hasty generalization:** There are few males in the nursing profession today because females are better at tedious, repetitive tasks and are more sympathetic than are men.

   Discussion: History, mistaken assumptions, stereotyping, prejudice, pay scales, and many other causes enter into this situation.

2. **Either/Or fallacy:** America: Love it or leave it.

   Discussion: Somewhat akin to hasty generalization in that such reasoning fails to take account of more than one cause; this kind of reasoning assumes only two alternatives for coping with a country's ills. Worse yet, it fails to take account of any causes of the ills.

3. **After this, therefore because of this:** Permissive child raising is common in affluent communities. Senseless vandalism is sharply rising in these affluent communities. Therefore, permissiveness causes vandalism in children.

   Discussion: Formally called *post hoc ergo propter hoc* fallacy, or *post hoc* for short, this kind of reasoning involves being misled by time sequence in establishing the cause of an effect.

4. **Insufficient cause:** Jean-Paul does not express himself well verbally at kindergarten because he comes from a bilingual family.

   Discussion: Some research does indicate that children raised in a bilingual home have expression problems in the early grades. But there may be other reasons for Jean-Paul's problem. He could have a hearing impediment, he might be uninterested, he might have a low maturity level, or he might be anxious in a new school situation. This problem of reasoning from insufficient cause is also akin to hasty generalization.

5. **Mistaking the nature of a cause:** Herman falls asleep every day in English class; it is obvious that he is bored.

   Discussion: Herman's teacher attributes his sleeping to boredom; actually Herman is recovering from mononucleosis.

Exercise 12-3 Recognizing Pitfalls in Causal Analysis

From your own experience or observation, supply an example for each of the problems in cause and effect reasoning.

1. Hasty generalization

2. Either/Or fallacy

3. Post hoc fallacy (after this, therefore, because of this)

4. Insufficient cause

5. Mistaking the nature of a cause

The Thesis Statement

The lead-in and the thesis for the Cause and Effect paper vary little from those of other rhetorical modes. The key words, however, for this paper are *causes, effects; reasons, results.* Notice that in each example, the key words are italicized for you.

Lead-In and Thesis (No Minor Inferences Stated)

Airplanes are used today more than ever before as a safe, fast, and comfortable way to travel. People trust airlines with their lives everyday, trusting the Federal Aviation Administration to certify that the planes have been maintained and that they are mechanically free from hazardous conditions. Nevertheless, there were sufficient *causes* discovered by the FAA to explain why 273 persons had to die on a DC-10 before the airline made any changes.

Throughout history there have been many outrageous events and many controversial issues. Some events are termed "fatal errors" while other seem to have numerous causes. An analysis of the attack on the USS Stark in which 37 sailors were killed indicates that there were several major *causes.*

Lead-In and Thesis Statement (With Minor Inferences Stated)

While birth control has become widely accepted by women today, it is alarming to see the large number of sexually active teenagers who fail to use contraceptives. As a result, unwed teenagers face the loss of an education, increased dependency on welfare, and an increase in physical and psychological problems.

STEP 5   Recognizing Cause and Effect Analysis in Research

You are probably aware by now that most causal analysis involves moving out of the area of personal experience and moving into the area of research. Right now you can give yourself a little practice in causal analysis (and possibly gain some insight into yourself as well) by working up a cause and effect paragraph on one of the questions presented in the opening of this chapter. For instance, you might find out once and for all why you can never get your papers in on time, if that's your particular problem.

However, as you work through Part 2 of this book, you will be writing a limited research paper that will be concerned with one aspect of a social, economic, or political problem in America. Subject matter of this nature cannot be investigated without careful attention to causes and effects, and such investigation cannot be undertaken without careful training in the basics of library research. You will receive this training in Part 2, and the writing suggestions dealing with cause and effect analysis will be delayed until after you have had this training. By examining the model on page 369 of Part 2, you can see how one student used cause and effect analysis in her paper "Anorexia Nervosa. "

In working through the various stages of this book, you have been working with expository methods one at a time. In working with an extended definition, you saw how mixed expository methods work together to communicate information to a reader. The experienced writer who is dealing with extensive exposition of a subject uses a combination of all the expository methods.

Depending on the subject you choose, your research paper will include most of the expository methods you have studied—analysis by classification and division, definition, possibly process analysis, comparison and contrast, and, of course, analysis by cause and effect. But what makes the research paper different from a simple theme? In addition to the fact that you use mixed expository methods, you will present not only the problem, but also the possible solutions to the problem.

STEP 6   Writing the Cause and Effect Paper

John Dunne enters college with no definite career plans in mind although he is interested in the medical held. He has heard that doctors earn hundreds of thousands of dollars each year; and there is no doubt in his mind that they do, judging from his own medical bills within the past year. He decides to investigate the medical field as a possible career and as his subject for a research paper. While reading the first substantial article on the subject, he discovers that a number of doctors have left the profession, and he wonders why. He then decides to pursue this problem. He finds that applications to medical schools have dropped 26 percent since 1975 and that schools are anticipating an additional ten percent drop. John does a computer search and finds a number of sources. He checks two: one in the June 29,1987, issue of *Newsweek* entitled "Med Schools Learn Humility" and one in the 1994 *Occupational Outlook Handbook.* He photocopies the articles, reads them analytically, underlining or highlighting those portions of the article that deal with causes and effects and annotates those portions with subject headings that summarize the information on the note card.

Writing Note Cards for the Cause and Effect Paper

First, the student writes a bibliography card for each article he reads. He cites causes and effects and makes sure that he writes specific topic heads.

> *Examples:*
>
> Vague topic head:
>   Reasons for dropout: financial
> Specific topic heads:
>   Reasons for dropout: cost of tuition
>   Reasons for dropout: lack of scholarships
>   Reasons for dropout: lack of federal loans

By writing specific topic heads instead of vague ones, the student will be able to classify his note cards easily by the major and minor inferences when he is ready to write the outline. In fact, the outline will depend upon the notes, and it will not matter from what source the information will have come. For instance, his outline may begin to take the following shape:

I. Reasons for fewer applications to medical schools
   A. Increased cost of education
      1. Cost of tuition $20,000 or more a year
      2. Lack of scholarships
      3. Fewer federal loans
   B. Lack of academic scholarship by students
      1. Poor high school preparation
         a. In physical science
         b. In reading discipline for studies
      2. Little self discipline for studies
         a. Rejection of traditional values
         b. Adherence to "me" generation values

II. Reasons for dropping out of medical schools
   A. Fear of AIDS
   B. Specific concerns
      1. Working conditions
         a. Sixty hours a week or more
         b. Twenty-four hour shifts
      2. Neglect of family
      3. Lower salary
         a. In comparison to business
         b. In comparison to investment banking
      4. Increased debt loads of $33,000 to $66,000 at graduation
   C. Cost of medical malpractice insurance
   D. Shift towards group malpractice insurance
      1. Result: loss of autonomy
      2. Result: drop in salary

As the student continues to research the subject, he will keep in mind the fact that he will add information to the notes he has already written; and he will often use the same topic heads to add information that is similar.

Model Outline: Cause and Effect Paper

The topic outline was written by a student who chose as the subject of her research paper the reasons for and the effects of the emergence of the young urban professionals during the 1980's. You can tell from her outline that causal analysis is an essential part of her research paper.

THE YUPPIES: A GENERATION OF MATERIALISTS

Thesis Statement: The 1980's reflected a period of peace and prosperity and a diminished interest in improving social conditions resulting in a generation of young urban professionals with their increasing obsession of materialism, their pessimism, and their renewed faith in business and profit.

I. Result: Obsession with materialism
  A. Reasons specified by surveys
    1. Financial security
        a. Percent from 1984
        b. Percent from 1967
    2. Worry over economic future
        a. Rising unemployment rate
        b. General decline in the economy
            (1) Knowledge of Proposition 13
            (2) Knowledge of government cutbacks
    3. Less concern of government and big business
        a. Neither liberal nor conservative
        b. Business careers rather than social service ones
  B. Evidence of materialism
    1. Willingness to work long hours
    2. High combined salaries
        a. Average of $25,000 a year
        b. Usual salary of $100,000
    3. High purchasing power
        a. Latest gadgets
            (1) Food processors and bread making machines
            (2) Computers
            (3) Video recorders
        b. Designer clothes
            (1) The need to display labels: Guess, Vanderbilt
            (2) The disregard for price
        c. Natural materials
            (1) Cotton, linen, silk, and wool fabrics
            (2) Natural wood furniture
        d. Expensive automobiles
            (1) BMW
            (2) Mercedes
            (3) Jaguar
    4. Use of credit cards
        a. To buy desired products
        b. To travel throughout the world
        c. To pay for services
    5. Expensive housing
        a. Renovations of housing for profit
            (1) Haight Ashbury district
            (2) Select neighborhoods in Philadelphia
        b. Purchase of $300,000 condominiums
II. Result: Pessimistic attitude
  A. About government issues

    1. Conservative views
    2. Distrust of government
        a. Not doing enough to control pollution
        b. Not doing enough to protect consumers
    3. Demand cuts in government spending
    4. Lack concern for poor and elderly
  B. About the military
    1. To avoid a nuclear war
    2. To avoid military involvement overseas
  C. Reasons for their attitudes
    1. Disillusionment with the leadership
        a. During the Vietnam War
        b. During the Watergate cover-up
        c. During campaigns for various political positions
            (1) For office of the President
            (2) For congressional seats
    2. Current economic pressures
    3. Breakdown of the family unit
    4. Overpowering influence of television
    5. Receiving inflated grades in high school and college
III. Result: Renewed faith in business and profit
  A. Self-oriented concern
    1. Reasons for their lack of concern for others
        a. Failure of schools and colleges to challenge students to become more generous
        b. Failure of the Yuppie to believe in anything other than profit
    2. Effects of their self interests
        a. Are non ideological
        b. Are unimaginative
        c. Are anti-philosophical
        d. Show apathy towards poverty, hunger, oppression
  B. Committed to their careers
    1. Go to health spas for business and money, not health
    2. Work sixty-hour weeks
    3. Seek positions with salaries of $100,000 or more

Concluding Statement: While the young urban professionals want to be rich to pursue the American Dream, their lack of concern for others through the demand for federal cuts in public service and for decreased monies for education may well deny the American Dream to many others.

Susan Swails

The second outline was written by a student who chose for the subject of her research paper the problem of "Stutterers in Our Elementary Schools." You can see from her outline that causal analysis is an essential part of her research paper.

STUTTERERS IN OUR ELEMENTARY SCHOOLS

Thesis statement: Stuttering, an increasing problem in elementary school children, if not. corrected early, can result in severe frustration, withdrawal from society, and abnormal psychological development.

I. Causes of stuttering
   A. Physiological abnormalities
      1. Abnormal movements of two muscles in the middle ear
         a. Simultaneous contraction of muscles
         b. Reduced intensity of sound
         c. Cutout of auditory feedback signal
      2. Oral abnormalities
         a. Teeth
            (1) Condition: badly spaced or misaligned
            (2) Result: poor articulation
         b. Hard palate
            (1) Condition: unusually high or very narrow
            (2) Result: distortion of sounds
   B. Psychological abnormalities
      1. Early childhood disturbances
         a. Birth of baby brother or sister
         b. Absence of a parent for extended time
      2. Parent-child relationship disturbance
         a. Lack of affection
         b. Severe reprimanding
         c. Overdomination by parents
            (1) Continually correct child's speech
            (2) Continually speak for him
            (3) Permit siblings to speak for him

II. Result: Severe frustrations
   A. Rejection by peers
      1. Child laughed at
      2. Child isolated from class during play with peers
   B. Rejection by teacher
      1. Child isolated during reading sessions
      2. Child isolated during speech sessions
   C. Inability to express clearly personal views
      1. Stutters 10 percent of words spoken
      2. Stutters on first word of sentence
      3. Uses fragmented sentences
      4. Substitutes convulsive movements
         a. Shutting or blinking of eyes
         b. Sudden jerking of hands and/or legs
         c. Contorting of facial expressions

III. Result: Withdrawal from society
    A. Avoids oral communication
    B. Develops inferiority complex
       1. By continual suppression
       2. By continual correction
       3. By continual persecution
IV. Result: Abnormal psychological development in school
    A. Becomes behavior problem in school
       1. Disrupts class for attention
       2. Refuses to cooperate during activities
    B. Maintains low maturity level
       1. Will not practice articulation
       2. Will not master phonetic skills
    C. Displays buried hostility
V. Solutions for stuttering children
    A. Home therapy
       1. Manage own affairs
       2. Speak for self
       3. Blow off steam
       4. Encourage warm parental relationship
    B. Classroom therapy
       1. Teacher consults with speech therapist
       2. Teacher improves child/peer relationships
       3. Teacher encourages child's oral expression
    C. Clinical therapy
       1. Vocal therapy
          a. Articulation principles
          b. Articulation reorganization
       2. Listening skills
       3. Mechanical devices
          a. Pacemaster
             (1) Times speech by metronome
             (2) Controls pace of speech
          b. Klein Speech Rectifier
             (1) Produces sounds through microphone over larynx
             (2) Allows speaker to hear himself better
          c. Computer
             (1) Compares reference from memory banks
             (2) Allows speaker to make consistent decisions
             (3) Prevents distraction by others
          d. "Dial-a-Therapy"
             (1) Corrects speech patterns by phone
             (2) Diagnoses problem and treatment

Concluding statement: Each of the over 1,500,000 elementary school children who stutter can be helped by parental guidance, classroom cooperation, speech therapy, and mechanical devices. Such attention given early will save them from abnormal personal and academic development.

Photograph 12.1 (Photo by Stephen Grasso)

Photograph 12.1 suggests a topic for a Cause/Effect paper: the increased number of highway accidents. The student might research causes for the increase as well as the effects on society in terms of lives lost, new legislation, and financial loss.

Part

II

Finding and Using Information: The Basics of the Research Paper

Photograph II.1 (Photo by Stephen Grasso)

Stage

I

Beginning the Research Paper

1. Choosing a Subject
2. Limiting the Subject
3. Understanding the Purpose of the Research Paper

So far you have been relying primarily on personal experience for source material for your papers. Your subject matter has been drawn from jobs, hobbies, sports, school, travel, family, friends, cultural activities, organizations, and social life. In drawing on this source material, you were involved in observation, participation, conversation, and perhaps interviews.

Photograph II.1.1 (Photo by Stephen Grasso)

285

The next step is to move beyond reporting personal experiences into an area of research. As we read periodicals, listen to the radio, or watch television, a number of questions come to mind. For instance, we may hear a report about the increased number of school dropouts, and we wonder why the public has lost faith in the public school systems. A number of other questions may come to mind: "What has happened to the moral and ethical values in America?"; "What troubles are encountered by robot manufacturers?"; "How has the use of robots affected labor?"; or "Why have companies who use robots for heavy industrial application show an increase in profits?"; "Should journalists and politicians be compelled to disclose the names of confidential sources should public interest demand that they do?"; "What are the causes of the recent air disasters or near disasters?"; "Are the skies too crowded or do drugs and alcohol play a part?"; "What impact has electronic evangelists had on organized religion?"; "How can heterosexuals cope with the AIDS epidemic?"; "Why have incidents of child abuse been increasing despite parenting classes?"; "What happened to the flower children of the 1960's?"

Each of those questions suggests other questions that are related, and the more you find out about one problem, the more alert your natural sense of inquiry will become to other social, political, economic, and ecological events, discoveries and changes that are going on all around you. But awareness is not enough. If you are to participate in discoveries, changes, and problem solving, you will need to gather information. Information, the basis of all understanding, must first be collected, then sorted, and finally arranged carefully before it can be used.

The research paper is a project designed to help you master basic investigation skills and apply these skills to basic methods of exposition. A subject for a research paper can be almost any aspect of life in the past or present. Your subject for this first research paper, however, may be one aspect of a social, economic, political, or ecological problem in the United Slates. Because you will be using basic research sources and developing a very limited topic, your final product will be a modified research paper.

In thinking, reading, and writing about your subject, you will be drawing heavily on the composition skills you have already developed: subject limitation, thesis development, inference/fact distinction, classification and division, process analysis, cause and effect analysis, definition, and comparison and contrast analysis. In addition, you will be applying your newly acquired investigation skills and demonstrating your understanding of standard documentation procedures.

Objectives of the Modified Research Paper

There are four primary objectives of the modified research paper:

1. The first objective is to select a worthwhile subject to investigate and to limit that subject to a specific topic.
2. The second objective is for you to develop a working knowledge of some basic research sources (see p. 307).
3. The third objective is for you to learn note taking procedure so that you can make full use of your sources in a limited amount of time. You can do this by assembling your own sourcebook, a collection of articles on a particular subject. Your own sourcebook will contain articles which you find to be most useful and which you make copies of, articles

from magazines, newspapers, and pamphlets or bulletins, and any other pertinent items such as photographs or records or interviews. Assembling your own sourcebook will help in several ways:

a. You will be able to do more analytical reading of your sources because you can underline and annotate each source. This analytical reading will assist you because you will be able to take fewer and more precise notes and save yourself time.

b. You will be able to work at your own pace and wherever you wish because you will not have to do all of your note taking in the library.

c. You will have your complete sources at hand to refer to should a question arise when you are writing the final paper.

4. The fourth objective is for you to write a documented paper which will make use of the composition skills you have already developed.

Procedure for the Research Paper

In preparing this paper, you can follow a series of stages and steps which will help organize your time and the research material.

1. Assembling a preliminary bibliography

2. Reading for an overview of the subject

3. Selecting the most helpful sources for their specific topic and assembling them in a sourcebook

4. Assembling a working set of note cards

5. Writing an extended definition of your topic

6. Writing fact enumeration ("hard data") on your topic

7. Writing about causes and effects on the topic you have selected and proposing solutions

8. Writing an extended introduction and formulating a thesis

9. Classifying the information from the note cards into major and minor points

10. Preparing a working outline from the classified note cards

11. Writing a rough draft

12. Preparing the final documented paper with title page; formal outline; text; and bibliography/works cited

13. Preparing a five minute oral presentation of your findings and recommendations

STEP I Choosing a Subject

The first step in any research project is to select a general subject and limit it as soon as possible to a specific subject. Personal interest may lead you to a topic. For example, you may wish to compare and contrast present day heroes with those of the past or investigate police tactics aimed at minimizing the use of deadly force. You may wish to explore the reasons that crimes among those with diplomatic immunity have risen and determine what solutions are possible. Following is a list of questions raised by students:

1. With toys such as the new computer war games are manufacturers now forming public opinion rather than producing toys to entertain children?

2. Have television shows really contributed to increased violence among children?

3. Should television commercials be approved by a Review Board before being aired?

4. Scientific research is very helpful, but should we continue to give Federal grants to studies such as the one which cost $25,000. to find out how people react to a picture in a barnyard?

5. Should we continue to control construction along the coastal areas in the United States since waterfront property is being destroyed.

6. Should no-fault divorce be eliminated?

7. Have the no-fault divorce laws helped or hindered women?

8. Who should be permitted to adopt?

9. Has school busing helped the African-American student?

10. Should adopted children be encouraged to find their biological parents?

11. Is the volunteer armed forces really working?

12. What are the issues that concern environmentalists?

13. Should teachers be required to take competency tests?

14. What are the causes of homelessness?

15. Do we really graduate students from high school who cannot read or write?

Exercise 2-1 Choosing a Subject

Submit a list of at least five questions that you have had on your mind concerning some social, political, religious, scientific, or historical aspect. Select one question that interests you the most. Read a substantial article on the subject. Write a bibliography card for the source and annotate the card. Place a xerox copy of the article in your source book.

STEP 2   Limiting the Subject

The earlier that you limit your subject to a specific topic, the more efficient your research will be The following subjects are too broad: crime, socialized medicine, nutrition, television, computer crimes, the Iran-Contra Affair, teenagers.

Assume that you are interested in politics as a broad subject. You would need to limit your subject to only one aspect. You may wish to investigate the theory that in the United

States there will be a greater division of classes caused by educational needs to perform the job rather than economic needs.

As a student studying ecology, you may limit your subject to a particular area of the country. A student in California may wish to choose the topic of land erosion as a result of mud slides, while a student in Florida may wish to limit the topic to beach erosion along the Atlantic coastline in South Florida.

In selecting and limiting your subject, you will want to take care to avoid certain pitfalls.

Prejudging the Subject

You may be interested in a subject and have already formed an opinion about it. For instance, one student who selected as the subject effects of smoking marijuana already had decided that smoking marijuana was no worse than drinking alcohol and had decided that the Federal government should legalize the drug. However, when he began to research the subject, he found that there were still too many problems with the drug and that new evidence indicated that some children born of addicted parents who smoked only marijuana were born with severe defects. Had the student continued to maintain his position in his paper, reporting only the favorable aspects, he would have committed a research blunder known as "bending the thesis." He would have defeated the whole purpose of research, which is to investigate a subject, to report objectively all information about it, to propose solutions, and to draw a logical conclusion.

Choosing an Inconclusive Subject

You will want to avoid choosing a subject about which there is too little information and about which you cannot draw a conclusion. For instance, public school-based health clinics are controversial because they dispense contraceptives and counsel teenage students on sex and birth control. Although a few schools in the country do have school-based health clinics, it is still too early for any conclusive information to be available. We may not know how effective the clinics may be in providing counseling to stop teenage pregnancy and to prevent students from becoming potential dropouts for at least a decade. Another subject that you might select because it is timely is the effect athletic scholarships have on students with educational deficiencies. However, if you think about it, you will realize that in this case, too, there will be very little objective evidence available since many athletic departments would risk divulging information about their athletes nor would the students who receive not only money to attend the college or university, but also bonuses in the form of new cars and money. Still another example of an inconclusive subject would be that of letter grades versus comments by the teacher for elementary school children.

STEP 3   Understanding the Purpose of the Research Paper

Stage 2 will guide you in your search for information. First, however, you need to understand what a research paper is **not**. It is not a general summary of one book or a single periodical article an a subject. It is not a string of quotes from several sources joined together with a few of your own—conjunctions and transitional devices. It is not personal opinion based only on personal observation. It is not just a report of the findings of others on a subject, nor is it merely a collection of facts.

What is it then? The research paper is the end result of a careful investigation of a subject which is important to you. Extended research papers, such as those you will be writing in upper division college work or in business or professional situations, cover previous knowledge on a subject as well as current information. In the case of this limited research paper, your investigation of a topic will be directed primarily toward gathering and presenting current information on the topic.

Based on the information you gather, your paper will present a carefully formulated thesis. The paper will then demonstrate the thesis by presenting proof details in the form of facts gathered from reading about the subject, interviews, radio and television broadcasts, personal letters of inquiry, and visits to and observation of locations pertinent to the topic. Finally, the research paper draws a conclusion—one based not only on the judgment of experts, but on your own evaluation of the subject. However, this evaluation is always based on objective evidence. If the research paper involves a problem, then it will conclude with proposals for solutions. Again, these proposals are based not only on those suggested by the experts, but also on your own ideas which you have formulated through researching the subject.

Following is a list of titles of some papers written by composition students:

Nutrition: The New Food Pyramid
The Right to an Education: The Illegal Immigrant
The New Homeless with the Downsizing of America
The Rifle — Once a Protector, Now Man's Enemy
The Fatherless Families
Television Cameras in the Courtroom
The Working Poor and Health Care
Financial Problems of the Elderly—America's New Poor
Effects of Divorce on Children
Suffer Little Children: A Report on Child Abuse
The Overpaid Athletes: Are They Worth Their Salaries?
The Battle Against Childhood Leukemia
The New Natural Wonder Drug Melatonin: How Effective Is It?
Spinal Cord Injuries
Problems of the Immigrant Family
The Jury System: Is It Outmoded?
The English-only Controversy
Consumer Concerns: The Food We Eat
The Abduction of Children by Parents
Television Talk Shows: The New Age of Sleaze
The Stereotyped Image of Italian Americans: The Great Myth
The Backlash Against Immigration
Computers and the Road to Isolation

Stage	
2	# Finding Sources

1. Distinguishing Between the Preliminary and Final Bibliography
2. Assembling the Preliminary Bibliography

Once you have selected a subject, your next step is to begin a systematic search for information. Information can be gathered from various sources which include general references (encyclopedias, dictionaries, yearbooks, and statistical abstracts), books, magazine and newspaper articles, bulletins and pamphlets, letters, radio and television broadcasts and interviews. This list constitutes the bibliography.

STEP I Distinguishing Between the Preliminary and the Final Bibliography

The Preliminary Bibliography

There are two bibliographies for any research paper, the preliminary bibliography and the final bibliography. The preliminary bibliography is a complete list of all the sources you have collected for investigation of your subject. These sources are often written on index cards. As you examine these sources, you will find that some are helpful in researching your topic while others, which had promising titles, contain information you are not sure you can use. If you have been instructed to present your **works consulted,** you will list all of these sources. It is quite likely, though, that you will be asked to write a **selected bibliography** or to present your **works cited.** If such is the case, those cards listing sources of doubtful value are set aside. The remaining cards constitute your working bibliography.

The Final Bibliography

The final bibliography consists of the sources actually used in your paper. These will be acknowledged at the end of the paper. This final bibliography is usually entitled **selected bibliography** or **works cited** because it lists only those sources from which you drew the specific information that appears in your paper and which your document with footnotes that give credit to these sources. The bibliography for a completed research paper appears on pages 419–420.

STEP 2 Assembling the Preliminary Bibliography

Your search must establish whether there is sufficient published information on your subject One source, even if it is a complete book, does not constitute sufficient information for a research paper. Even for a very short paper you will need at least five different sources. One student found that a topic for which there was insufficient published material was "The Disadvantages of Food Stamps." This student found only one article, and that article mentioned only one disadvantage— too much red tape connected with the food stamp program. Since the student still wanted to investigate the subject of food stamps, he had to broaden the scope of his subject rather than limit it to "disadvantages." If you find that you have chosen a subject for which there are no periodical articles and you cannot enlarge the subject, then you have to change subjects.

Assuming, however, that you have in your early search determined that there is sufficient material from a variety of sources, it is now time to begin making a preliminary bibliography. Before you begin compiling the bibliography, you will need to familiarize yourself with the correct bibliography form for each type of source. You will need to know how to prepare the collection of note cards, which constitutes the preliminary bibliography, and how to prepare the entries which appear on your bibliography sheet at the end of your paper. You will notice from your examination of the bibliography for the research paper on "The Formative Years: Effects of Television" that the sources are entered alphabetically. You will save time and effort if you take this listing of bibliography forms along with you to the library and prepare the cards properly at the outset. Then, when you are ready to assemble the final bibliography, you will need only to alphabetize your cards and copy them onto your bibliography sheet.

Varying styles for bibliography and documentation exist. To indicate the various styles available in different disciplines, a few manual and handbook titles are presented below.

ART
Writing about Art.
BUSINESS
Writing Business and Economics Papers, Theses and Dissertations.
ENGINEERING
"Recommended Practice for Style of References in Engineering Publications."
HISTORY
Historian's Handbook: A Key to the Study and Writing of History.
LAW
A Practical Manual of Standard Legal Citations: Rules, Rationale and Examples of Citations to Authority for Lawyers, Law Students, Teachers, and Research Workers.
MATHEMATICS
A Manual for Authors of Mathematical Papers.
MUSIC
Writing about Music: A Style Book for Reports and Theses.

PSYCHOLOGY
American Psychological Association Publication Manual
SCIENCE
Committee on Form and Style: CPE Style Manual.
CHEMISTRY
Handbook for Authors of Papers in the Journals of the American Chemical Society.
PHYSICS
Style Manual for Guidance in the Preparation of Papers for Journals Published by the American Institute of Physics.

This list of titles is not exhaustive. It merely provides the reader with some idea of the variety of manuals and handbooks available in the professions.

In contrast to handbooks (such as the above) which deal with specific disciplines, the *MLA Handbook for Writers of Research Papers* provides the writer with information that allows that writer to do papers for a number of disciplines. Therefore, the following bibliography entries are based upon MLA recommendations.

Bibliography Forms
Books

1. Book with one author

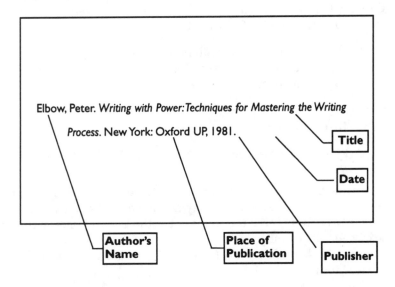

- The first line begins flush with the left margin.
- Write the author's last name first in order to arrange the last name alphabetically in the final bibliography. Then it concludes with a period.
- Any lines after the first are indented five spaces.

- Each line is double-spaced.
- Titles of books must be italicized. If your printer does not italicize well, **your instructor may require you to underline your titles.**
- Publication information is next. It consists of the place of publication followed by a colon, then the name of the publisher followed by a comma, and the date of publication followed by a period. Only the city is given. If the city is **not** in the United States, write both the name of the city and the name of the country.
- The abbreviation **UP** means university press.

2. A book with two authors

Gelb, Arthur, and Barbara. *O'Neill.* Cambridge, Eng.: Harper, 1987.

Schick, Frank L., and Renee Schick. *Statistical Handbook on U.S. Hispanics.* Phoenix: Oryx, 1991.

- When there are two authors, invert the first author's name but do **not** invert the second author's name. The second author's name is preceded first by a comma and second by the word **and.**

   Parenthetical Documentation. The sentence following shows how to cite two authors paraphrased.

   ⇒ O'Neill's biographers indicate that the three people that closely associated with Carlotta O'Neill, his wife, after O'Neill's death were his literary agent, his lawyer, and his curator (Gelb and Gelb 951).

   > CAUTION: When working with publications having more than one author, do not rearrange the names. Keep the names in the same sequence as they are in the book's title page.

3. A book with three authors

Millett, Fred B., Arthur W. Hoffman, and David R. Clark. *Reading Poetry.* 2nd ed. New York: Harper, 1968.

- The last name of the author is presented first. Other authors' names that follow are presented in the same sequence as they are found on the title page.
- Only the city is given, but if the city is not in the United States, write both the name of the city and the country.
- The above publisher's full name, Harper & Row Publishers, is shortened to conform to the latest form.

   Parenthetical Documentation: This sentence shows how to cite the preceding authors when citing a direct quotation.

   ⇒ "Kinesthetic imagery are most commonly carried by verbs" (Millett, Hoffman, and Clark 56).

4. A book with more than three authors

Hubbell, Jay B., et al. *Eight American Authors: A Review of Research and Criticism.* New York: Norton, 1963.

- When there are four or more authors for the same book, use et al. (and others) after the name of the first author.
- Norton is the shortened form for the publisher W W. Norton & Company, Inc.

   Documentation for a quotation of more than three lines.

⇒   From his own day to the present Hawthorne has been fortunate in his crit-

   ics. Such contemporaries as Poe, Melville, and Whipple took him seriously

   enough to write carefully formulated discussions of him, and later a number

   of perceptive readers, not the least of whom was Henry James, wrote at

   length about him. (Hubbell 134)

- ◆ This shows how to cite a direct quotation running more than four lines.
  - ◇ Indent the quotation ten spaces from the left,
  - ◇ Double-space each line.
  - ◇ Double-space from the text to the quotation.
  - ◇ Use the block style (all lines line up from the left).
  - ◇ Do not use quotation marks.
  - ◇ Place the period at the end of the quotation, not after the citation.

5. An edited book

Bevington, David, ed. *The Complete Works of Shakespeare.* 4th ed. Dallas: Scott, 1980.

- When referring to edited selections, use the editor's name.
- On the other hand if you are referring to a particular play within the edited edition, then the author's name will be given—e.g. Shakespeare, William.
- Following the editor's first name is a comma and the abbreviation ed. (editor) which is not capitalized. '
- If a book is a second, third, fourth, or later edition, then the edition number must he noted following the title.
- Scott is the proper MLA designation indicating Scott, Foresman and Company.

   Parenthetical Documentation: When writing a summary, cite a section from an edited book in one of the following ways:.

⇒ According to Bevington in his "General Introduction," Robert Greene's written attack was evidence of his envy of Shakespeare's increasing success (lvii).

⇒ Robert Greene's written attack was evidence of his envy of Shakespeare's increasing success (Bevington. General Introduction. lvii).

◆ In this text the "General Introduction" is in Roman numerals.

◆ Since the editor's name and the source are included in the paraphrase, only the page number is necessary in the documentation.

6. A book with two editors

Peary, Gerald, and Roger Shatzkin, eds. *The Modern American Novel and the Movies*. New York: Ungar, 1978.

- The abbreviation **eds.** is not capitalized when it is placed after names.
- The abbreviation **eds.** means more than one editor.
- The abbreviation **ed.** is used for one editor only.

Parenthetical documentation: When writing a paraphrase, you may cite a section from an edited book in the following manner.

⇒ Peary and Shatzkin make the observation about the film *Intruder in the Dust* that Chick is seen only once in a large group of people, thus increasing the idea of detachment (182).

◆ The editors' names are mentioned in the sentence.

◆ Therefore, only the page number is needed for the documentation.

7. A book with corporate authorship

The American Psychological Association. *Publication Manual of The American Psychological Association*. Washington: American, 1994.

- An organization or a group may be the corporate author rather than individual(s) or editor(s) as in the above example.

Parenthetical Documentation: A corporate authorship should be cited in the following way:

⇒ Good writing cannot cover up unskilled research (The American Psychological Association 2).

- The **full** corporate name must be given the first time.
- The second time that a corporate name is given, it may be shortened.
  - ◆ If the shortened version of the corporate name is easily confused with another title cited in the paper, the shortened version may not be used.
  - ◆ An example of the shortened version may be as the following: (American Psychological 2).

8. An essay in an edited edition

Rose, Mark. "Hamlet and the Shape of Revenge." *Shakespeare 's Middle Tragedies. A Collection of Critical Essays.* Ed. David Young. Englewood Cliffs: Prentice, 1993.

- The name of the author is presented.
- Then the title of the essay used is written.
- The title of the book follows.
- The editor's name preceded by **Ed.** (editor) follows the book title. **Notice:** If there are two editors the word **and** separates the names.
- The publication information is next.
- After the date, the page numbers for the entire article are given when the researcher is specifying a single article or essay from the complete work.

    Summary Documentation: A summary is cited in the following manner.

    ⇒ Hamlet and Oedipus have similar problems because their wills are restrained. Hamlet's restraint [he calls it imprisonment] in Denmark is self-imposed, but it is also tied to his personal relationships (Rose 7–8).

    ◆ The documentation is the same as the paraphrased documentation.
    ◆ The difference between summary and the paraphrase is that the summary covers a larger amount of material, and that material is shortened.

9. A translated book

Friedrich, Johannes. *Extinct Languages.* Trans. Frank Gaynor. New York: Barnes, 1993.

- The name of the translator follows the title of the book.
- The title **Trans.** (translator) precedes the name of the translator.

    Direct Quotation: A direct quotation of up to three lines should be documented in the following manner:

    ⇒ "Only the Nile Valley, about 500 miles long but only a few miles in width, is arable land. but extremely fertile at that, nurtured by the floods of the Nile, and flanked by the barren desert on both sides" (Rose 1-2).

    ◆ The quotation ends with the final quotation marks.
    ◆ After two spaces the parenthetical space has the author's name and the pages' numbers.
    ◆ Finally at the end of the parentheses, the final punctuation mark follows.

10. A work of several volumes

Janson, H. W. *History of Art.* Ed. Anthony Janson. 3rd ed. 2 vols. Englewood Cliffs: Prentice, 1986.

When using two or more volumes in a multi-volume set, include the total number of volumes before the publication information.

- Follow this order:
  - ◆ Where there is both an editor and an author, the editor's name is stated after the title. The title **Ed.,** precedes the editor's name and is capitalized.
  - ◆ Normally if there is an edition number, it is written after the title. However, if there is an editor, the edition number then follows the editor's name.
  - ◆ The complete number of volumes precedes the publication information. Notice that **vols.** when following a number is not capitalized (e.g. 2 vols.).

  ⇒ Janson's first volume begins with the ancient world and ends with Gothic art as he discusses Gentile Da Fabriano's inclination for large paintings. His second volume beginning with the Renaissance concludes with a discussion of the modern photography employed by David Hockney which attempts to transcend the usual single focus (Janson, vols. 1-2).

  - ◆ When referring to an entire volume or several volumes of a work do not cite page numbers.

---

11. A book that is one of several volumes

Janson, H. W. *A History of Art*. Ed. Anthony Janson. 3rd ed. Vol. 1. Englewood Cliffs: Prentice, 1986. 2 vols.

- If the volumes were completed over a number of years, give the inclusive dates (e.g. 1980- 1983).
- If you used only one volume of the set, place the volume before the publication information.
- Notice that the designation **Vol.** is capitalized when it is placed before a number (e.g. Vol. 1).

Parenthetical Documentation

  ⇒ Janson observed that although Trajan conformed to the Roman tradition of not wearing a beard, his successors did sport beards according to the Greek fashion. (1:186)

  - ◆ The first number is the volume number.
    - ◇ Notice that the abbreviation vol. is **not** used here, nor is the word *volume*.
  - ◆ Following the colon, type the page number.
  - ◆ Since the name is given in the documented sentence, it should not be repeated within the parentheses.

---

12. The Bible

The Bible. New American Standard Version.

- Note that no italicizing is used for sacred books.

Direct Quotation

⇒ "Like apples of gold in settings of silver/Is a word spoken in the right circumstances" (Prov. 25: 11).

◆ The / (virgule) indicates that there is a break between lines in the original.
◆ Prov. is the standard abbreviation for the book of Proverbs.
◆ The first number (25) indicates the chapter.
◆ The second number (11) following the colon indicates the verse.

13. A reprinted edition

Garland, Henry, and Mary Garland. *The Oxford Companion to German Literature.* 1976. London, England: Oxford UP, 1984.

- The original publication date is placed after the title.
- The latest publication date is placed at the end of the bibliography entry.
- Follow the usual format for the rest of the publication information.

Parenthetical documentation combined with a direct quotation

⇒ Goethe remained aloof from Schiller for a while; however, after Schiller managed to break through Goethe's aloofness, Schiller "inaugurated a lasting intellectual friendship" (Garland and Garland 291).

◆ Within a parenthetical statement a student may incorporate a direct quotation.
◆ The section containing the direct quote will have the proper quotation marks.
◆ Since the whole documentation comes from one source, that source is given at the conclusion.

14. Reference Books

A signed encyclopedia article

Hauck, A. "Constantine The Great and His Sons." *The New Schaff-Herzog Encyclopedia of Religious Knowledge.* 1952 ed.

- Since an encyclopedia is arranged alphabetically, volume numbers and page numbers are not important.
- However, the date of the particular edition is important since encyclopedias are updated with new information periodically.
  ◆ The term **ed.** stands for edition.

Parenthetical documentation

⇒ Constantine received the title Constantine the Great after crushing Greek and Roman paganism (Hauck).

◆ Alphabetically arranged encyclopedia articles do not require page numbers.

An unsigned encyclopedia article

"Alcoholism." *The Concise Columbia Encyclopedia.* 2nd ed. 1989.

- If no author's name is given, begin with the title of the article.
- Do not include volume numbers and page numbers for encyclopedias.

15 Dictionary

"Lachrymose." *Webster's Third New International Dictionary Unabridged*. 1966 ed.

- Dictionaries are treated much like the encyclopedia.
  - ◆ The defined term is in quotation marks.
  - ◆ The full title is then given.
  - ◆ The date of the edition is last.

  ⇒ The term lachrymose is mournful as when an individual weeps or is sorrowful over a person or an event (Webster).

  - ◆ If no other dictionary is given. the above is sufficient, since information is alphabetically arranged.
  - ◆ If you have used a dictionary with a similar title, then enough information will have to be given to distinguish which dictionary is intended (e.g., *Webster's New World*).

16. Government Publications

Bureau of Economic and Business Research. *1994 Florida Statistical Abstract*. 28th ed. Gainesville: Fla. UP, 1994.

U.S. Department of Commerce. *Statistical Abstract of the United States*. Washington: GPO, 1996.

- Government publications usually begin with a corporate authorship.
- UP refers to university press.
- GPO means government printing office.

17 An Unsigned Magazine Article

"A Guilty Verdict for Brothers in Arms." *US News & World Report* 1 Apr. 1996: 17.

- Where no author of a magazine article is given, begin with the title of the article.
- Enclose the article title with quotation marks.
- In **weekly** magazines, the date begins with the day.
- If it is a **monthly** magazine. omit the day of the month.
- Conclude the date with a colon.
- Page number follows the date.

  ⇒ The court convicted the two brothers Erik and Lyle Menendez who were attempting to win their case by alleging that they murdered their parents because they were abused ("A Guilty Verdict" 17).

  - ◆ When the author's name is not given, begin with the title of the article.

A shortened version of the article's title may be given if it can easily be recognized in the bibliography. The article's title should be encased in parentheses.

18. A signed magazine article

McMurray, Scott. "A Fast Ride to the Top." *U.S. News and World Report* 18 Mar. 1996: 55–56.

- Begin with the author's last name followed by a comma.
- The author's first name is followed by a period unless there is a middle initial.
- The rest of the information is the same as the preceding magazine entry.
- Do not include volume numbers or issue numbers with magazine bibliographies.

19. Newspaper article with author

Herschman, Bill. "Freedom Would Rule at Charter Schools." *Sun Sentinel* 28 Apr. 1996: 1A+

- This article began with the title followed by "By Bill I. Hirschman." This type of beginning is called "a byline."
- Whenever there is a byline, begin the bibliography entry with the author's last name first as usual.
- The number 1A+ indicates that the article began on page one.
- The section number is A.
- The symbol + indicates that the article is not sequential. It will skip several pages before it continues.
- This same symbol may also be used for magazine articles that skip pages.

20. An Unsigned Newspaper Article

"Air-traffic Control Glitch Causes Delays in Flights." *Sun Sentinel* 28 Apr. 1996: 15A.

- Many newspaper articles do have a writer's name attached to it.
- If there is no name, begin the bibliography with the title of the article.
- Associations such as Associated Press (AP), United Press International (UPI) or Reuters, which are mentioned after titles of articles, are **not** entered into the bibliography.
  - ⇒ Because of radio problems at a traffic center just north of Jacksonville, pilots could not talk to the control tower thus causing flight delays of up to an hour and thirty minutes ("Air Traffic" 15A).
  - ◆ The title of the article may be shortened.
  - ◆ Both the page number and the section number are given.

21. A Journal with Continuous Pagination

Mirskin, Jerry. "Writing as a Process of Valuing." *CCC* 46(Oct. 1995): 387-410.

- The explanation for the title *CCC*, which stands for College Composition and

Communication, is given below it.

- Continuous pagination means that the page numbers continue from the first volume to the last volume of the set.
- Notice that only the volume number (46) is given before the date.
- The pages in this article are consecutive.
- A very large number of journals have continuous pagination.

⇒ Mirskin, during his discussion about writing, made the following observation: "The French Symbolist poets, toward the end of the nineteenth century, and the American and English poets of this century, especially after World War 1, began the period of the intensive use of free verse (qtd. in Mirskin 393).

◆ In the article, Mirskin has quoted what Abrahams had to say about poets.
◆ The term **qtd.** in the parentheses means quoted.
◆ The number in the parentheses is the page number where the article is found.

22. A journal with separate pagination

Kranzelok, Edward P. "Management of Acute Poisoning Emergencies." *Emergency Medical Services* 16.6(1987): 26+.

- Separate pagination indicates that each issue of the journal begins anew with page numbers beginning with page one and running consecutively to the end.
- Both the volume and the issue numbers are given as indicated in **16.6.**

23 Television Show

"Search for Immortality," *Next Step.* Narrs. Paul Robin and Phil Cowin ABC. WPBF, Palm Beach 8 May 1996.

- The title of the movie or production in quotation marks is first.
- Then the name of the program italicized is next.
- The narrator or narrators are then mentioned.
- The name of the network follows.
- The call letters are listed.
- Last is the date of the broadcast.

⇒ According to an ABC televised program, some individuals have paid thousands of dollars so that after death they will have their bodies frozen and placed in a metal tube. They hope that scientists will someday find a way to restore their bodies to life. The term for this process is called "cryonics" ("Search").

◆ You may shorten the title.
◆ The shortened title must begin with the word by which it would normally be alphabetized if it were not shortened.
◆ May, June and July are not abbreviated.

24. Radio

Morning Edition. Narr. Bob Edwards. PBS. WLRN, Miami. 29 July 1988

- Begin with the name of the program.
- If a person's particular work is being mentioned, begin with the individual's name—e.g. Hemingway, Ernest. *The Sun Also Rises.*
- The rest of the information is similar to that used for television.

25. Pamphlets

Pamphlet with a personal author

Bowen, Otis R. *What You Should Know about AIDS.* Washington: GPO, n.d.

Pamphlet with corporate authorship

Broward County Public Health Unit: Health Education Section. *What Everyone Should Know about AIDS.* South Deerfield: Channing, 1983.

- The abbreviation **n.d.** means no date.
- Treat the pamphlet entry the same way as a book entry.

26. Bulletin

Koehler P.G. *Pantry Stored Food Pests.* Cooperative Extension Service Bulletin ENT-5, n.d.

- If there is a bulletin number, include it.
- If there is no date, use n.d.

27. Interview

Personal

Haker, James A. personal interview. 28 Apr. 1996.

Published Interview

"How to Influence Press Coverage." *U.S. News and World Report* 19 Feb. 1996: 54+.

- In a personal interview the name is given.
- The phrase "personal interview" follows.
- Then it concludes with the date.
- The published interview depends upon whether it is published in a book, magazine, newspaper, or journal.
  - ⇒ When six press relations experts were interviewed, one of the questions asked was how a citizen can penetrate the bubble around the press. Michael Deaver responded: "The best advice you can give to somebody when they're dealing

with the media is don't think about these people as journalists, because they aren't. They're in the entertainment business, and that's how you get their attention" ("How to Influence" 54).

28. Letter

O'Connor, Sandra Day. Letter to the author. 2 May 1996

- The name of the person who wrote the letter is given first.
- The phrase "letter to the author" is referring to the writer using the letter.
- Finally, the date is given.

Computer-Based Programs

29. CD ROM

"Eudora Welty." *The New Grolier Multimedia Encyclopedia.* 6th release. CD-ROM. Danbury: Grolier, 1993.

- If the author's name is given, write the last name first.
- If the author's name is not given, begin with the title.
- Since this is an encyclopedia article, enclose the title with quotation marks.
- The title of the product is italicized.
- If there is mentioned an edition, release or version, include that.
- Include the publication type (CD-ROM).
- Next, include the city where published.
- Then insert the name of the publisher.
- Last, include the year of the publication.

30. Diskette Information

Strunk, William and E.B. White. *The Elements of Style.* Vers MS-DOS. Diskette. Carmel: Microlytics, 1979.

- If the author's name is given, write the last name first.
- If the author's name is not given, begin with the title.
- The title of the product is italicized.
- If there is mentioned an edition, release or version, include that.
- Include the publication type (Diskette).
- Next, include the city where published.
- Then insert the name of the publisher.
- Last, include the year of the publication.

31. Computer Network

Johnson, Robert A. *Understanding Masculine Psychology.* Rev. ed. New York: Harper, 1989.
Online. Library of Congress. Selfnet. 14 May 1996.

- Begin with the author's name.
- Give the title of the text.The term **Rev. ed.** means revised edition. If it has an edition number use that instead-e g. **5th ed.**
- Remember to put a colon after the place of publication.
- Next, insert the publisher.
- Then include the date.
- Include the publication medium (Online)
- State the place where the electronic information is.
- Give the name of the network.
- Last state the date when the material was accessed.

For additional information on how to cite sources in your paper, see pages 361–364.

Index from Encyclopedia Americana 1995 edition. Reprinted by permission.

In the preparation of your bibliography, you will develop a working knowledge of the basic kinds of sources necessary for any investigation:

the standard library card catalog
general and specialized encyclopedias
Reader's Guide to Periodical Literature
The New York Times Index
Essay and General Literature Index
yearbooks and statistical references

The following pages show you the actual steps taken by a student in his search for material on the general subject of "AIDS." You will see the reasons for the order in which he consulted each type of source and the way he determined the usefulness of each source.

General Encyclopedias

The best way to begin research on a subject is to locate an article on it in an encyclopedia; in this way you can get an overview of the subject. This overview will point out important characteristics, background, and major subdivisions of the subject. Often the overview reading in an encyclopedia will help you in narrowing your subject to a specific topic. The *Encyclopedia Britannica*, the *Encyclopedia Americana*, and *Collier's Encyclopedia* are three encyclopedias that are useful for college-level research because the articles in them are written by experts or teams of experts on a given subject.

You will save yourself time if you first consult the Index volume of any encyclopedia. When you do so, be flexible in looking up your classification of the subject. You may already be too limited. For instance, the student who looked up "Education of the Mentally Retarded Child" did not find the subject listed this way; he had to look in the index under the larger classification of "Child Development." He then found his topic listed as a sub-classification.

Reproduced on page 306 are entries from the index of the 1995 *Encyclopedia Americana*.

Discussion: There are a few problems that a student might have in looking up a subject like "AIDS." Since this word is an acronym (a word formed from the initial letters of each of the successive parts) the student should look up the complete name since information may be found under the heading of the acronym, or the complete name, or both. Furthermore, information may not be found in the original encyclopedia set because extensive discussions on this topic are relatively recent. However, begin with the encyclopedia index first. If the topic is not listed under a general heading such as disease, medicine, health, or a specific heading such as AIDS or Acquired Immune Deficiency Syndrome, then try one of the encyclopedia annuals that are published on a yearly basis.

Discussion: Notice in the 1995 *Encyclopedia Americana* index that the term *Immune Acquired Syndrome* is listed first but tells the student to look at the entry entitled *AIDS*. There the student is told the page numbers to look up. The index is for the full encyclopedia set; the student finds not only page numbers but volume numbers also where the information is listed.

If the student were to check volume 21 on page 592 first, this student would find the subject listed under one of the boldfaced headings. In this case the heading "Pediatrics" is what the student would find. Although the information about AIDS and children is short, it does supply information on the problem. and there are other topics that are useful in finding further information about the subject. Sometimes an encyclopedia article such as this one may have "see also" references at the end of the article, but it may also have selected bibliographies that serve as a springboard to put you on to other sources

Since this is an article that the student wishes to use for current statistical information in his or her paper. the student makes a bibliography card.

Bibliography Entry for an Encyclopedia.	Caplan, Karen M., M.D. "Pediatrics: AIDS and children."
	Encyclopedia Americana. 1995 ed.
Annotation	Has statistical information on the number of AIDS cases for the year.

Note that an annotation on a bibliography card is a short comment about the contents of a source. Annotating the bibliography card after examining the source is a good practice because the annotation will remind you about the contents and will indicate whether you think the source is definitely helpful, of possible use, or of no use.

The Card Catalog

Having read an overview article on your subject in an encyclopedia, you will want to find out now whether any books on your subject are available. Thus you will consult the card catalog, which indexes all the books in a library's circulating and reference collection, or an electronic index. Each book owned by the library is described and filed alphabetically. A book will be found listed in the card a catalog on four types of cards: author card. title card. subject card. and cross reference card.

At this point in your research it is unlikely that you know specific names of books on your subject; therefore. you will be looking for subject cards. The student researching AIDS found the following cards through subject headings

```
                    AIDS (Acquired Immune deficiency syndrome)
      R
      616.97          Tyckoson, David A.
                          AIDS (Acquired immune deficiency syndrome) /
                      by David A. Tyckoson.—Phoenix, Ariz.: Oryx Press,
                      1985.
                          60 p.; 28 cm.—(Oryx science bibliographies; v. 1 )
                      Includes index.
                      1 1 756451
                      ISBN 0—89774—203—6 (pbk.)

                      1. AIDS (Disease)—Bibliography.
                      2. AIDS (Disease)—Abstracts. I. Title
                      II. Series
      FFIB                          EDBBdc                    85-3061r85
```

Discussion: The title of this book is AIDS. It was written by David A. Tyckoson and published in Phoenix, Arizona, by the Oryx Press in 1985. The title, of course, indicates that the book might be useful, but further reading of the catalog card reveals that the book is only sixty pages long and that it contains bibliographies and abstracts. The book not only lists other sources, but it also has abstracts of various articles. The student writes a bibliography card, making sure to enter the call number so that when he is ready to examine the book, he will not need to return to the card catalog to find the location of the book in the stacks.

```
      R
      616.97
      T978a
                    Tyckoson, David A., AIDS
                    Phoenix, Ariz.: Oryx Press, 1985.
```

Notice the letter R above the call number, which indicates that this particular book does not circulate; it is kept at all times for use in he reference room only. Reference books, such as *Statistical Abstracts*, that are used frequently may be kept behind the librarian's desk rather than in the reference stacks so that the student may have quick access to it. Those cards will have an additional instruction: "Ask at Reference Desk" printed at the top.

The second card is indexed by subject heading, "Communicable diseases."

614.4	Communicable disease.
	Institute of Biology
	Biological aspects of the transmission of disease; edited by C. Horton Smith. Edinburgh. Published for the Institute of Biology by Oliver and Boyd [1957]
	viii, 184 p. 23 cm.
	Report of a symposium.
	Includes bibliographical references.
	I. Communicable diseases. I. Horton-Smith, Clifford,
ed.	
	II. Title
	RC112 I5 614.43 A 58-570
	Queens Univ., Kingston Ont. Library for Library of

Discussion: The book is a report of a symposium held by the Institute of Biology . Notice that no single author is given; this is an instance of a book with corporate authorship—the Institute of Biology—and edited by C. Horton Smith. The student notices that the date of publication is 1957 and concludes that the book will not be useful since the subject of AIDS is very recent; therefore, he does not write a bibliography card and continues his search.

Two additional cards with the subject heading of AIDS seem to be more useful to the student because one book gives the social aspects of the disease in the United States as well as public opinion, and the other was published in 1987.

	AIDS ((DISEASE)
808.4	
R32	AIDS/edited by Robert Emmet Long—New York: Wilson, 1987. 192 p. : 19cm—(The Reference shelf; v. 59, no. 3)
	Reprinted from various sources.
	Includes bibliographic references.
	15549792
	ISBN 0–8142–0751–3
	I. AIDS (Disease) I. Long, Robert Emmet. II. Series
FFIB	EDBBdc 85-3061r85

Discussion: The student notes that the book is on the reference shelf. Because the date of publication is 1987, the student feels that this might be a good book. He also notes that the book is edited and the articles are reprinted from other sources.

```
         AIDS (DISEASE)—UNITED STATES—PUBLIC OPINION
362.19
A468a     Altman, Dennis.
              AIDS in the mind of America / Dennis Altman.—
          1st ed.—Garden City, N.Y: Anchor Press/Doubleday,
          1986.
          viii, 228 p.; 22 cm.
          Bibliography: p. [1951-216.
          Includes index.
          12236432
          ISBN 0—385—19523—0

          1. AIDS (Disease)—Social aspects—United States.
          2. AIDS (Disease)—United States—Public opinion.
          3. Public opinion—United States. I. Title

FF1B                   EDBBdc                        85-15055
```

Discussion: The student researching AIDS notes that the author is Dennis Altman and that the book was published in 1986. Because the book has a bibliography, the student may assume that the author has used a number of sources to write the book. The title of the book is *AIDS in the Mind of America*.

Cross Reference Cards: The two types of cross reference cards are the "see" and the "see also" cards. A "see" card is the library's way of telling the researcher that the subject will be found under a classification different from the one the researcher is looking for.

```
          Acquired immune deficiency syndrome
             see

          AIDS (Disease)
```

A "see also" card suggests other related subjects that can be investigated. "See also" cards are filed after all other cards on the same subject. They are often a help in limiting the subject.

```
Immunologic diseases
    see also

ALLERGY

Collagen diseases

Immunopathology
```

Once the student has examined all of the cards in the card catalog for the subject being researched, he makes bibliography cards for those that seem most promising, making sure the call number of each book is on the bibliography card. He decides to check out one book: *Immune Disorders.*

```
616.97
133         Immune disorders.—Springhouse, Pa.: Springhouse
                Corp., c1985.
                192 p.: ill.; 29 cm—(Nurse's clinical library)
                "nursing 85 books."
                Includes bibliographies and index.
                11756061
                ISBN 0—91 6730-76—X

            1. Immunologic diseases.
            2. Immunologic diseases—Nursing.
            I. Series


FF1 B                        EDBB                  dc85—2699
```

Since the book is part of a series of eighty-five books from the Nurse's Clinical Library, the student feels that the information will be of value, for it may give symptoms of the disease as well as a description and a formal definition of the term.

To determine whether or not the book will be helpful, the student first examines the table of contents. The book lists fourteen chapters, beginning with the review of basic principles of immune disorders and ending with controlling gastrointestinal disorders. Skimming the table of contents, the researcher notes that there is not an entry for AIDS but that there is a subdivision: "Disorders of the Immune System." The student reads further and finds that a subtopic is "Overcoming Immune deficiencies." Since the researcher is not sure that the specific topic of *AIDS* is included, he looks in the index which gives him a more detailed listing and finds that the subject of acquired immune deficiencies is on pages 80-81 as well as on a number of other pages throughout the book. As the student continues to examine the book, he finds a bibliography that could be helpful.

For research projects that are limited, the student may not have time to do extensive reading but will want to examine the sources that are most useful for the paper. Therefore, if he does locate a book on the topic and the table of contents and the index indicate that a particular section is pertinent, he may want to use it.

Readers' Guide to Periodical Literature

The Readers' Guide to Periodical Literature indexes by subject (and sometimes by author) the contents of over one hundred magazines. The yearly bound volumes of *Readers' Guide* index articles from March through February every year. If the bound volume for the recent year is not yet in your library, you can still locate very current articles on your topic because the *Readers' Guide* keeps indexing articles all year and publishes them in paperback supplements semimonthly between September and June and monthly between July and August. Once you learn to use the *Readers' Guide*, you will be able to use other indexes for specialized fields because the formats of these indexes are the same as the format for *Readers' Guide*.

Reproduced here are excerpts from actual pages in the *Readers' Guide*. In his bibliography search on the subject of AIDS, the student looks first in the most recent index available. He finds four columns of articles on the subject. The articles are classified under various headings, including *Causes, Costs, Psychological Aspects, Religious Aspects, AIDS and Youth, Therapy, Statistics, Fund Raising, International Aspects, Legal Aspects, Mortality, Prevention, Psychological Aspects, Public Opinion, Religious Aspects*, and *Statistics*. In all there are twenty- nine categories, as well as a "See also" reference to specific categories.

Since the student is undecided, he skims the entries and selects two categories: "AIDS (DISEASE AND CHILDREN)" and "AIDS (DISEASE AND WOMEN) "

AIDS (DISEASE) AND CHILDREN
See also
AIDS (Disease) education
Children of AIDS patients
Pediatric AIDS Foundation
Honorary Giraffe (pediatric AIDS specialist J. Oleske) J.Glausiusz. il por *American Health* v14 p24-5 N '95
Should an AIDS test be required for all pregnant women? A. Engeler, il *Glamour* v93 p 58+ N '95
This is what you thought: should HIV tests be mandatory for pregnant women? [results of survey] il *Glamour* v93 p153 S '95
AIDS (DISEASE) AND WOMEN
"Could I have AIDS?" P. Lister, il *Redbook* v186 p112-15+ N '95
A Kennedy and his flock [Irish Catholic priest M. Kennedy's assertion that woman with AIDS deliberately infected men in Dungarvan] C Tóibín. il *The New Yorker* v71 p36 O 2 '95
Living with AIDS. B. Mirsky. il *Sassy* v8 p92 O '95
Should an AIDS test be required for all pregnant women? A. Engeler, il *Glamour* v93 p 58+ N '95
So much to lose; ed. by Kathryn Casey, A. Getty. il pors *Ladies' Home Journal* v112 p38+ S '95
This is what you thought: should HIV tests be mandatory for pregnant women? [results of survey] il *Glamour* v93 p153 S '95
A weekend with HIV-positive women. D. Danna. il *Glamour* v93 p112 S '95

Women & the HIV epidemic: no individual solutions [Uganda] E. Reid. map *Choices (New York, N.Y.)* v4 P30-2 Ag '95

Women, AIDS and budget cuts. *America* v 173 p3 O 28 '95

However, since the student is still undecided, he scans the titles of the articles listed in both categories. Neither category interests the student; however, at this point he decides to focus his paper on the vaccines available.

Vaccines and vaccination

An AIDS mystery solved [Australian HIV survivors offer hope for effective vaccine] J. M. Nash. il *Time* v146 p100-1 N 20 '95

Attenuated retrovirus vaccines and AIDS. K. K. A. Van Rompay and others. *Science* v270 p1213-22 N 17 '95

A benign strain of the virus [research by John Mills] *Newsweek* v126 p 80 N 11 '95

Into another hot zone [interview with D. Francis] por *Men's Health* v10 p42 N '95

Mutated HIV could serve as vaccine [Australian survivors] L. Seachrist. *Science News* v148 p308 N 11 '95

New clues found to how some people live with HIV [Australian survivors] J. Cohen. il *Science* v270 p 917-18 N 10 '95

Thailand weighs AIDS vaccine tests. J. Cohen. il *Science* v270 p904-7 N 10 '95

Under the subject heading, he sees three articles that appear to be promising. He makes proper bibliography cards for these citations in *Reader's Guide*. In order to do so, he must understand what the various parts of the citation mean. Here is an explanation of the first article.

"An AIDS mystery solved" is the title of the article

" (Australian HIV survivors offer hope for effective vaccine) " is the subtitle. "J.M. Nash" is the author.

"il" means that the article is illustrated.

"Time" is the name of the periodical containing the article . It is in volume 146 on pages 100–101.

"N.11 '95" is the month, day, and year.

The student now consults the examples of bibliography forms (pages 293–305) to see how to write a proper bibliography card for a signed article. The *Reader 's Guide* citation converted to bibliography form would look like this:

Nash, J. M. "An AIDS Mystery Solved." *Time* 20 Nov. 1995:

100-1.

Taken from READER'S GUIDE TO PERIODICAL LITERATURE, 1996. Reprinted by permission.

The student can now begin his working bibliography by writing cards for those articles that he plans to use.

Assignment 1: Beginning Your Preliminary Bibliography

Find one useful article from a general encyclopedia, one or two books, and at least four articles from *Reader's Guide* on your subject. Be sure to consult the paperback supplements of *Readers' Guide* so that you locate the most current articles on your subject in periodicals. If you are looking for some history and background on your subject, you can skim through bound volumes of the *Readers' Guide* for as many years back as you care to go. Checking the list of examples for bibliography forms, make proper bibliography cards for each of these sources.

Newspaper Indexes

New York Times Index: The *New York Times Index* is the major newspaper index and most libraries subscribe to the *New York Times* newspaper on microfilm. The index can be helpful to you in three ways:

First, the *New York Times* is the most comprehensive newspaper in the United States; the index, therefore, can direct you to articles on innumerable subjects.

Second, the *New York Times Index* not only lists articles by subject, but also gives short summaries or abstracts for articles of special importance. These summaries will give you a good idea of what the article is about, and you can eliminate some without having to read the articles themselves on microfilm.

Third, the *New York Times* serves as an index to the reporting of events in other newspapers since international, national, state, and even some local news stories are covered on the same day or during the same period of time.

The yearly volumes of the *New York Times Index* list articles from January to January of each year. Supplements to the index come out in paperback twice a month, and the index is usually ready six weeks after the issue of the paper itself. Therefore, the New York Times Index is one of your best guides for locating current information on a subject.

Excerpts from actual pages of the *New York Times Index* are reproduced below. First, the student looked under "Acquired Immune Deficiency Syndrome." The entry with the term AIDS in parentheses heads a long list of articles. A brief excerpt is reproduced below.

Acquired Immune Deficiency Syndrome (AIDS)

Grandparents nationwide have become unexpected victims of AIDS epidemic; increasing numbers are being forced into traditional roles, but with new twist, namely, of caring for adult children with AIDS and for grandchildren, many also dying of disease, who are left behind; statistics suggest more will be caring for children as disease increasingly affects entire families. Federal Centers for Disease Control report proportion of heterosexual AIDS cases decreased from 66.5 percent to 46.6 percent between 1985 and 1993, while that attributed to intravenous drug use among women and heterosexual men increased from 17.4 percent to 27.7 percent; studies show about 30 percent of newborns born to HIV-positive mothers end up infected themselves: photos (m), N 21, A, 1:2

Federal judge in Toledo, Ohio, rules Dr. Charles Hull violated Americans with Disabilities Act when he refused to treat 29-year-old Fred Charon at hospital because he had AIDS (S), N 22,A,16:4

Dr. Christine Katlama of France reports that experimental cocktail of AZT and new drug, 3TC, has produced pronounced short-term anti-HIV effect, says combination caused sustained reduction in virus in blood; tells of her finding at second International congress on drug Therapy in HIV Infection in Glasgow; her study of 129 HIV-positive patients is consistent with second study, of 223 patients, by Dr. Schlomo Staszewski in Germany (M), N 22,C,3:3

Group of HIV-positive artists plans to gather on steps of Metropolitan Museum to tell their stories of creating art from their experiences with AIDS (S), N 25, C,30:3

The entry gives brief summaries of articles that are available. Following these, the *Times Index* helps the researcher by listing articles of special interest in boldface print, and any article in boldface is generally followed by a summary.

Pres. Clinton names Patricia S. Fleming new White House director of AIDS policy; former Health and Human Services official succeeds Kristine M. Gebbie, who resigned 11 months ago; Fleming photo; black AIDS group welcomes appointment of black woman (s), N 11,A,20:1

Pedro Zaomora, well-known AIDS educator and cast member of MTV's The Real World, dies of AIDS at age 22; his photo; Zamora, Cuban who tested positive for HIV at age 17, was sought-after speaker on disease; students comment at his Florida alma mater, Hialeah High School (S), N 12,1,8:1

A look at one of the summaries tells the student that it would be useful to read the whole article about grandparents on microfilm. The last line of the entry gives specific location information about the article. The (M) indicates that the article is of medium length. The article can be found in the Nov. 21 issue of the *New York Times* on page 1, column 2 of section A. You will notice that unlike the citations in *Readers' Guide,* the year is not given. You must refer to the cover of the *New York Times Index* for the year, which in this case is 1994. You cannot make the complete bibliography card for this article until you actually see it on microfilm because the exact headline is not given in the citation. The space for the title is left blank and filled in when the article is read on microfilm or on the computer.

<u>The New York Times</u>

21 Nov. 1994, sec. A:1:2

Excerpts from *The New York Times Index*. Reprinted by permission.

Local Newspapers: Nearly every city newspaper has an index of its own. However, instead of indexing articles in a book, the newspaper maintains a room referred to as the *morgue* or the *library* where articles are classified and filed, often in long envelopes, by names and by subject These files are available to the public for use in the newspaper's library, along with machines for making photocopies of articles. Newspaper employees attempt to keep these files current, within two weeks of the newspaper's publication. The newspaper library also keeps on microfilm copies of all editions of its newspaper.

If you have narrowed your subject to a local aspect of the problem, you plan to explore in your research paper, your local newspaper library will be a valuable source of material.

NewsBank

NewsBank is a current reference service that not only indexes articles from newspapers and periodicals, but also allows researchers to access information from microfiche. The articles are indexed on microfiche in two ways: the "citation only" and the "citation with index terms." The "citation only" includes an abstract.

NewsBank, inc. - NewsBank Reference Service Plus - Citation Only

---

MICROFICHE LOCATOR CODE: NewsBank   1996 HEA 8:F12

SOURCE: Journal Star (Peoria, Illinois)

DATE: February 24, 1996
ABSTRACT: An experimental gene therapy treatment for HIV-positive
               individuals, which was developed at Northern Illinois
               University, is approved for clinical trial.

The "citation with index terms" has an abstract as well as the Index terms.

NewsBank, inc. - NewsBank Reference Service Plus - Article with Citation

---

MICROFICHE LOCATOR CODE: NewsBank   1996 HEA 8:66

SOURCE: (Newark, New Jersey) Star-Ledger

DATE: February 18, 1996
ABSTRACT: The development of a new class of drugs to combat AIDS, the
               protease inhibitors, is described, and the potential for profit
               is examined.

INDEX TERMS:

```
NewsBank:    AIDS (DISEASE)
             treatment
             protease inhibitors
```

However, the most user friendly and most widely used base is the NewsBank index to periodicals. Not all libraries subscribe to this service, however. Here are several listings from that index. A key to the abbreviations of all listings is provided by NewsBank.

> **Beating the odds.** (people surviving with AIDS) (includes related articles) Susan Brink, Traci Watson and Mike Tharp. U.S. News & World Report, Feb 12, 1996 v120 n6 p60(8). Mag Coll.: 82H0617. Bus. Coll.: 92N2018.
> —Abstract available—
> **Jungle fever.** (bone-marrow transplants from baboons to humans as potential cure for AIDS) Rachel Gotbaus. The Advocate, Sept 5, 1995 n689 p34(3)
> —Abstract available—
> **Killer cells may be clue to HIV baby's recovery.** Jeremy Webb. New Scientist, April 8, 1995 v146 n1972 p6(1)
> —Abstract available)

Yearbooks

Statistics and miscellaneous facts about various events and agencies are published annually in several sources. The sources are known as yearbooks.

Statistical Abstract of the United States: The Statistical Abstract, as it is commonly called, is published by the United States Government, and it includes a wide range of subjects. The table of contents of the statistical abstract is very comprehensive, but if you cannot find your particular topic listed there, consult the index.

Here the student finds that there are several different statistical tables that report information about the disease. Turning to page 139, he finds the chart reproduced on the next page, a good example of the type of statistical table you are likely to find in the source.

These charts often have a notation under the heading which bears directly on the figures given in the tables. For example, under the title of table No. 211, the student reads "figures should be interpreted with caution." He notes that the source for the data is from the U.S. Center for Disease Control and that the figures are only important because they indicate trends of the various diseases reported.

The student also notes that there are not figures for the years between 1970 to 1985 because, according to the second explanatory footnote, AIDS "was not a notifiable disease until 1984." Since the figures are only those reported to the Center for Disease Control, the statistics may be incomplete. Because statistics on this subject are always changing, the student should probably find the most recent ones available in current periodicals.

The bibliography entry for any of these yearbook sources is prepared in the same manner as an entry from a general encyclopedia. The bibliography card for the chart in *Statistical Abstract* is as follows:

No. 211. Specified Reportable Diseases—Cases Reported 1970 to 1993

(Figures should be interpreted with caution. Although reporting of some of these diseases is incomplete, the figures are of value in indicating trends of disease incidence. Includes cases imported from outside the United States. See *Historical Statistics, Colonial Times to 1970*, series B 291–303, for related data.)

DISEASE	1970	1980	1985	1988	1989	1990	1991	1992	1993
AIDS [1]	(NA)	(NA)	8,249	31,001	33,722	41,595	43,672	45,472	103,691
Amebiasis	2,888	5,271	4,433	2,860	3,217	3,328	2,989	2,942	2,970
Aseptic meningitis	6,480	8,026	10,619	7,234	10,274	11,85	14,526	12,223	12,848
Botulism	12	89	122	84	89	92	114	91	97
Brucellosis (undulant fever)	213	183	153	96	95	85	104	105	120
Chickenpox (1,000)	[3]	190.9	178.2	192.9	185.4	173.1	147.1	158.4	134.7
Diphtheria	435	3	3	2	3	4	5	4	–
Encephalitis									
Primary infectious [4]	1,580	1,362	1,376	882	981	1,341	1,021	774	919
Post infectious	370	40	161	121	88	105	82	129	170
Haemophilius influenza	[3]	[3]	[3]	[3]	[3]	[3]	2,764	1,412	1,419
Hepatitis B (serum) (1,000)	8.3	19.0	26.6	23.2	23.4.	21.1	18.0	16.1	13.4
A (infectious) (1,000)	56.8	29.1	23.2	28.5	35.8	31.4	24.4	23.1	24.2
Unspecified (1,000)	[3]	11.9	5.5	2.5	2.3	1.7	1.3	0.9	0.6
Non-A, non-B (1,000)[5]	[3]	[3]	4.2	2.6	2.5	2.6	3.6	6.0	4.8
Legionellosis	[3]	[3]	830	1,085	1,190	1,370	1,317	1,339	1,280
Leprosy (Hansen disease)	129	223	361	184	163	198	154	172	187
Leptospirosis	47	85	57	54	93	77	58	54	51
Lyme disease	[3]	[3]	[3]	[3]	[3]	[3]	9,465	9,895	8,257
Malaria	3,051	2,062	1,049	1,099	1,277	1,92	1,278	1,087	1,411
Measles (1,000)	47.4	13.5	2.8	3.4	18.2	27.8	9.6	2.2	0.3
Meningococcal infections	2,505	2,840	2,479	2,964	2,727	2,451	2,130	2,134	2,637
Mumps (1,000)	105.0	8.6	3.0	4.9	5.7	5.3	4.3	2.6	1.7
Pertussis [6] (1,000)	4.2	1.7	3.6	3.5	4.2	4.6	2.7	4.1	6.6
Plague	13	18	17	15	4	2	11	13	10
Poliomyelitis, acute [7]	33	9	7	9	9	6	9	6	3
Psittacosis	35	124	119	114	116	113	94	92	60
Rabies, animal	3,224	6,421	5,565	4,651	4,724	4,826	6,910	8,589	9,377
Rabies, human	3	–	1	–	1	1	3	1	3
Rheumatic fever, acute [8]	3,227	432	90	148	144	108	127	75	112
Rubella [9] (1,000)	56.6	3.9	0.6	0.2	0.4	1.1	1.4	0.2	0.2
Salmonellosis [10] (1,000)	22.1	33.7	65.3	48.9	47.8	48.6	48.2	40.9	41.6
Shigellosis [11] (1,000)	13.8	19.0	17.1	30.6	25.0	27.1	23.5	23.9	32.2

– Represents zero. NA Not available. [1] Acquired immunodeficiency syndrome was not a notifiable disease until 1984. Figures are shown for years in which cases were reported to the CDC. Beginning 1993, based on revised classification system and expanded surveillance case definition. [2] Beginning in 1980, includes foodborne, infant, wound, and unspecified cases. [3] Disease was not notifiable. [4] Beginning 1980, reported data reflect new diagnostic categories. [5] Includes some persons positive for antibody to hepatitis C virus who do not have hepatitis. [6] Whooping cough [7] Revised. Data subject to annual revisions. [8] Based on reports from States: 38 in 1970, 37 in 1980, 31 in 1985, 29 in 1988, 28 in 2989, 30 in 1990, 23 in 1991, and 26 in 1992 and 1993. [9] German measles. [10] Excludes typhoid fever. [11] Bacillary dysentery. [12] Newly reported active cases. New diagnostic standards introduced in 1980.

Source: U.S. Centers for Disease Control and Prevention, Atlanta, GA, *Summary of Notifiable Diseases, United States, Morbidity and Mortality Weekly Report*, vol. 43, No. 32, August 19, 1994.

"AIDS Cases Reported by Patient
Characteristic: 1981 to 1994."
Statistical Abstract of the
United States 1995: 140.

Should the student wish additional statistics, he may turn to page 140 under "Health and Nutrition." There are two additional charts. The first one listed, NO. 212, again cautions the researcher because the comparisons may "reflect improvements in the 1988 design rather than true changes in hospital use." Also, the source for this information is the National Center for Health Statistics.

Health and Nutrition

No. 212. Selected Measures of Hospital Utilization for Patients Discharged With the Diagnosis of Human Immunodeficiency Virus (HIV): 1985 to 1993

(See headnote, table 189)

MEASURE OF UTILIZATION	UNIT	1985	1989	1990	1991	1992	1993
Number of patients discharged [1]...	1,000	23	140	146	165	194	225
Rate of patient discharges [2]........	Rate	1.0	5.7	5.9	6.6	7.6	8.8
Number of days of care	1,000	387	1,731	2,166	2,108	2,136	2,561
Rate of days of care [2].............	Rate	16.3	70.2	87.7	84.1	84.3	99.9
Average length of stay [3]	Days	17.1	12.4	14.9	12.8	11.0	11.4

[1] Comparisons beginning 1989 with data for earlier years should be made with caution as estimates of change may reflect improvements in the 1988 design rather than true changes in hospital use. [2] Per 10,000 population. Based on Bureau of the Census estimated civilian population as of July 1. Population estimates for the 1980's do not reflect revised estimates based on the 1990 Census of Population. [3] For similar data on all patients, see table 189.

Source: National Center for Health Statistics, Vital and Health Statistics, series 13.

The third chart, shown on the following page, has other information concerning the disease. Not only are AIDS cases reported by individual states, but they are also listed by age, sex, and race/ethnic groups.

Editorial Research Reports

A specialized index, the printed Report is issued on Friday, four times a month, and is published by the Congressional Quarterly, Inc. Each report treats a subject that is in the current news or may be in the near future In the first part of the book are listed all reports issued in 1990. The index, however, lists reports for the past ten years.

Under the heading of AIDS, there are four subject headings: "AIDS Dilemmas," "AIDS: Spreading Mystery Disease," "AIDS Update," and "Good News and Bad about AIDS." Year, volume, and page numbers are also given.

World Almanac and Book of Facts: One of the most useful collections of miscellaneous information is the *World Almanac*. It contains statistics on educational, financial, industrial, religious, and social subjects. In addition, it includes lists of historical events and statistics on

No. 213. AIDS Cases Reported, by Patient Characteristic: 1981 to 1994

(Provisional. For cases reported in the year shown. For data on AIDS deaths, see table 130. Data are subject to retrospective changes and may differ from those data in table 211.)

CHARACTERISTIC	Total	1981–1985	1986	1987	1988	1989	1990	1991	1992	1993	1994
Total [1]	427,392	15,331	13,083	21,503	30,703	33,631	41,762	43,776	45,964	103,360	78,279
Age:											
Under 5 years old	4,711	201	155	271	443	494	583	530	615	680	739
5 to 12 years old	1,184	23	27	56	127	103	144	149	142	202	211
13 to 29 years old	78,838	3,224	2,794	4,382	6,261	6,703	8,087	7,827	7,918	18,671	12,971
30 to 39 years old	195,304	7,214	6,078	9,826	14,176	15,555	18,994	20,026	20,760	47,148	35,527
40 to 49 years old	103,894	3,215	2,685	4,661	6,539	7,351	9,764	10,655	11,632	26,609	20,783
50 to 59 years old	31,319	1,143	966	1,594	2,142	2,418	2,940	3,248	3,442	7,455	5,971
Over 60 years old	12,142	311	378	713	1,015	1,007	1,250	1,341	1,455	2,595	2,077
Sex:											
Male	368,920	14,247	12,028	19,666	27,417	29,973	36,871	38,087	39,608	86,802	64,221
Female	48,472	1,084	1,055	1,837	3,286	2,658	4,891	5,689	6,356	16,558	14,058
Race/Ethnic group:											
White [2]	214,061	9,125	7,769	13,253	17,050	18,597	22,378	22,163	22,507	48,039	33,180
Black [2]	146,159	3,981	3,392	5,435	9,141	10,292	13,250	14,684	16,103	38,424	31,457
Hispanic	62,419	2,133	1,810	2,608	4,236	4,371	5,685	6,446	6,789	15,642	12,699
Other/unknown	4,753	92	112	207	276	371	449	483	565	1,255	943
Leading States											
New York	83,197	5,295	3,804	4,010	6,945	5,991	8,368	8,135	8,322	17,383	14,944
California	78,064	2,498	2,524	5,188	5,692	6,449	7,373	7,713	8,821	13,690	12,136
Florida	43,978	1,066	1,031	1,633	2,650	3,448	4,018	5,471	5,066	10,958	8,617
Texas	3,712	830	949	1,666	2,214	2,382	3,317	3,053	2,930	7,492	4,879
New Jersey	25,089	952	781	1,516	2,461	2,235	2,457	2,296	,2024	5,374	4,993
Illinois	14,255	344	347	628	984	1,120	1,269	1,612	1,887	2,960	3,104
Pennsylvania	12,754	337	305	665	852	1,072	1,223	1,233	1,347	3,192	2,528
Georgia	12,228	285	303	518	841	1,098	1,229	1,468	1,399	2,842	2,245
Maryland	10,534	229	190	457	549	711	983	972	1,201	2,520	2,722
Massachusetts	9,254	296	286	454	708	750	839	959	863	2,698	1,401
District of Columbia ..	7,129	285	237	466	504	496	733	711	710	1,588	1,399
Louisiana	6,611	177	165	334	402	507	701	822	825	1,439	1,239
Ohio	6,509	95	214	342	504	492	692	631	778	1,577	1,184
Virginia	6,308	174	158	244	350	397	748	682	780	1,623	1,162
Michigan	6,240	104	151	212	455	505	580	636	741	1,821	1,035
Washington	5,922	173	170	324	341	525	752	583	564	1,558	932
Connecticut	5,754	167	180	255	413	432	427	565	649	1,754	912
Missouri	5,635	82	73	241	410	443	580	658	713	1,722	713
North Carolina	5,419	90	81	209	277	446	571	602	585	1,371	1,187
Colorado	4,571	126	166	226	325	388	365	431	406	1,322	816

[1] Includes other States not shown separately, and persons whose residence is unknown. [2] Non-Hispanic. [3] States with at least 2,000 total cases reported through 1994.

Source: U.S. Centers for Disease Control and Prevention, Atlanta, GA, unpublished data.

political organizations and on society in general. An alphabetized index is at the front of each volume. The *Almanac* is considered a reliable source and is kept up to date.

Facts on File: Indexed twice monthly, this reference is cumulated throughout the year. It is a digest of news classified under such headings as World Affairs, National Affairs, Foreign Affairs, Latin American Affairs, Finance, Economy, Arts, Science, Education, Religion, Sports, and Miscellaneous.

Information Please Almanac: This source classifies miscellaneous information with a subject index. Specialists write the articles about books, sports, theater, movies, music, art, and so on. In addition, there are entries with statistical and historical information and other general information.

Statesman's Year-Book: This manual is a concise, reliable record of descriptive and statistical information about the governments of the world.

Essay and General Literature Index

This reference source is an index to essays and articles published in books. Since you cannot find individual essays by subject listed in the card catalog, you must use the *Essay and General Literature Index* to find information in essays collected in books.

Published once every six months, this index is cumulated in a hard cover volume at the end of each calender year; and every five years the yearly volumes are bound in a single volume. Not all essays published during a year are indexed, however. Only those appear which the editors consider the most important.

The *Essay and General Literature Index* is divided into two parts. The first part indexes the essays by subject, listing the author and the title of the essay and the book in which it appears. Reproduced below is an example of an entry for the subject of "AIDS."

> **AIDS (Disease)**
> Amis, M. Double jeopardy: making sense
> of AIDS. (In Amis, M. The moronic inferno
> p. 87-98)

What does this entry mean?

> M. Amis is the author of the essay.
> "Double Jeopardy" is the title of the article.
> The moronic inferno indicates the name of the book in which the essay will be found.
> p. 87-98 is the inclusive page reference for the essay about "making sense of AIDS. "

The second part of the *Essay and General Literature Index* lists complete information about the books in which the essays appear. The student will now have to consult the card catalog or the book itself to find the place of publication so that he can complete a bibliography card. The bibliography card will be an example of the form for an essay in an edited collection.

Specialized Encyclopedias

One of the most useful sources for detailed or technical information on a subject is a specialized encyclopedia. A look in the card catalog under "Encyclopedias" or a walk around the reference room of a library will show you the wide range of encyclopedias on special fields. Just a few of the many specialized encyclopedias you will find are the *Encyclopedia of American Politics*, the *Encyclopedia of Banking and Finance*, the *Encyclopedia of Cybernetics*, the *Encyclopedia of Education*, the *International Encyclopedia of the Social Sciences*, the *Encyclopedia of Oceanography*, and the *Encyclopedia of Religion and Ethics*.

The student researching acquired immune deficiency syndrome consults the *McGraw Hill Encyclopedia of Science and Technology*. Like other indexes the subject is listed under "acquired immune deficiency syndrome." The index volume directs the student to articles on the subject of "AIDS" on pages 66 to 69 and 378–379, according to a listing of the articles (a portion shown below).

> Acquired immune deficiency syndrome (AIDS) 66—69* 379
> chorioretinitis 68
> diarrhea 68 69
> fever and weight loss 68
> history and epidemiology 67-69
> immunologic profile 69
> Kaposi's sarcoma and other tumors 69.

The asterisk indicates the page reference to the titles of articles. The student consults the article on pages 66–69, and writes a bibliography card for the source.

Manchere, Abe M. "Acquired immune deficiency syndrome
 (AIDS)." *McGraw Hill Encyclopedia of Science and Technology*
 1985 ed.

At the end of the article there is "see" reference for background information as well as a bibliography for the entry.

Since the article is three pages long, the student will be able to get specific information about the disease. In addition, the article gives a strict definition of the term AIDS adopted by the Centers for Disease Control (CDC). The author's name is listed at the end of the article in brackets: [Abe M. Manchere].

The Vertical File

You are now familiar with the basic research sources in any library. There is, however, one more source which you will want to know about. This is the vertical file. Many college and city libraries keep a filing cabinet which contains folders of newspaper and magazine clippings and pamphlets and bulletins. These materials are arranged by subject. Some libraries keep a separate vertical file for the articles that pertain to their state. Librarians try to keep the vertical file current, particularly on subjects of great general interest. It is a good idea to end your bibliography search with a look at the vertical file.

Assignment #2: Completing the Preliminary Bibliography

Add to the bibliography cards you already have by consulting *The New York Times Index*, one or more of the yearbooks, the *Essay and General Literature Index*, and a specialized encyclopedia. Finally, check the vertical file. Obtain any pamphlets and bulletins related to your topic. You may not be able to find information on your topic in all of these sources, but the careful researcher investigates all of them during the preparation of the preliminary bibliography.

Reviewing Your Preliminary Bibliography

As you look over your preliminary bibliography, you will see that you have obtained your information from two types of reference sources—direct and indirect. Direct reference sources include general and specialized encyclopedias, yearbooks, general and specialized dictionaries, and the vertical file. They are called direct sources because you get your information directly from them. Indirect sources, such as the card catalog, the periodical indexes (*Reader's Guide* and *The New York Times Index*), and the *Essay and General Literature Index* are called indirect reference sources because they do not contain the information itself but direct the researcher to the books, magazines, and newspapers where he can find the information.

Once you have learned to use these basic reference sources, you will be able to use other important indexes for more advanced research. These indexes on specialized subjects will direct you to specialized publications. Some of the indexes are *Applied Science and Technology Index*, *Cumulative Index for Nursing Literature*, *Education Index*, *Social Sciences and Humanities Index*, and *Business Periodicals Index*.

Electronic Information for Bibliography

There are some services that are now providing information about library materials or sources that are available not only within a given community but outside of the community as well. Some of the libraries are *Online* which allows a researcher to look for material on a given subject to see what books, magazines or other sources of information may be within a particular library. This information. in some cases, may range from your local library up to the Library of Congress. For example, the universities and community college systems in South Florida have an Online system, entitled Seflin, which provides information linking thirteen local libraries within the area as well as libraries outside of the state. When you choose the catalog from one of these libraries, there are further choices to be made, such as indexes for magazine articles, other databases including electronic encyclopedias, remote library catalogs, health indexes, and library news and events.

Because an individual wanted to gather information on extremist cults using violence, he looked through the indexes and found a radio program dealing with his subject. The following is what he found under the title of "Cults" in a source entitled *Journal Graphics*.

—————————————Journal Graphics —————————

Host/Reporter: Correspondent
Headline: Extremist Cults Use Violence to Achieve Utopian Vision
Program name: Morning Edition (NPR)
Network: National Public Radio
Summary: History professor and author Paul Boyer says that extremist religious groups that sponsor violence share certain characteristics, such as a sense of catastrophe and apocalypse combined with a utopian vision.
Section: News; Domestic
Show topics: Cults
        Terrorism & Hostages
        Psychology
Guests: PAUL BOYER
Air date: 03/23/1995
Show #: 1569 Segment: 11
Program Type:
636 words

The above information is a summary of the program. The source informs the student that he may have the full transcript of the entire program if the student will write to the station.

There are several considerations that the student must make before deciding whether to use a source such as the one mentioned above. The most obvious consideration is whether this will supply the information needed for the paper. But an even more important consideration whether the author or the narrator can be classified as an expert. He or she should be an expert in the particular subject under discussion. Therefore. he or she should have the education, the training and the experience to qualify. Furthermore, if the author or narrator is an expert, he or she will be recognized by other experts in an area of study.

Students who check sources can strengthen their written quality. **Not all information gathered from electronic networks is acceptable for formal expository writing.**

Stage	Assembling the Sourcebook
3	

Assembling the Sourcebook

1. Determining Whether Sources Are Authoritative
2. The Systematic Assembly of the Sourcebook

A sourcebook, sometimes called a casebook is a collection of information on a particular topic. The sourcebook for your research paper is your collection of photocopied articles, clippings from your own newspapers and magazines, bulletins, pamphlets, and any other pertinent material you have found in your research.

STEP 1   Determining Whether Sources Are Authoritative

Before selecting the sources you will actually use from your preliminary bibliography, you need to determine whether those sources are authoritative. Simply because something is in print does not necessarily mean that it is true, that it is accurate, or that it is presented objectively. Suppose, for instance, that you had two pamphlets or bulletins about water pollution in a river in your state. Perhaps a major manufacturing company has been guilty of polluting the river and has put out a pamphlet concerning its efforts to assist in correcting the problem. The pamphlet may be informative, but you are more likely to get unbiased and completely objective information from a bulletin or pamphlet issued by a neutral investigating agency or commission.

In addition to judging probable objectivity, you will want to check the date of publication of any source to see how old the information is. You might want to use older sources if you are establishing the history or the progress of a problem, but you will also need current information for investigation of an American social problem.

You begin research by checking encyclopedias first not only because you can get a good overview of a subject, but also because the articles in encyclopedias are written by experts in their fields. Sometimes the article is signed at the end; sometimes only the author's initials appear, and you must refer to the list of initials at the beginning of the volume for the author's name. An unsigned article is written by the research staff.

Books published by university presses are often reliable sources because they are written by individuals or groups that have conducted extensive research. Another way of checking the authoritativeness of a book is to find out what the writer has done in the past and what he is currently doing. For instance, *Crime in America* was written by Ramsey Clark, former attorney general of the United States. Dr. Morris Chafetz, who wrote a book about alcoholism in 1962, is now director of the Department of Health, Education and Welfare's National Institute on Alcohol Abuse and Alcoholism. Biographical references such as those found in the *Who's Who* series can help you to determine an author's background and his qualifications to write on a particular subject.

Articles published in technical and professional journals are more scholarly and often more specific and derailed than those published in magazines for wider audiences. However, since you may be using these less technical magazines for your first research project, you should rely on those periodicals that are considered the most accurate and objective.

STEP 2 The Systematic Assembly of the Sourcebook

Now, with your preliminary bibliography assembled and with some understanding of what constitutes authoritative material, you can begin to assemble your sourcebook. This can be done just as systematically as you prepared your bibliography.

1. Select the encyclopedia article that you think is the most informative on your topic and then make a photocopy of it. At the top or on the side of the article, write the complete information about the source which you have obtained from the bibliography card.

2. Next, examine the books for which you have made bibliography cards. If a scan of the introduction and the table of contents of a book indicate that the book is of no use to you, return it to the stacks and remove the card from your set of preliminary bibliography cards. If, however, you find that several pages or perhaps a chapter of a book is useful, make a photocopy of only those pages you are sure you will use. Identify these materials here as you did the encyclopedia article by transferring the information from the bibliography card.

3. Now check the periodical indexes. Check the magazine articles for which you have made bibliography cards. Scan each article rapidly to determine whether it contains information that bears on your topic. Copy only those articles which you are sure that you can use. Identify each article by transferring the information from the bibliography card onto the top or side of the first page of the article. If you are undecided about the usefulness of an article, then annotate the bibliography card and set it aside for the time being. Later, if you decide you need this information, a review of your annotated bibliography cards will remind you where to find it. Now add your copies of magazine articles to the sourcebook.

4. After consulting general encyclopedias, the card catalog, and magazines, then consult the other sources. In the case of the *New York Times*, you will have to read the article on microfilm or CD-ROM. Some libraries have microfilm copying machines; if your library does not, you will have to take notes directly from the microfilm. If this

is the case, then wait until you have had instruction in note taking before you investigate the *New York Times*.

5. Now follow the same procedure for yearbooks and statistical sources, for the *Essay and General Literature Index*, and for the specialized encyclopedias as you did when you investigated the other sources.

6. Finally, add to your sourcebook any pamphlets, bulletins, newspaper and magazine clippings, and other miscellaneous information you have found on your topic. You are now ready to begin taking notes.

Stage 4 | Taking Notes

1. Making a Note Card
2. The Information on the Note Card
3. Writing the Paraphrase, the Summary, the Précis
4. Restricting the Subject Before Taking Notes
5. Taking Notes
6. Expanding Information from a Note Card
7. Stating the Preliminary Thesis
8. Setting Up the Preliminary Outline

Note taking is the operation by which you extract from your sources the specific information that develops your topic. Notes are theories, facts, illustrations, and examples about your topic. The information on note cards is to the research paper what the list of proof details is to the theme. It is just as important to be systematic in your note taking as it is to be systematic in the preparation of your bibliography. If you follow the steps to efficient note taking, you will enjoy research; and you will save yourself a great deal of time in the preparation of your final paper.

STEP 1 Making a Note Card

Notes are written on index cards. These cards can be three by five inches or four by six inches. Some writers prefer to use larger cards for their notes because it is easier to keep them separate from the three by five inch bibliography cards. Some writers feel that using the smaller cards forces them to carefully digest the information from their sources and consequently to take briefer notes. Whatever size you choose, you will need to observe the rules of note taking.

1. Enter only one type of information on each card. You may have as many cards as you wish with as many different types of information as you find pertinent to your topic.

2. Make sure that every note card carries a subject heading which classifies the infor-

mation on that card. You do this so that when you are ready to write your outline, you can assemble all the note cards in groups according to their subject headings regardless of what source they came from. To organize your themes, you grouped your proof details by classifying them according to what they had in common. You are grouping your note cards in the same way. If you prepare good note cards with properly classified headings according to the subject matter contained on each card, your outline will practically write itself.

3. Enter on every note card the source and the exact page reference for the information. The methods for entering the source are explained in detail in Step 2, *The Information on the Note Card.* Following these rules will give you some distinct advantages in preparing your research paper.

    a. As you arrange your cards by subject headings and put them in the order in which you will present the information in your paper, you will see that the subject headings form a preliminary outline.

    b. As you look over your note cards planning ways to arrange them, you will detect gaps in information in the various categories of discussion. With further research you can make additional note cards and add them to the appropriate category.

    c. If you should come across new or additional information on your subject, you need only to enter that information on a note card and add the information under its proper classification.

    d. If you decide to rearrange major subject headings or proof details for a more effective order, all you need to do is shift your cards as you see fit. Thus, when your note taking is completed, you will be able to arrange and rearrange the note cards simply by shuffling them rather than by writing outline after outline.

    e. Because your source and page number are entered on the note card, you can cite the reference without returning to the original source material.

STEP 2 The Information on the Note Card

In addition to understanding the purpose of a note card, you need to understand the kinds of information that are put on note cards, the types of notes, and the parts of a note card.

Kinds of Information

A student doing research for the first time often has difficulty taking notes from his sources. He must decide what notes to take and how much of the material to quote directly. If you keep in mind the fact that the notes are to your research paper what the list of proof details is to a theme, you will have a better understanding of what kinds of information to extract from your sources. In other words, you will be gathering evidence in the form of facts, theories, opinions, examples, and illustrations that support your topic.

Types of Notes

There are three ways to transfer information from an original source to a note card:

1. **The paraphrase.** For a paraphrase you read the original material carefully, select those portions that bear on your topic, and restate them in your own words. Most notes are written in the form of a paraphrase.

2. **The direct quotation.** You already know that a research paper is not a series of quotes strung together with a few conjunctions and transitions. Too much direct quoting suggests to the reader that you have not thought through carefully enough the information that you have gathered in your research. However, there are several very good reasons for using direct quotations in a research paper:

   a. Sometimes the wording is so original or the style is so distinctive that to paraphrase it would be to lose its essential impact. If you decide to quote such a passage, be sure that you take it down on your note card in the exact wording of the original, making sure to put quotation marks around it.

   b. Sometimes the material you come across is of such a technical or scientific nature that paraphrasing it would either distort the meaning or make the meaning unclear. In this case it is best to take the material down on the note card directly as it appears in the original again making sure to put it in quotation marks.

   c. There are times when you will want to quote a work or a phrase because no synonym exists which would give the exact meaning intended by the author.

   d. Direct quotations from an authority on a topic help to give weight to your own conclusions about it.

   e. If your research reveals that there are conflicting theories or conflicting information on a subject, then direct quotes from representatives of both positions will help to clarify the controversy and will also give objectivity to your discussion of the differences.

3. **The combination note card.** The combination note card contains both paraphrase and direct quotes. As you paraphrase material, you may find it necessary to include a word, a phrase, or a sentence of direct quotation for one or more of the reasons given here.

STEP 3 Writing the Paraphrase, the Summary, the Précis

The Paraphrase

There are times when it is necessary for a writer to reword information in his own words. For instance, English writer Charles Lamb and his sister Mary decided to paraphrase Shakespeare's plays so that children could understand them. *Tales from Shakespeare* used contemporary language of Lamb's day. During the twentieth century E. Nesbitt retold twenty of

Shakespeare's plays in a book entitled *Beautiful Stories from Shakespeare* retaining a few of the original dialogs for the reader although no quotation is more than half dozen words. Like these authors, when students take notes for research papers, they prefer writing the information in their own words so that they do not simply string together a series of quotations or present a "patchwork" of several authors' styles. In a research paper, anything that is not common knowledge must be footnoted since the idea is not original with the student writer. A paraphrase may be as long as the original material, but the difference is that the idea, opinion, or fact presented by an authority on the subject is rewritten in the language of the student writer.

The Summary

At other times, writers prefer to summarize a longer article in order to record the main ideas of an article or a book. Usually when the summary is of a legal document or case, the results of a scientific study, or a technical one, it is called an *abstract*. Regardless, both are brief statements of the main ideas which are concise and comprehensive. In the same class are *digests*, summaries of literary works, such as the *Masterplot* series in which *Anna Karenina* by Leo Tolstoy is critiqued and condensed in two and a half pages of text. Summaries are also used at the end of a chapter to review the major points for the reader. In writing note cards for summaries, the student must remember to summarize only those articles that are of doubtful importance. If, however, the student feels that he will need more information, he can always review those note cards, go to the original source, and take more comprehensive notes. Sometimes related summaries are used in explanatory footnotes. Nevertheless, summaries must also be documented when they are used as an explanatory footnote. If the author is not well known, both the title of the article and the author's name and title may also be used.

The Précis

A third method is one in which the original material is not reworded or summarized, but it is instead "cut down." Précis, known as a formal summary, is written in complete sentences. Like the word *precise, précis* means "accurate, very correct, very exact." For instance during the reign of Queen Elizabeth I of England, the précis was used frequently; for often Queen Elizabeth relied on her envoys or advisors to read the numerous foreign documents associated with the affairs of state and then relate to her the essential information in an oral précis. The speaker reduced the original document to about one third of its original length, maintaining the exact style and vocabulary of the author of the document. In this way there was no chance for the envoy to inject his own interpretation or to change the tone of the contents intended by the original writer, always a danger in an age when beheading was the order of the day. When a student writes a précis, he retains the author's style and tone, presents the material in nearly the same order as the original, often quoting one or two words.

Following are three examples, one for each of the methods. The original paragraph is from a paper on "Early Student Life."

Original

In 1620 in New England, there were no towns, no schools, no colleges. The colonists' principal task was to carve a life out of the wilderness and to fulfill a patriotic sense of the community they had formerly shared in England, or as John Winthrop counseled: "We must delight in each other." Childhood was barely recognized, for after the age of six, children were expected to behave as adults and were seen as subjects moving towards full maturity. This attitude prevailed until 1636 with the founding of Harvard College. When higher education came, the college students were considered to be the only adolescents in a society that knew no adolescence. 109 words

The Paraphrase

New England in 1620 had no towns, schools or colleges, for the colonists were to build homes and develop a sense of a patriotic community, sharing in each other's lives. Children over six years of age were expected to act as adults. It was not until 1636 with the founding of Harvard College that there was an exception to that attitude. The first classes of college students were considered to be adolescents although that term was not recognized during that period. 81 words

The Summary

Colonists in New England (1620) had two purposes: to build homes and develop a patriotic sense of the community. Childhood ended at age six. There were no adolescents until the founding of Harvard College in 1636 when the first adolescents were the students. 42 words

The Précis

New England colonists in 1620 had no schools, towns, or colleges, for their "principal task was to carve a life out of the wilderness" and " fulfill a patriotic sense of the community of as John Winthrop said, to" . . . delight in each other." Childhood extended to age six, and only the classes of college students, beginning with the founding of Harvard College in 1636, were considered adolescents in a "society that knew no adolescence." 74 words

Using the Précis for an Oral Report

The précis can be used effectively for anyone who must give an oral report on a subject For instance, before giving a report on a modified research paper, one student prepared a summary of her paper in précis form. First she reduced each one of her major paragraphs: the introductory paragraph, the three developmental ones and the concluding paragraph. She used only the main points of her paper, eliminating detailed illustrations and examples. She wrote the précis on a 4 x 6 card.

Alcoholism: The Effects on the Newborn

Various studies have shown that children born to alcoholic mothers have functional disorders, structural abnormalities, and mental drawbacks. Functional disorders consist of newborns being born as alcoholics and suffering from withdrawal symptoms, liver defects. and congenital disease. Structural abnormalities range from the newborn's having a small head size to their being two thirds of a normal baby's weight and measuring 20 percent shorter at birth. Infants suffer from mental drawbacks due to their living in an alcoholic environment and having a low I.Q. The study of fetal alcohol syndrome is still a new field of research. However, doctors aware of deformities caused by alcohol are suggesting early termination of the pregnancy of alcoholic women.

The student then can use the notes from the card to discuss the major and minor points of the subject that was researched.

Parts of a Note Card

Every note card must have four types of information on it. The experience of competent researchers is that there are built in safeguards in recording the information on a note card in the following order:

1. The exact source from which the information comes
2. The specific page on which the information was found
3. One type of information
4. The subject heading which classifies that information

In "Step 1, Making a Note Card," you learned the reasons for procedures three and four. It is important for you to understand that the first two items of procedure are also essential, because you will have to document (identify the sources of your information) in the in-text documentation. There are several ways of recording the source information on a note card. The cards illustrate two of the more commonly used forms.

MLA format

In the upper right hand corner of the note card, the source from which the information comes is written according to the MLA internal citation format.

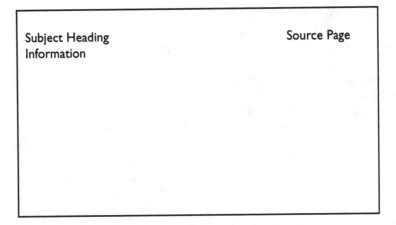

The specific page on which the information was found is placed next to the source.

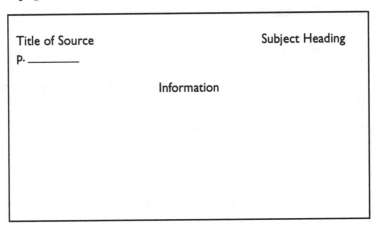

Source card title

Some students prefer to put the title of their source, or a shortened version of the title, on the left. The specific page reference is written below the title of the source.

Regardless of the method you use, always check your note card to make sure that it carries the source and the specific page reference before you go on to take another note.

STEP 4   Restricting the Subject Before Taking Notes

Once you have your working bibliography and your sourcebook assembled, you are ready to start taking notes. From the overview reading of your selected sources, you have general knowledge about your topic. Before you begin note taking, however, you need to decide on a specific limitation of your topic so that you will not spend time taking unnecessary notes. From preliminary reading, the researcher on AIDS discovered that there were numerous limitations of the subject: effects of the disease, legal issues, AIDS educational programs, discrimination in education and business, and changes that have come about as a result of the spread of AIDS. Once the topic was limited to the changes, the student found at least three major classifications under this topic: changes in government policies and legislation, changes in social attitudes, and changes in health care for the victims.

The student had decided to limit his topic to the AIDS virus since the death toll appeared to be rising and since most authorities on the subject felt that the AIDS epidemic may well be the singularly most important social and political issue during the next decade. Also, since the epidemic had now spread to 112 countries, the student felt that it was important to explore what changes had already come about because of the fear of AIDS. In a short research paper, the student realized that he could not write about all of the world wide changes; he, therefore, limited the changes to those in the United States that appeared to be the major ones. At this point serious note taking can begin.

STEP 5 Taking Notes

Looking over his working bibliography, the researcher on AIDS decides to begin his note taking with an article from *Time* entitled " 'You Haven't Heard Anything Yet.' " Taking out the bibliography card for this article, he writes an appropriate bibliography card. Here is the bibliography card:

```
Wallis, Claudia, and Dick Thompson, " 'You Haven't Heard

    Anything Yet,'" Time 16 Feb. 1987: 45-56.
```

The student now begins to take notes from his copy of the article. Reprinted below is a portion from the article from page 54.

Today's plague is a very different beast. AIDS works its way through a population slowly, over a period of ten years and even decades. It also tends to kill slowly, laying waste the immune system so that patients fall prey to a debilitating succession of infections. Unlike the plague of Guy's era, it is spread only through the most intimate forms of human contact, sexual contact, sexual intercourse, childbearing, the sharing of contaminated blood or needles.

Yet as the AIDS death toll climbs and statisticians project its probable course into the next decade, comparisons with history's greatest killers begin to make sense. "If we can't make progress, we face the dreadful prospect of a worldwide death toll in the tens of millions a decade from now," warned Health Human Services Secretary Otis Bowen at a recent gathering of the National Press Club. Such earlier epidemics as typhus, smallpox and even the black death will "look very pale by comparison," he continued. "You haven't read or heard anything yet."

As the student takes notes, he knows that the notes can be abbreviated or written in a shortened form because the writer will then expand the notes by writing them in full sentences, developing the ideas, and tying in those ideas with ones written previously. The main point is that the notes should be accurate and complete enough so that you can make sense of them when you are ready to write the first draft.

From the article " 'You Haven't Heard Anything Yet,' " the student begins to take these notes:

Subject heading	Dev. in comp. to other diseases Wallis & Thompson 54	**Source**
Paraphrase	Unlike other diseases and plagues, AIDS does not develop in a few days or even a year. It might take years or decades for the disease to spread. Tends to kill slowly.	
	(Note: Bubonic plague 1348. French surgeon Guy de Chauliac of Avignon. Patients died within five days.)	

At the bottom of the note, the student reminds himself to explain what is meant by "other diseases and plagues" and the comparison to those. These facts were mentioned in the first two paragraphs of the entire article.

The warning by the Secretary of Health and Human Services is written in a direct quotation because there is no way to effectively paraphrase the medical information. Notice that an omission within a direct quote is indicated by an ellipses (three spaced periods). For complete information about ellipses, see page 440.

Subject
heading

Paraphrase
cites the
authority

Direct quote

Statistics: expectation of death toll   Wallis & Thompson 54   Same
source

Warning by Otis Brown, Secretary of Health and Human
Services:

"If we can't make progress, we face the dreadful prospect of a
worldwide death toll in the tens of millions in a decade from
now." . . . "even the black death will 'look very pale in comparison.'"

The next note includes information that the student knows from general knowledge:
patients get cancer and pneumonia.

New subject
heading

Effects of the disease   Wallis & Thompson 54   Same
source

Destroys the immune system. Patients get cancer, pneumonia.

New subject
heading

Ways of getting AIDS   Wallis & Thompson 54   Same
source

Spread by "sexual intercourse, childbearing, the sharing of contaminated blood or needles."

The student transfers to his note cards all of the essential information from his first source and then moves on to the other sources. He may key each bibliography card to his sources. He finds one source that he is not certain he will need; however, he writes a bibliography card for it and then annotates it in the event he will need the information later. The student codes the source since it is the seventh article that he found while researching the subject.

```
                                                                    7

  "Hope for Babies of Women with AIDS," Insight
      27 July 1987: 53

  (The article discusses the possibility of using the drug AZT to treat
  fetuses of women who have AIDS."
```

Because the student has his own photocopies of each article, he is able to annotate its contents in the margins. This kind of analytical reading can save you from taking more notes than necessary.

Reading Analytically

Reading analytically can save the student much time for the process can allow him to take more precise notes, write specific subject headings on his note cards, organize his note cards more effectively, and write the outline. Before beginning to take notes from a source, scan the article quickly to determine whether or not there is information in the article that will help you. If you determine that the article is a good source for you, then photocopy it so that you can underline portions of the article and annotate the underlined information with key phrases. By doing so you will actually be writing topic heads for your note cards.

A student working on reasons why there is a concern for the depletion of the ozone level wanted to get background information for his paper. He found an article in *Newsweek*, "Psst! Aerosol Alternatives," in the May 9, 1977, issue. In the article, authors Peter Gwynne, Henry McGee, and Dan Shapiro mention that researchers are trying several substitutes for the aerosol container. The student decides to use this information and then find if any of the substitutes were effective. He begins the process of analytically reading:

Substitute: *pump spray*	One simple replacement is the pump spray in which the user supplies his own pressure by pushing on a plunger. The pump is sound environmentally, but it often produces a weak	
Disadvantage: *pump spray*	and very wet spray. Consequently, researchers have focused on several chemical substitutes for chlorofluorocarbons:	*Chemical* *substitutes*
	Carbon dioxide. This gas produces a wet spray, and its use is	

confined to larger cans because it requires more pressure.
Nitrous oxide. It is good for whipped cream, but it doesn't
dissolve well in other products.
Hydrocarbons. Shaving cream dispensers and spray paints use
butane, propane and isobutane as propellants—and these

*Current use
of aerosols*

chemicals have already been adapted for some cosmetic
aerosols. But their spray isn't as fine as that produced by
chlorofluorocarbons, and they catch fire—although a solvent
addition known as methylene chloride reduces their
flammability.

*Disadvantages
of
hydrocarbons*

When the student completed the analytical reading of this one page article, he found that he had written eleven note cards. Other subject headings included "Reasons for ban," "Prevention measures: Warning label," "Products affected," "Stages of the ban," and others.

Once the student has underlined the article and annotated the information, he will then be ready to take notes from the article. Some notes may be direct quotes, some may be paraphrases, and some may be a combination of a quote and a paraphrase. For instance, the student may write the following note card:

Chemical substitutes   Gwynne, McGee and Shapiro 99

Carbon dioxide
Nitrous oxide
Hydrocarbons

These are ones that were being tested in 1977 as possible substitutes for the aerosol.

(Check current information to update the use of the substitutes.)

At the bottom of the note the student reminds himself to check the current status of the chemical substitutes.

Plagiarism

However, before beginning note taking, you should understand what plagiarism is and how to avoid it. Plagiarism is the act of submitting as one's own work the ideas, words, or conclusions of another as if the work submitted were the product of one's own thinking rather than an idea or product that came from another source. Most beginning writers document direct quotations from sources but believe that if the information has been reworded, that it need not be documented. You must remember that even if you paraphrase the information, the ideas, conclusions, and specific information came from another source and, therefore, must be documented carefully. Plagiarism consists of the following:

1. Failure to credit paraphrased materials.

2. Failure to credit quoted materials.

3. Use of another's ideas as one's own.

4. Duplication, in part or whole, of another student's themes or projects.

Information may be included in a paper without documentation if it meets all of the following conditions:

1. The information is common knowledge.

2. The information is written entirely in the words of the student; that is, the information is in the form of generalities and conclusions the student has drawn as a result of the research.

Often the student who is taking notes for the first time from original material lends to borrow heavily from the sources. Student researchers may do this unintentionally because they lack the experience in note taking. Sometimes the plagiarized material is evident because the researcher lifted the original material almost in its entirety. In other cases, the plagiarized material is more subtle because the researcher changed the order of sentences and kept only a few of the original phrases.

Investigating the subject of "AIDS," a student discovers that some states have already proposed legislation that allows penalties to be imposed for anyone who consciously transmits the disease to another. The article by Richard Lacayon and others, "Assault with a Deadly Virus," is from the July 20, 1987, issue of *Time*, page 63 The student reads the following paragraph before taking notes:

> Other lawmakers might sympathize. A survey project at George Washington University in Washington found that 25 of some 500 AIDS related bills introduced in state legislatures this year proposed criminal sanctions for conscious transmission of the disease. Florida and Idaho have made it a crime knowingly to expose another person to the virus. The possible penalties include prison terms of 60 days in Florida, six months in Idaho. A similar criminalization measure awaits Governor Edwin Edward's signature in Louisiana: penalties could range as high as a $5,000 fine and ten years in prison. A new Nevada law requires that anyone arrested for prostitution must take an AIDS virus test; those who test positive can be charged with a felony if picked up for prostitution again.

Obvious Plagiarism

Survey: AIDS related bills   Lacayon 63

A survey project at Geo. Wash. Univ. found that 25 of 500 AIDS related bills introduced in various state legislatures for 1987 proposed criminal sanctions for conscious transmission of the virus. The possible penalties include 60 days prison in Florida and six months in Idaho

Here the student follows nearly the same phrasing and the exact sentence structure of the original material. He eliminates a word here and there and substitutes "various state legislatures" for the original "in state legislatures" and "for 1987" for "this year." In addition, he has broken one of the rules of note taking: writing more than one piece of information for each note card. Although he will document the information, he has still been trapped into the act of plagiarism because he has not expressed the information in his own words.

Now look at this note card:

Survey: AIDS related bills   Lacayon 63

    A Geo. Wash. Univ. survey found that state legislatures introduced 25 of 500 bills that are AIDS related support criminal sanctions for a person's knowing he can transmit the virus to another. Possible penalties are prison terms of 60 days in Florida and six months in Idaho

---

Although the student did not follow the exact sentence structure of the original, he has plagiarized because he has used the same phrasing as the original. All the student has done is to rearrange and to change a few words; he has not reworded it. Compare the original text with this note card. Phrases such as "criminal sanctions" and "possible penalties" are still the exact wording of author Richard Lacayon. Notice, also, that the student includes more than one type of information.

A good practice for you to follow while you are taking notes is to read the original material carefully and then to look away from the material when you write your note card. In this way there is far less chance of plagiarizing. However, if you wish to use the exact phrasing, then you must enclose the material in quotation marks so that you will remember to do so when you use the information from that note card in your paper.

Suitable Note Cards

Observe how the student using the same material avoids plagiarism. Here are notes the student took from the same source. Notice that he has two different classifications of notes for the information.

```
Survey: AIDS related bills                    Lacayon 63

    Survey at Geo. Wash. U. 500 bills in state legislatures
for 1987 related to AIDS; 25 support penalties and consid-
er the virus to be a weapon.
```

```
Current penalties: By states                  Lacayon 63

Florida, prison terms of 60 days
Idaho, 6 months
Louisiana, pending Gov. Edwin Edward's signature—
    $5,000. fine and ten years
Nevada, felony if the prostitute tests positive for the AIDS
virus and continues to work as a prostitute.
```

Long Note Cards

At times, the information from a source may run over to a second card. If you have a long note, it is better to continue it on a second card rather than to write on the back of a card. When you use the cards to write the final paper, you will find that flipping cards over is awkward, and it is also possible to omit relevant information. The original material comes from page 63 of the article "Assault with a Deadly Virus."

Original Material

Imposing penalties and defining the behavior they are meant to prohibit poses a host of problems for prosecutors and lawmakers. "Criminal statutes must speak with clarity so that people can at least know if they are putting themselves at risk of prosecution," says Yale University Law Professor Harlon Dalton, co editor of *AIDS and the Law: A Guide for the Public*, which will be published next month by Yale University Press. Failure to provide such clarity, he warns, is a "violation of due process."

The last consideration has probably spared PFC Morris at least one additional headache.

Although Morris also had sexual relations with his fiancee, assault charges were not brought against him in that connection because the woman knew of his positive test results. But he already faces enough AIDS-related travails. If convicted, Morris could spend up to 17 years in the military prison at Fort Leavenworth, Kansas.

Suitable Note Cards

The student uses a combination of a direct quote and a paraphrase and notes on the first card that the information is continued on a second card. The student also uses single quotes for the information that was already quoted in the article and double quotes when the information is written exactly as it appears in the article in order to avoid plagiarism.

Problems for prosecutors and lawmakers   Lacayon 63

Legislators and prosecutors attempting to set penalties and the bounds of those who have the AIDS-related virus and who knowingly transmit it, face a number of problems " 'Criminal statutes must speak with clarity so that people can at least know if they are putting themselves at risk of prosecution,' says Yale University Law Professor Harlon Dalton, co-editor of *AIDS and the Law: A Guide for*

(cont'd)

Problems for prosecutors and lawmakers (cont'd)   63

the *Public*, published by Yale University Press. "Failure to provide such clarity, he warns, is a 'violation of due process.'"

The case of Private First Class Morris is discussed earlier in the article, and the student now takes notes to clarify the information found at the end of the article, for the case prompted prosecutors in the military to be among the first to enforce penalties and to determine that AIDS can be considered another weapon.

> Prosecuted cases: By the military   Lacayon 63
>
> PFC Adrian G. Morris, clerk-typist, stationed at Huachuca, Arizona, alleged to have assaulted two soldiers—one male, one female—court martialed. Screened by the army, he knew he was a carrier of the AIDS virus and the army considered him to have willfully transmitted the disease.

Other cases that had been prosecuted in civilian courtrooms are discussed in the article, and the student writes a note card for each of the cases, using a similar subject heading but making the sub heading more specific. For example, the heading on one card might read "Prosecuted cases: Los Angeles court."

At times, the student may find that related material is found on two different pages of an article, and he then wishes to write the information on one note card. The student then notes the individual pages after each specific note. The information comes from another article in *Time* in the June 15, 1987, issue, pages 56–58 The article, entitled "At Last, the Battle Is Joined," was written by J. D. Reed.

> Strategies in Europe for prevention   Reed 57–8
>
> The Netherlands began a government-sponsored campaign to advocate safe sex, and Britain allocated $32 million to produce and set up billboards across the country warning and advising their subjects (57).
>
> France to require testing before couples receive a marriage license (58)

STEP 6 Expanding Information from a Note Card

While you may now be able to write good note cards, you must also be able to use the information from the note card in the text of your paper. For example, suppose you were investigating reasons why health care in hospitals seems to be on the decline. One reason you find is the critical nursing shortage. After writing a bibliography card for the article by Matt Clark and others from *Newsweek*, "Nurses: Few and Far Between," from pages 59–60 in the June 29 issue, you write the following note card:

> Nationwide vacancies   Clark, et al. 59
>
>   Vacancies nationwide—6.5 percent to 13 percent . . .
> 1985-86
>
> Detroit, 1,200 vacancies; Dallas-Ft..Worth, 900.

It is obvious when the time comes for you to incorporate this information in your paper, you will not simply want to transfer the information from the note card as written, nor will you wish to use the words of the original writer. Instead, you will take the note you have written and expand the information into a sentence or more, making sure that the appropriate transition is used, as well as whatever general knowledge you have learned. For instance, the note may be expanded in this way:

> The quality of hospital care nationwide is in jeopardy as nurses leave the profession, citing as reasons ten and twelve-hour shifts and severe understaffing with one nurse to care for as many as sixteen patients. Statistics indicate that from 1985 to 1986 the percentage of vacancies doubled, from 6.5 percent to 13.5 percent. Two cities report alarming numbers of available positions. The Dallas-Ft. Worth area has 900 vacancies while Detroit has 1,200 (Clark et al. 59).

Notice that the student was careful to document this information by citing the author and the specific page.

Since health care will be a major topic for the research paper, the researcher completely investigates all facets of the subject. The student finds that the AIDS epidemic has affected government policy, social attitudes, and health care. As he works through his bibliography cards, he finds articles which discuss the changes that are already in effect and those that are projected. One of the more substantial articles, "The Big Chill: Fear of AIDS," from the February 18, 1987, issue of *Time*, pages 50–53 discusses the change in lifestyles and ways that heterosexuals are coping with the fear of the disease. The student already has the major inference for his thesis statement: changes in effect. With additional information he has gathered, after he completes note taking, he can complete his thesis.

STEP 7   Stating the Preliminary Thesis

Using the information he has found during his note taking, the student can now complete his analysis chart and state the thesis. He bases his thesis on a five-year projection cited by authorities. If he puts the chart on paper, it would look like this:

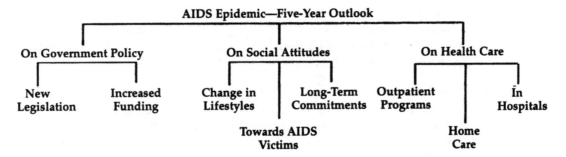

Thesis statement: As a result of these overwhelming statistics and as an attempt to avoid the catastrophe that is already evident in Central Africa, changes have begun in terms of government policies and legislation, social attitudes, and health care.

As the student classifies the information on a chart, he also begins to note sub topics and lists them under the main topics. For example, thus far, he has two sub points under "government policy." They are "new legislation" and "increased funding." As he continues to review his note cards, he will find other points.

STEP 8 Setting up the Preliminary Outline

The researcher is now ready to set up a preliminary outline. In a short paper this outline is constructed directly from the minor inferences of the thesis. In a longer paper, such as the research paper, you will find that there may be several types of information you would like to present to your reader before you develop the minor inferences of the thesis. For example, you may feel that the reader needs a good working definition of your topic or of several key terms connected with the topic. You may decide that a brief history of the problem you are discussing would be relevant. You may also decide that you want to impress the reader with the seriousness of your topic as not only an American social problem, but as also now a world-wide concern. Certainly you will want to conclude the paper with some possible solutions to cope with the problem—those suggested by experts and those you propose from your own conclusions. For example, one may be the preventative measures suggested for fetuses of women who are carriers of the AIDS virus. Here is the way the researcher set up his preliminary outline:

(temporary title)   **THE AIDS EPIDEMIC**

Thesis statement: As a result of these overwhelming statistics and as an attempt to avoid the catastrophe that is already evident in Central Africa, changes have begun in terms of government policies and legislation, social attitudes, and health care.

I.   Background information
     (Discuss the devastation in Central Africa and its relation to the AIDS epidemic

in America, mentioning Dr. Michael Gottlieb, who is credited with recognizing AIDS as a new disease in 1981.)

II. Extent of the problem

(Discuss the number of reported AIDS cases—those who test HIV-positive, those with ARC or the AIDS-Related Complex, and those with the AIDS syn drome—the findings of the Geneva-based World Health Organization and the National Institute of Allergy and Infectious Diseases.)

III. Changes in government policies and legislation

(Discuss the new and proposed legislation, such as mandatory blood testing, quarantine of victims, penalties for knowingly transmitting the disease, and the possibility of a national health insurance as well as increased funding for both scientific and medical research.

IV. Changes in social attitudes

(Discuss changing lifestyles and long term commitments, voluntary blood screening, and attitudes towards AIDS victims.)

V. Changes in health care

(Discuss comprehensive reforms in home care, in out-patient programs, and in hospital care, focusing on delivery of care, financing of programs, construction of care facilities, and alternative care facilities.)

VI. Treatment and possible solutions

(Discuss use of AZT drug, AIDS hot lines, medical advice for safe practices, American Foundation for AIDS Research, and other strategies.)

Concluding Statement: Unless a cure for AIDS is found before the next decade, deaths from AIDS will rank alongside the other major epidemics of the world, including the bubonic plague beginning in 1334 in Europe, the influenza epidemic of 1918–1919 and the polio epidemic from the mid 1940's to the mid 1950's.

Exercise 4-1: Practicing Note Taking

Unemployment in many fields continues to be a problem in the United States. In spite of strict government restrictions, discrimination because of age contributes to the problem. Assume that you are writing your research paper on age discrimination in employment. Among your sources is one that discusses the complaints from people over fifty who feel that age discrimination is still practiced despite the Age Discrimination in Employment Act of 1967.

Complete the following assignment:

A. Read the article analytically. Underline those portions that appear to be important. Annotate the information.

B. Make a proper bibliography card for the article. Complete the first three note cards with information which relates to the subject heading on each card and which corresponds to the type of note specified.

C. Now you are on your own. Finish taking notes from the article by completing the next four note cards, making sure that each carries the four essential parts of a note card. Under each card, indicate the type of note you have taken (paraphrase, direct quote, or combination).

Sun-Sentinel, Wednesday, March 27, 1996   3D

Older workers say there's bias

Unemployment rates show discrimination isn't rampant

By CAROL KLEIMAN
Chicago Tribune

Grow old along with me, the best is yet to be is the promise in a poem by Robert Browning.

It's a lovely sentiment, but the number of complaints from people older than 50 who say they are being discriminated against in hiring would indicate the sentiment does not reflect reality.

If what they say is true, their would-be employers are in violation of the federal Age Discrimination Act. Complaints filed under the act have increased to 17,401 in 1995 from 17,009 in 1994, according to the Equal Employment Opportunity Commission.

Speculation is that age discrimination fluctuates with the job market.

In November 1995, 26.7 million U.S workers older than 50 had jobs, according to Paul LaPorte, economist with the U.S. Bureau of Labor Statistics. At the same time, 915,000 people in that age group were unemployed but looking for work.

That means that 3.4 percent of workers older than 50 were unemployed, a figure lower than the national 5.3 percent unemployment rate for workers 16 years and older for the same period.

Unemployment rates of older people suggest that discrimination isn't rampant, but official complaints have risen.

That's why inside tips on how to get a job are important.

According to the experts, one way to find a job when you're considered "old," is to "work through an agency that can help you."

That's the advice of Ernestine Jones, co-director,

with Shirley Johnson, of the South Austin Job Referral Service in Chicago, a non-profit agency that finds jobs for 350 Austin residents of all ages with more than 200 companies each year.

To place older job seekers, the agency works with Operation Able, a national group devoted to helping seniors.

So what older job-seekers get jobs?

"Those who are reliable, willing to adapt to change and have a great work ethic," said Jones, who in 1979 was one of the founders of the free referral service.

The agency has placed older workers in manufacturing and general office work.

"Stay patient," Jones urges older job seekers. "Learn new skills, particularly computers. Be confident."

But no matter how confident you are, older workers still have to overcome prejudice, according to the American Association of Retired Persons.

AARP asked 400 human resource executives what older workers can do to improve their image.

Their advice:

■ Cut back on your resume. Cite only relevant skills and experience.

■ Demonstrate flexibility, such as learning new skills.

■ Get coaching on interviewing skills, particularly if you haven't looked for a job for many years.

■ If you're looking in a new industry, acknowledge that you may have to start at an entry level.

"Older workers say there's bias," by Carol Kleiman. © Copyrighted Chicago Tribune Company. All rights reserved. Used with permission.

Exercise 4-1A: Practicing Note Taking

Note Card (paraphrase)

Statistics—percent of workers over 50 unemployed

Note Card (Combination: Quote and Paraphrase)

Statistics—complaints filed

Bibliography Card

Note Card (Direct Quote)

Contrary opinion concerning complaints

Exercise 4-1B

Type of Note:

Type of Note:

Type of Note:

Type of Note:

Preparation: Taking and Using Your Own Notes

1. Correct Documentation
2. Preliminary Writing

You are now ready to take notes from your own sources. In order to understand better the relation between your note taking and the actual writing of your paper, three very short papers may be written as your note taking continues. The papers will be drawn from different types of sources and will make use of different types of development for expository writing. This advance preparation has several distinct advantages:

1. You will understand how a writer comes to eliminate some notes, how related notes are combined, and how the wording of the notes is often changed as the paper is written.

2. You will gain practice in the preparation of the various forms of documentation which give credit to your sources.

3. You will have an opportunity to review the several types of expository development and to see how they are combined and used in a longer paper.

4. You will also see whether there are any gaps in your note taking. If there are, this will be the time to review the cards you had set aside from your preliminary bibliography. If you cannot use any of the sources listed on these cards, then you will need to get other sources, add them to your working bibliography, and do further note taking.

These short papers will not necessarily be used in the order you write them, nor will they be used in their entirety. However, you will certainly be able to transfer a great deal of this writing to the developmental paragraphs of your final paper.

STEP I Correct Documentation

Internal documentation is the current preferred notation for direct quotations, paraphrases, and summaries. However, some forms of writing still require endnotes or footnotes; therefore, proper footnote and endnote information is still useful.

Footnote Forms

Notice that a footnote for a book differs from the bibliography form in six ways. Footnote form for a book with one author:

[1] Allan Bloom, *The Closing of the American Mind* (New York: Simon, 1987) 148.

Bibliography form for this book:

Bloom, Alan. *The Closing of the American Mind.* New York: Simon, 1987.

The differences:

Footnote Form

1. The footnote is indented five spaces from the margin. If the footnote runs beyond one line, single space and begin other lines flush with the margin. Double space between footnotes.

2. The footnote carries an Arabic number called a superscript. It corresponds with the footnote number in the text of the paper.

3. The author's first name is first. A comma follows the author's full name.

4. No punctuation is placed after the title of the book because the parentheses follow the title.

5. Parentheses enclose the publication information.

6. The page reference, which indicates the page(s) where the reference is found, follows the parentheses immediately with no intervening puncutation.

Bibliography Form

1. The bibliography entry begins flush with the left margin. If the entry runs beyond one line, double-space and indent all other lines five spaces.

2. The bibliography, which appears alphabetically on the bibliography page, is not numbered.

3. The author's last name comes first, followed by the first name, which concludes with a period.

4. A period follows the title of the book.

5. Parentheses do not enclose publication information.

6. The bibliography entry for a book does not give page references.

Endnote Form

1. Title the page ENDNOTES.

2. Center the title one inch from the top.

3. Indent first line five spaces from the left margin.

4. Type the note number with no punctuation slightly above the line. After the number, leave a space and type the number.

5. Double space all endnotes.

6. Number all pages.

ENDNOTES

As the title ENDNOTES suggests these notes appear on a separate page after the paper has ended. Begin the page with the title ENDNOTES or NOTES centered about one inch down from the top of the page. Then double-space and begin entering the required information.

To enter the information properly, use the correct form. First, indent five spaces from the lefthand margin, and insert the number for the first entry so that the number is raised one half space above the line. Do not punctuate the number. After the number, make sure that there is a space between it and the first letter of the first word. If the endnote exceeds one line, begin the second line at the left-hand margin. Double-space each entry in the endnote; this is different from the footnote which is single-spaced between each entry.

1. A book with one author

[1] Peter Elbow, *Writing with Power: Techniques for Mastering the Writing Process* (New York: Oxford UP, 1981) 75.

2. A book with two authors

[2] David J. Pittman and Charles R. Snyder, *Society, Culture, and Drinking Patterns* (New York: Wiley, 1983) 130.

3. A book with three authors

[3] Ken Williams, Bob Kernaghan, and Lisa Kernaghan, *Apple II Computer Graphics* (Bowie: Prentice, 1983) 19.

4. A book with more than three authors

[4] Donald Greenburg, et al., *The Computer Image: Applications of Computer Graphics* (Reading: Addison 1982) 92.

5. An edited book
One editor

[5] David Bevington, ed., *The Complete Works of Shakespeare* 3rd ed. (Dallas: Scott, 1980) 599–600.

Two editors

[6] Gilbert Gels and Ezra Stotland, eds., *White Collar Crime and Theory and Research* (Beverly Hills: Sage, 1980) 221.

6. A book with a corporate authorship

[7] Al-Anon Family Group, *Living with an Alcoholic With the Help of Al-Anon* (New York: Headquarters, 1981) 32.

7. An essay in an edited edition

[8] Michael Fabre, "The Man Who Lived Underground," *Richard Wright: A Collection of Critical Essays*, Eds. Richard Mackey and Frank E. Moore (Englewood Cliffs: Prentice, 1984) 71.

8. A translated book

[9] Michael Fabre, *The Unfinished Quest of Richard Wright*, Trans. Isabel Barzun (New York: Morrow, 1973) 32.

9. Several volumes
A work that is one of several volumes

[10] H.W. Janson, *History of Art*, Ed. Anthony Janson, 3rd ed., 2 vols. (Englewood Cliffs: Prentice, 1986) 1:721.

10. The Bible, a specific book (Genesis)

[11] Gen. 2:12

11. A reprinted edition

[12] Henry Garland and Mary Garland, *The Oxford Companion to German Literature* (1976; London, England: Oxford UP, 1984) 354.

12. Encyclopedia
A signed encyclopedia article

[13] Lewis Penner, "Child Abuse," *The World Book Encyclopedia*, 1983 ed.

An unsigned encyclopedia article

[14] "Alcoholism," *The World Book Encyclopedia*, 1983 ed.

13. Abstract

[15] "Reported Child Neglect and Abuse Cases by Division: 1978-1984," *Statistical Abstract of the United States: 1987*, 107th ed.

14. Yearbooks and Almanacs

[16] "Sixth Man Received Artificial Heart," *Facts on File*, 1986.

[17] Paxton, John, ed., "Health and Welfare," *The Statesman's Yearbook*, 122nd ed., 1985-1986.

[18] "Alcoholism—No. 1 Drug Problem," *Reader's Digest and Yearbook*, 1987.

15. Periodicals
An unsigned magazine article

[18] "Sexy Premiums: Feminists vs Insurance Firms," *Time* 20 June 1983: 62-63.

A signed magazine article

[19] Ezra Bowen, "Are Student Heads Full of Emptiness?" *Time* 17 Aug. 1987: 56-57.

16. Newspaper

[20] "Jet's Hijackers Put on Their 'Death Shrouds,' " *Fort Lauderdale News* 12 Apr. 1988: A1.

17. Journals
A journal with separate pagination

[21] Edward P. Kranzelok, "Management of Acute Poisoning Emergencies," Emergency Medical Services 16.6 (1987): 31.

A journal with continuous pagination

[22] Schwartz, Michael Walker. "Potassium Imbalance for CE Credit," *AJN* 80 (1987): 1297.

18. A radio or television show
Television

[23] *The ABC's of AIDS*, Mod. Art Carlson, Prod. Brian Gandinsky, ABC Special, WPLG, Miami, 29 July 1987.

Radio

[24] *Morning Edition,* Nar. Bob Edwards, PBS, WLRN, Miami, 15 Mar. 1988.

19. Pamphlets
Pamphlet with personal author

[25] Otis R. Bowen, *What You Should Know About AIDS* (Washington: U.S. Dept. of Health, n.d.).

Pamphlet with corporate authorship

[26] Broward County Public Health Unit: Health Education Section, *What Everyone Should Know About AIDS* (South Deerfield: Channing, 1983).

20. Bulletin
Bulletin with an author

[27] Koehler, P.G. *Pantry and Stored Food Pests* (Gainesville: Florida Cooperative Extension Service Bulletin ENT-5, n.d.).

21. Public Document
Government Publication

[28] United States. Department of Social and Health Services, *Candidiasis* (Washington: GPO, 1981).

• If the publication has page numbers, the exact page number is recorded after the parentheses.

22. Interview

[29] William F. Buckley, personal interview, 13 Apr. 1988.

[30] Milos, Jakes, "Jakes: 'We Simply Need Restructuring,' " *Time* 18 Apr. 1988: 42.

23. Letter

[31] F. Lee Bailey, letter to the author, 11 Apr. 1988.

These are the basic documentation forms. You will need to know three other particulars about documentation before you begin to write them: (1) what to document, (2) how to place and space the documentation, (3) other forms of documentation.

What to Document

Understanding why you document is the first step in understanding what to document. There are two primary reasons for documenting information. The first is to give full credit to your sources— let the reader know that the information you have presented was not original with you. The information may be in the form of statistics gathered and interpreted, conclusions and insights derived by authorities on the subject, and opinions by others. The second reason is to give your reader an opportunity to follow up your sources if he wishes to find out more about the topic. The following types of information must be documented.

a. Direct quotations
b. Paraphrases of opinions, facts, and conclusions that belong to others
c. Statistics
d. Charts, photographs, diagrams, tables, and other graphic devices prepared by others as well as any graphic illustrations you have prepared from information provided by others
e. Information obtained through interviews, letters, radio commentaries, film or television documentaries, or tapes and records

You do not need to give credit for information that is considered general knowledge. Consider whether your reader would be likely to know a particular kind of information from a standard reference book. Would the reader have known it from general education, from observation, or from the media? For example, the fact that Lee Harvey Oswald was alleged to have assassinated President John F. Kennedy in 1963 is common knowledge or that Elvis Presley's mansion in Memphis is called Graceland. However, a fact that would need to be documented is the one concerning Maurice Barboza, a former American Bar Association lobbyist from Virginia, who got a bill signed for a memorial that would honor those 5,000 blacks who served in the American Revolution.

How to Cite Sources in Your Paper

There are several ways to document references. Documentation notes may appear at the bottom of each page where the information is cited as footnotes, or they may be collected and placed at the end of the text as endnotes. The new Modern Language Association (MLA) style of documentation replaces footnote and endnote numbers with a parenthetical reference within the text of the paper at the specific point of reference. Here, for example, is an in-text reference:

> A few years' worth of monthly payments would eventually surpass the expertise of purchasing a system outright (Dunn 130).

Notice that the author's last name is used with the page number where that one piece of information was found. The period follows the parenthetical citation. If the text had a footnote or endnote, it would be as follows:

A few years' worth of monthly payments would eventually surpass the expense of purchasing a system outright.[1]

Notice that the notes are numbered with Arabic numerals consecutively, beginning with 1. The numeral is raised one-half line and it is placed after the final punctuation in a sentence. The footnotes or endnotes are numbered sequentially to correspond to the note numbers in the text. If a page has three notes, then they may be placed on the bottom of that page. Do not carry a footnote over from one page to another. If you place footnotes at the bottom of the page, you may separate them from the text with an eight to fifteen space bar line two double spaces below the last line of your text, beginning at the left margin. Begin the first footnote a double space between this bar line. Single space footnotes but double space between them. For example, a series of three footnotes would appear as follows:

----

[1] Donald H. Dunn, "Dish Antenna Prices Come Down Out of the Sky," *Business Week* 30 Apr. 1984: 130.

[2] Ronald B. Kaatz, *Cable: An Advertiser's Guide to the New Electronic Media* (Chicago: Graian Books, 1982) 10.

[3] Alex Ben Block, "An eye in the Sky," *Forbes* 5 Nov. 1984: 197.

If you choose to use endnotes, you can collect your notes in numerical order and place them on a separate page at the end of your paper just before the bibliography page. Use the raised index numeral and space the endnotes in the same manner as if you were placing them at the bottom of each page. Some writers prefer this method as it simplifies the typing of the paper.

How to Use the Internal Citation Method

In the MLA internal citation system, there are several rules to follow. The important part is that the text reads smoothly and that the references do not interfere with the reading. If you can mention the author's name and work within the text do so. For example:

Thomas E. Baldwin and Stevens McVoy in *Cable Communications* report that in 1985 there were over 5,500 cable system, 36 million subscribers, and 42 percent of the available viewers using cable services (9).

Since the authors' names are incorporated in the text, only the page number needs to be cited. On the other hand, if the writer has written more than one article, you will need to cite an abbreviated title as well as the author's name and the page.

Direct Broadcast Systems (D.B.S.) do not, however, receive normal satellite programs; the only programs they receive are those broadcast specifically for D.B.S. units (Clifford "Direct" 75-7).

In this case, because the information was summarized from three pages, the writer cites all three.

When the writer quotes another author within the text other than the author of the source, the writer uses the abbreviated qtd. in the citation.

> According to one professor, "Alexander W. Austin, professor at the University of California, conducts an annual survey of college freshmen" (qtd. in "Graduates of the 80's" 87).

If the source cited has no author's name, then just the abbreviated title of the article and the page number is cited.

> Among the new technologic gadgets is the Calorie Watch that monitors a runner or jogger and gives a "calorie-burn" report ("This Watch" n.p.).

Since the information was part of a two-page series of advertisements inserted in the August 10, 1987, *Insight,* entitled "The Lifestyle Resource," no pages were cited. However, in the same issue there was an article on China's one-child policy. Information from that source may appear as follows:

> China is beginning to evaluate its policy of permitting couples to have only one child. According to surveys, researchers have found a me-generation of spoiled children with severe personality problems ("China May Regret" 35).

How to Note Sources Previously Cited in Full

Once you have provided full reference information for a source, subsequent footnotes or endnotes referring to that source may be shortened. Documentation practices favor the use of the author's last name followed by a comma and a specific page reference. In the absence of an author, you can use an abbreviated or shortened title followed by the specific page reference. These subsequent citation forms are used instead of the Latin abbreviation *Ibid* (in the same place), *op.cit.* (in the work cited), and *loc.cit.* (in the place cited). Here is an example of a complete initial reference and a subsequent citation of the same work:

> [1] David Brock, "A Regal Battle to Reign," *Insight* 10 Aug. 1987: 9.
>
> [2] Brock 12.

If you have more than one book or article by the same author, then add a shortened version of the title after the author's last name. The student using these citations was drawing from a series of articles written by Martin Clifford.

> [3] Martin Clifford, "Direct Broadcast Satellites, *Radio Electronics* June 1984: 75.
>
> [4] Martin Clifford, From Freedom to Receivers," *Radio Electronics* June 1984: 67.
>
> [5] Clifford, "From Freedom" 68.

If you have material from two authors with the same last name, then in the shortened citations you would give the first initial and the author's last name: J. Swails and S. Swails.

The Content or Explanatory Footnote

Simple citations are known as reference notes. There is, however, another type of documentation, known as the content or explanatory note. You may find that the occasion arises where you have material which is related but not directly pertinent to a point being discussed. If you think that the reader would profit by having this additional information, you can discuss it in a brief explanatory note. In a paper with internal citations, the notes themselves are treated as footnotes and are referred to by using consecutive numbers throughout the paper. If the paper is using the footnote or endnote system, the explanatory note is treated as one of the footnotes or endnotes.

[1] In order to emphasize the tragedy AIDS has brought to the United States, the editors of *Newsweek* in their August 10, 1987, issue published a yearbook of photographs of the 302 men, women, and children who died of the AIDS epidemic in a one-year period. The victims range in age from 13 months to age 87 and come from all walks of life. The cover story "The Face of AIDS: One Year in the epidemic" was the magazine's eighth cover story on AIDS in four years.

[2] Obviously since *Newsweek* has published eight cover stories, it would appear that those eight reports would give a researcher an opportunity to examine other facets of the disease from causes and treatments to impact on the victims, their families, and the doctors who care for them.

STEP 2   Preliminary Writing

Preliminary Writing Assignment 1: Defining Your Topic

Review "Extended Definition" (Part 1, Stage 9). From your source book, select the articles you have photocopied from the general and specialized encyclopedias. Take notes from these sources.

After you have taken notes, write a short paper of extended definition on your topic. In some cases a topic may be only one word—"Custom," "Lottery," "Discipline." More often than not, the topic for a social problem will be more than one word. Examples of such topics are "Fatal Attraction," "Medical Malpractice, " " Young Urban Professionals," "Political Prisoners," " Human Rights. "

Work out a formal sentence definition of your term and then extend the definition in as many ways as you think necessary so that the reader will fully understand the term.

Document this short paper with the appropriate citations. Following is an example of one student's extended definition on the word *pirate*. The topic for his research paper was the hijacking of the Trans World Airlines Flight 847 by Palestinian radicals.

PIRATE, PRIVATEER, OR BUCCANEER?

Piracy has been called one of man's three oldest professions (Bottinger 2). Although mankind has harnessed the power of the atom, walked on the moon, and accomplished an infinity of technological feats, piracy acts of all types still appear throughout the world. The most traditional modern act of piracy, the boarding and overtaking of a ship, was accomplished when members of the Palestinian Liberation Organization (PLO) held the Italian cruise ship *Achille Lauro* under their control. However, the hijacking of the Trans World Airlines Flight 847, also by Palestinian radicals, is an act of piracy. Although these are just two examples of the latest exploits of contemporary pirates, they clearly illustrate that piracy is far from becoming a term used solely in history textbooks. Nevertheless, in order to understand our society's extant pirates better, it is worthwhile to examine the origins and the very early applications of the word *pirate*.

A pirate is a person who robs at sea or who plunders the land from the sea. The word, like so many others, originates from the Latin *pirate*, which means "to attempt, attack, and assault." Although no one can be certain of the exact origins of pirates, there are numerous accounts from the early civilizations of the Middle East and later the Romans, indicating that they had to contend with piracy in the Persian Gulf and the Mediterranean Sea (Gosse 951). However, it was not until late in the fifteenth century, with the discovery of the New World and its monumental riches, that piracy would flourish to unprecedented heights (Bonner 449). In the early sixteenth century countries like Portugal and Spain began to transport to Europe the riches they had amassed in the newly discovered lands. With the introduction of mercantilism as the dominating economic policy, the Iberian countries began relying heavily on the riches of the new world to provide much needed income to their royal coffers. By the 1600's, a sundry of galleons heavily laden with gold, silver, and other valuables began criss-crossing the Atlantic Ocean (Gosse 951). If the Spaniards had not become so zealous in protecting their new found riches, the buccaneers might never have evolved into pirates.

However, there is a distinction between the eighteenth century buccaneers and their pirate descendants. The word *buccaneer* is derived from the French words *boucan*, "a grill for curing meat," and *boucaner*, which means "to dry meat on a spit or barbecue" for use in ships at sea. Buccaneers were sea wanderers who plundered ships in the Caribbean Sea from the late 1500's to the early 1700's. The first buccaneers were hunters who lived in the West Indian Islands and made a living by supplying passing ships with meat and other provisions (Alden 545). They also robbed the Spanish galleons. The British, who at that time were at war with the Spaniards, protected their own ships with privateers who sailed under the Union Jack and not a "Jolly Roger," the emblem for the pirate flag (Bottinger 48–49). Many privateers had been pirates before offering their services to England; and when their privateering commissions expired, they reverted to the old professions as free-lance pirates. Still, many pirates never acted as privateers, for they were the descendants of the buccaneers (Lyndon 21). Later, in an effort to eliminate the unwanted presence of the French in the New World, Spain slaughtered all wild cattle from the Caribbean Islands. Left with no other alternative to make a living, the buccaneers were forced to find a new occupation: attacking the ships of all nations and making their name synonymous with piracy.

Unlike the fictional pirate seen in movies and portrayed in novels, the historical one resembled neither type. The real pirates were drunkards, desperados who were pressed into service because of their poor home life, the injustice of the period, low wages, hard labor, or their desire for sudden wealth and a life of danger. Dressed in rags, they spent money as fast as they stole it and had little regard for material objects (Bonner 449). Although the historical pirates are known for their ruthless behavior, they sometimes showed compassion, respect, and benevolence towards their victims. In 1918 when Captain William Greenaway and his seven companions refused to join the mutineers, they were cast ashore naked and without provisions on Green Key, a Bahamian island. Sometime later the pirates returned with provisions of flour, salt, gunpowder, muskets, axes, knives, pots and pans as well as three hunting dogs used to catch wild hogs (Bottinger 54–55).

Welsh born pirate Bartholomew Roberts permitted no gambling on board, no young boys or women. Seducing a woman meant death (Bottinger 51). The fictional pirates seen in novels such as *Treasure Island* and *Kidnapped* often have a swarthy complexion with a black bushy beard and a huge mustache. They wear a turban made of a large handkerchief or a large black hat. Some wear black eye patches, have a hook for a hand or a wooden peg for a leg, and are usually envisioned burying treasure or dueling on board. All seem to have a parrot who screeches "pieces of eight." These pirates wear a huge gold earring which frames a fierce- looking face. Hollywood often portrays them as elegant cavaliers with trimmed beards and curly hair and dressed in silk and brocade. Usually the damsel they kidnapped falls in love with them. According to William Bonner, unlike the fictional pirate, the historical ones were considered outlaws who seldom lived long (449).

Because pirates became so numerous and successful during the late seventeen and eighteen centuries, that period became known as the Golden Age of Piracy (Bottinger 6). Henry Every; Bartholomew Roberts; Edward Teach, known as Blackbeard; and Captain Kidd all rose to notoriety through their flamboyant behavior and brazen actions which eventually became legendary (Gosse 952). In time these pirates, or buccaneers as they were also known, gradually became an endangered species. It was just a matter of time before the pirates of the past who posed a threat to the ships on the high seas would evolve into the modern day pirate—the hijacker—who threatens the ships of the air—Newton Berwig.

BIBLIOGRAPHY

Alden, John R. "Buccaneer." *The World Book Encyclopedia*. 1972 ed.

Bonner, William. "pirate." *The World Book Encyclopedia*. 1972 ed.

Bottinger, Douglas. *The Seafarers: The Pirates*. Alexandria: Time-Life Books. 1978.

"Buccaneer." *Oxford English Dictionary*. 1933 ed.

Cook, Chris. "Buccaneers." *Dictionary of Historical Terms*. New York: Peter Bedrick Books, 1983.

Gosse, Philip. "Pirate and Piracy." *The Encyclopedia Britannica*. 1966 ed.

Lyndon, James G. *Pirates, Privateers, and Profits.* Upper Saddle River: N.J.: The Greg Press, 1970.

" Pirate. " *Oxford English Dictionary,* 1933 ed.

Notice the statements in this paper that do not need documentation.

1. The formal definition and the etymology which can be checked in any dictionary
2. The mention of the hijacking of Flight 847, which is known by most educated people
3. The statement that Spain slaughtered cattle to eliminate the presence of the French, which many history books report

Notice, also, that when articles from reference books are listed in the Bibliography, the entry does not have the page numbers. The writer of the paper listed all references used in the paper although not all are cited.

Preliminary Writing Assignment 2: Enumerating Data

Select from your sourcebook your statistical and yearbook sources and take notes on them. Statistics indicate just how widespread a particular problem is. For example, both child abuse and rape are found in almost every community and among every class of Americans. Statistics answer the questions who, where, when, how, why, under what conditions, and to what extent.

Write a paragraph enumerating statistics about your topic. If the statistical and yearbook sources you have selected do not give you sufficient information, scan your magazine and newspaper articles for statistics. If you still do not have enough "hard data" to answer the questions who, where, when, how, why, under what conditions, and to what extent, then you know that you will have to do some more research. It is better to find this out now than on the day you are writing your first draft for the paper.

The Topic Sentence for Data Enumeration

All topic sentences follow the basic pattern—a limited subject and one controlling inference. The topic sentence for the Data Enumeration Paragraph has an additional detail, a word that indicates to the reader that a statistical paper will follow. Following are suitable topic sentences written for Data Enumeration papers. The specific word(s) that indicates the type of rhetorical mode is (are) underlined.

1. Not only do statistics indicate that fifty million Americans will get cancer in their lifetime, but also that cancer is one of the leading causes of death today.
2. The rate of alcoholism among adolescents is rising steadily.
3. Violent juvenile crime is on the upsurge.
4. Based on police reports and family court records, the extent of wife beating is shocking.

Following is an example of a student's enumeration paper. His topic is "Cable Viewing Versus Satellite Viewing."

COST OF CABLE RECEPTION

From city to city and from cable company to cable company, the costs of cable reception vary. The expenses, which include installation, basic subscription rates, and premium channel costs, become long-term expenses since the viewer never finishes paying for the service. Nevertheless, the number of cable television subscribers served in 1986 was 37.5 million, a considerable increase from 1981 when there were 18.3 million ("Utilization of Selected Media" 531). The number of homes with cable television during the same year was reported to be 42,820,780 (" U.S. Television Sets" 362). In actuality the subscriber does not buy cable service, but instead rents it. The cable lines and the channel selector box are always the property of the cable company and never belong to the viewer. Nationally, the rental charge for cable service averages $275 per year ("Cable TV" 547). This average may be on the decline, however, for the basic yearly rate projected for 1995, according to the 1988 *Statistical Abstract*, is $227 (532). In the early stages of organizing cable service in many towns and cities, competing cable companies had promised a vast multitude of services in order to be granted sole rights to provide cable service to the specified area's viewers. Many of these companies have not been able to live up to their promises of two way communications, 130+ channel availability, and diverse business oriented channels. These companies have reduced their rates due to the reduction of promised services (MacNeice B2).

Cable systems do have their short-term expenses, also. Since cable service is rented on a monthly basis, the monthly bill can be considered as a short-term expense. This cost averages between $17 and $22 a month on a nationwide basis (Kaatz 18, MacNeice 213). This monthly rate can also be reduced with the deletion of premium channel service, such as Home Box Office, Showtime, Cinemax, and The Movie Channel. These premium channels usually cost an average of $9 per month in addition to the basic cable rates which average from $4.95 for listed service to $13.95 ("Cable TV" 552). In some areas the basic cable service offers all local channels in addition to several "super stations," such as WTBS in Atlanta, WOR in New York, and WGN in Chicago (Kaatz 18).—Joe Swails

WORKS CITED

"Cable and Pay TV—Summary, 1955 to 1985, and Projections, 1990–1995." *Statistical Abstract of the United States 1987:* 532+.

Kaatz, Ronald B. *Cable: An Advertiser's Guide to the New Electronic Media.* Chicago: Graian Books, 1982.

MacNeice, Jill. "Cable TV Picture Darkens." *The Miami Herald.* 3 May 1984: B1-2.

U. S. Television Sets and Stations Received." *World Almanac and Book of Facts 1988:* 362.

" Utilization of Selected Media: 1950 to 1986. " *Statistical Abstract of the United States 1987:* 531.

Vital to any kind of research is an analysis of the causes and effects of a particular problem. Without such an analysis, no remediation and no solutions are possible. Review "Cause
and Effect Analysis" (Part 1, Stage 12, pages 263–281). Complete note taking from all of your
sources. Write a short paper about the causes and effects of your topic. Following is a limited cause and effect analysis on the topic of anorexia nervosa.

ANOREXIA NERVOSA

Anorexia nervosa is a psychosomatic illness that effects one out of every ten girls. It
is called a young woman's disease because one percent of all women in the United
States between the ages of twelve to twenty-five are afflicted ("Anorexia" 47). Fewer
than 10 percent are male (Brody 6). However, it was not until the death of pop singer
Karen Carpenter in 1983 that many began to realize that anorexia nervosa, sometimes
called "the starving disease," had become epidemic. The instances of severe weight loss
is now so common that causes for the disease may not at first be recognized as contributing reasons.

Nevertheless, researchers note that the various causes of the eating disorder are
important. Author Barbara Kinoy in her book *When Will We Laugh Again? Living and
Dealing with Anorexia Nervosa and Bulimia* writes that "anorexia nervosa occurs when
the child is overprotected . . . the family members are excessively involved with one
another" (26). The parents may also set incredibly high standards of achievement.
These expectations may deny children a sense of personal identity. In some cases children are expected to earn high grades, participate in extra curricular activities, hold a
part time job, and enjoy a social life. Kinoy notes that children may be obsessed with
weight control to please parents, to be perfect (12). According to *U.S. News and World
Report*, the anorexic is the " 'perfect little girl'—bright, pretty, artistic, a model student,
well-behaved. She is the focus of a close-knit family" ("Anorexia" 47). Nevertheless,
competition for a parent's love is only one cause.

There are other reasons. A reaction against an unstable home life, a domineering
mother, or an alcoholic father are others. The anorexic may not be able to control the
people or events in her home, but she can control her own life. Karen Strunk of
Arlington Heights, Illinois, agreed that controlling her diet and her body allowed her to
control and manipulate her family ("Anorexia" 47). In addition, anorexics have a distorted image of their own body. Even when they are quite thin, they see themselves as
fat. A former anorexic, Barbara Robinson, an emaciated eighty- five pound twenty-
seven-year-old, was convinced that she would look better if she lost ten pounds
(Seligmann 60). Dr. Arnold Anderson, a psychiatrist at John Hopkins Medical Center,
sees patients who weigh only sixty-five pounds and who believe that they "feel a little
heavy" (Seligmann 60). A feeling of rejection, a "disappointing experience with a
boyfriend," or a lover's quarrel may be other reasons (Kinoy 33).

While young girls have a preoccupation with food and dieting to reach a desired
weight, young male and female athletes have other reasons: not making an athletic
team. Both gymnasts and wrestlers experience this concern. Dr. Charles Tipton of the
University of Iowa, conducted a study of 747 high school students over a seventeen-
day period to determine the eating pattern of wrestlers (Amdur 12). He found that

University of Iowa, conducted a study of 747 high school students over a seventeen-day period to determine the eating pattern of wrestlers (Amdur 12). He found that "there was an average weight loss of seven percent of body weight on the day of certification (or about 10 percent) for 150-pound wrestler" (12). Varsity wrestler Marc Friedberg said that one teammate at Northern Valley High School in Old Tappan, New Jersey, "frequently lost 14 pounds on the day of a match." Friedberg cited taking laxative and water pills as well as induced vomiting were practices used by athletes before weighing in (12).

While these causes are serious and dangerous, sometimes leading to death, they are only the beginning stages of the disease.

WORKS CITED

"Anorexia: The 'Starving Disease' Epidemic." *The New York Times*. 30 Aug. 1982: 47-48.

Amdur, Neil. "The Toll Conditioning Can Take on Athletes." *The New York Times*. 6 Mar. 1983, sec 5: 1,12.

Brody, Jane E. "Personal Health," *The New York Times*. 14 July 1982, sec. 3:6.

Kinoy, Barbara P. *When Will We Laugh Again? Living and Dealing With Anorexia and Bulimia* New York: Columbia UP, 1984.

Seligmann, Jean et al. "A Deadly Feast and Famine." *Newsweek*. 7 Mar. 1983: 59–60.

Stage 6 | Beginning the Paper

1. Writing the Introductory Paragraph

Having completed note taking and preliminary writing and having gained some experience with documentation, you are now ready to begin writing your final paper.

STEP 1 Writing the Introductory Paragraph

In the short essay the lead-in is usually only a few sentences. These sentences, followed by the thesis statement, make up the introductory paragraph. In the longer paper you will be able to write a more extended introductory paragraph. You will inevitably get some good ideas for your introductory paragraph as you are taking notes from your sources. You may include one or several of the following in this paragraph: startling statistics, a description, a narration of an incident, a series of questions to be answered, a formal definition, a significant quotation, or a very brief history.

Here are some introductory paragraphs written for research papers. The first is by the writer researching effects of the AIDS virus.

Example #1

AVOIDING THE AIDS CATASTROPHE

At first AIDS appeared to be confined only to certain groups. In Central Africa it was called the "slim disease." In the United States it was termed the "gay disease" that also afflicted drug addicts and a few hemophiliacs who might have received a transfusion of blood with the AIDS virus, spread to heterosexuals and carriers (Reed 57). Thus far, according to the World Health Organization in Geneva " 100 million will become infected during the next ten years" (Wallis 54). In the United States more than 30,000 cases were reported in 1987 (54); however, if the epidemic continues to spread at the current rate, by 1991 there will be 270,000 cases of AIDS in the United States alone and

179,000 deaths (Morganthau 30). Unfortunately the real total of AIDS cases may be much higher since many cases go unreported and since the figures are based on current trends. As a result of these overwhelming statistics and as an attempt to avoid the catastrophe that is already evident in Central Africa, changes have begun in terms of government policies and legislation, social attitudes, and health care.

Note that the writer carefully documents information from three sources:

Morganthau, Tom et al. "The AIDS Epidemic: Future Shock," *Newsweek* 24 Nov 1986: 30–39.
Reed, J.D. et al. "At Last the Battle Is Joined," *Time* 15 June 1987: 56–58.
Wallis, Claudia and Dick Thompson. "You Haven't Heard Anything Yet," *Time* 16 Feb 1987: 54–56.

Example #2

POLLUTION IN NEW RIVER

Fort Lauderdale, Florida, with its 270 miles of scenic waterways, is known as the Venice of America. One of the major waterways is New River, which winds through the downtown part of the city and on through the residential areas. A trip up the dreamy New River with its ever-changing scenery is a real tropical experience. Along the banks of the river are rare trees and flowering plants and exotic birds such as flamingos and macaws. The thick green lawns of the waterfront homes meet the river's edge. Once, the only pollution of this river was a gull's wing. Today, New River is seriously contaminated. The causes of this pollution are three: plant distribution of chemically treated effluent, dumping of raw sewage, and intrusion of salt water. The effects of this unfortunate pollution are unsanitary water for recreation, poisoned marine life, and unsafe water for irrigation.

Example #3

SHOPLIFTING AND THE SENIOR CITIZEN

He was sixty-eight years old, married with three grown children, all who lived in other states. On the desk in the security's office were his wallet with $87.00 and a bottle of store-brand aspirin, 100 tablets, which sold for seventy-nine cents. He sat quietly, answering the questions put to him by the young store detective. Both the police and his wife had been called. When they arrived, they were told that he had purchased groceries, paid for them, but had been seen slipping the small bottle of aspirin in his sweater pocket. The man sat there denying that he had ever taken the aspirin. "Why should I?" he said. "I just paid $39.28 for these groceries." Yet, this senior citizen did commit a serious form of larceny, one which is on the increase in America, especially among the elderly. Although the apprehension of shoplifters is a common occurrence in many stores, there are still more shoplifters who are successful than those who are caught. It was believed that the age of shoplifters was from 12 to 50; however, today it is not uncommon for the senior citizen to be apprehended and prosecuted. Shoplifting affects merchants, who lose millions of dollars a year in stolen merchandise; and it affects the consumers, who must pay higher prices for the goods they buy. In order for the public to understand the reasons for this new wave of shoplifters, it is important to have a profile of the shoplifters, their reasons for shoplifting, and ways other than with a prison sentence or a fine to prevent their repeating the crime.

Example #4

PIRATES OF PAST AND PRESENT

Piracy has been called one of man's three oldest professions (Bottinger 2). Although mankind has harnessed the power of the atom, walked on the moon, and accomplished an infinity of technological feats, piracy acts of all types still enjoy immense popularity around the globe. Trans World Airlines Flight 847 was a victim of air pirates when it was hijacked by Palestinian radicals. The most traditional act of piracy, the boarding and overtaking of a ship, was accomplished when members of the Palestinians Liberation Organization (PLO) held the Italian cruise ship *Achille Lauro* under their control. Although these are just a few examples of recent exploits of contemporary pirates, they clearly illustrate that piracy is far from becoming a term used solely in history textbooks. However, a distinction between eighteenth century buccaneers and contemporary hijackers should be emphasized. Buccaneers acted primarily as thieves who committed acts of piracy primarily for personal gains. These pirates, although being notorious for their ruthless behavior, many times also displayed compassion, respect, and benevolence towards their victims. Recent incidents such as the heinous killings performed during the Egypt Air hijacking have clearly shown that contemporary pirates do not exhibit any sign of mercy, like their predecessors. Many of these air pirates are driven by religious fanaticism which knows no limits. These terrorists will go to any extreme in order to make a religious or political statement. Nevertheless, since air piracy still poses a serious threat to commercial aviation worldwide, it is worthwhile to examine the origins and early applications of the term *pirate* while comparing it to contemporary usages

Newton Berwig

The writer cites one reference for the introduction, a book by Douglas Bottinger and the Editors Time-Life Books, *The Seafarers: The Pirates*, Alexandria, Va.: Time-Life Books, 1978. The other information in the introduction is from general knowledge and the conclusions the writer drew from his own knowledge and from his research.

Example #5

BEATRICE FOODS: PROFITS DOWN, ANXIETY UP

Mergers and acquisitions of many large corporations are under close scrutiny by business analysts. While some analysts show minor concern over the growing trend of conglomerates, others are very disturbed over the trend because of its effect on the economy of this country. We know that Coca-Cola has merged with Wine Spectrum, Sara Lee with Hanes, Allied with Bendix, and Beatrice Foods with a multitude of companies. Economists agree that power, efficiency, and high profits appear to be the prime motivation behind these mergers. However, it is unclear whether or not efficiency and higher profits are actually realized by many of the companies involved in the acquisitions. Still, the real furor among experts involves the area of power. Author Stephen Rhoades is concerned that our system of "competitive" capitalism is moving towards "monolithic" capitalism, a system by a few large, diversified companies (ix). These mergers should produce companies that are more productive and stronger, but Yale Brozen writes that there is an inordinate fear of monopoly (400), for the average consumer no longer knows with whom he is doing business; for example, few people know that Heinz has merged with Weight Watchers. The criticism, nevertheless, has not deterred executives from merging their companies, nor has it stopped backers from investing their money. There are few mergers that do work. However, no company has rivaled Beatrice Foods, a multinational conglomerate. Suddenly, Beatrice, which had always preferred to remain hidden in the shadows, began to advertise, sponsor sports events, and put its name before the public, causing many people to speculate that Beatrice is not as sound today as it has been for the last thirty years. In order to evaluate how stable the Beatrice Company is, it is important to understand the conglomerate's history, growth pattern, and current condition.

Janet K Beline

The student's reference included the following: Yale Brozen, *Concentration, Merger, and Public Policy*, New York: MacMillan, 1982, and Stephen A. Rhodes, *Power, Empire Building, and Mergers*, Lexington: D. C. Heath Co., 1983, as two sources for the introduction. Because the subject of conglomerates was too broad, the student chose to research Beatrice Foods, a name with which she became familiar through the television media.

Example #6

TODAY'S NEW GENERATION

They carried flowers or placards; they were the hippies, the flower children, the campus protesters of the 1970's. Today they are Yuppies, young urban professionals committed to careers and money; they are DINKS: Double Income, No Kids. Both are part of the me- oriented, I-want-it-now generation. Their dreams are for money and social status and for climbing the executive ladder. Their heroes are those who have achieved their dreams. Some prefer a lifestyle without children, free to travel, to accumulate wealth, and to avoid the emotional and financial pressures that come with the rearing of children. Those who have children provide them with designer clothes, computers and video recorders, and private schools. It is the Yuppies who have set the new middle class values, seen through their increasing obsession with the materialistic world in working diligently to acquire material possessions. As college students they were concerned about nuclear wars, political conventions, and social problems.

However, the 1980's reflected a diminished interest in improving social conditions and an attitude of self concern. Evidence of this new attitude is shown by an increasing obsession with the materialistic world, a renewed faith in business and profit, and growing pessimism about governmental issues and about the military.

Susan Grasso

Writing Assignment 1: The Extended Introductory Paragraph

Using one or several of the methods for extended introductory paragraphs listed on page 371, write the introductory paragraph for your own paper. Conclude the paragraph with your thesis statement.

Writing Assignment 2: Preparing the Outline

You know that by the time you form your thesis statement you already have a preliminary outline. Now group your cards according to the major subject headings. These subject headings correspond to the minor inferences in your thesis and when developed will form the major sections of your paper. Within each group of subject headings, arrange the cards according to the order in which you want the proof details to appear.

If you discover that you have cards that you cannot use because they contain duplicate information or irrelevant information, set them aside. Do not discard them because some instructors like to see unused note cards and unused bibliography cards so they can follow your process of selection and limitation.

Once you have decided on the final order of your note cards, number them on the bottom. These numbers will correspond to the in-text citations in your paper. A bonus to numbering the note cards is that if they should get out of order you can quickly reassemble them.

Now review the form for the standard topic outline (pages 156–57). Also study carefully the outline for the model research paper on "The Formative Years: Effects of Television" on page 391.

Then write your own outline.

Stage 7 Writing the Rough Draft

1. Using the Note Cards
2. Checking the Rough Draft

STEP 1 Using the Note Cards

With a detailed outline and a complete set of note cards arranged to correspond to the outline, you will have little trouble writing the first draft of your paper. Using the outline as a structural guide and the note cards to supply the supporting details, you can begin to write. Since you have already written the introduction, you can begin the first draft with your first developmental paragraph.

Writing is a very personal process. Some people like to rough out the whole paper rapidly, waiting for revision to check grammar, sentence structure, punctuation, and general style. Others prefer to develop one section of the paper at a time, polishing and revising each section before going on to another section. Whichever method you use, you will find that following a few hints for rough draft procedure will make the writing go smoother.

1. Watch the development of your paragraphs carefully. Make sure that you have a topic sentence for each which contains a controlling inference. Work in the raw material from your notes in a smoothly flowing and unified way. The following pages illustrate how the student researcher on "The Formative Years: Effects of Television" worked her note cards into her paper. One page of her research paper is reproduced on page 379. Opposite the page are the note cards she worked with. Notice how this information was incorporated in the paper.

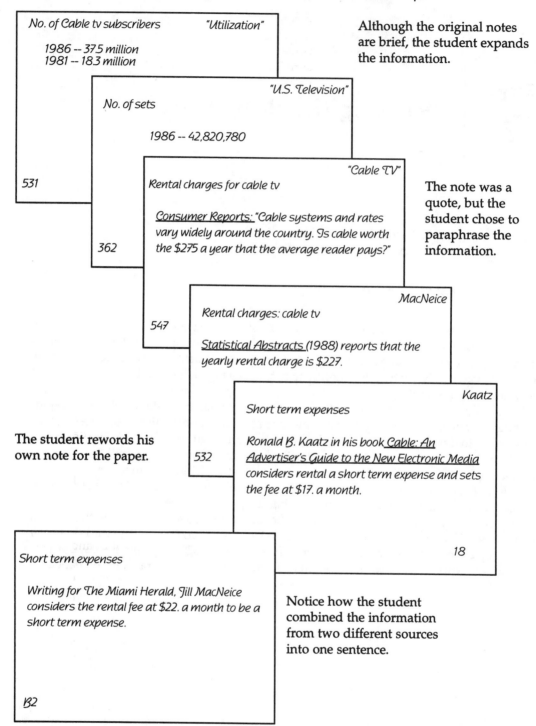

No. of Cable tv subscribers   "Utilization"

    1986 -- 37.5 million
    1981 -- 18.3 million

531

Although the original notes are brief, the student expands the information.

"U.S. Television"

No. of sets

    1986 -- 42,820,780

362

"Cable TV"

Rental charges for cable tv

<u>Consumer Reports:</u> "Cable systems and rates vary widely around the country. Is cable worth the $275 a year that the average reader pays?"

The note was a quote, but the student chose to paraphrase the information.

547

MacNeice

Rental charges: cable tv

<u>Statistical Abstracts</u> (1988) reports that the yearly rental charge is $227.

Kaatz

Short term expenses

Ronald B. Kaatz in his book <u>Cable: An Advertiser's Guide to the New Electronic Media</u> considers rental a short term expense and sets the fee at $17. a month.

532

The student rewords his own note for the paper.

18

Short term expenses

Writing for <u>The Miami Herald</u>, Jill MacNeice considers the rental fee at $22. a month to be a short term expense.

Notice how the student combined the information from two different sources into one sentence.

B2

From city to city and from cable company to cable company, the costs of cable reception vary. The expenses, which include installation, basic subscription rates, and premium channel costs, become long-term expenses since the viewer never finishes paying for the service. Nevertheless, the number of cable television subscribers served in 1986 were 37.5 million, a considerable increase from 1981 when there were 37.5 million ("Utilization of Selected Media" 531). The number of homes with cable television during the same year was reported to be 42,820,780 ("U.S. Television Sets" 362). In actuality, the subscriber does not buy cable service, but instead rents it. The cable lines and the channel selector box are always the property of the cable company and never belong to the viewer. Nationally, the rental charge for cable service averages $275 per year ("Cable TV" 547). This average may be on the decline, however, for the basic yearly rate projected for 1996, according to Statistical Abstract, is $227 (532). In the early stages of organizing cable service, competing cable companies had promised a multitude of services to the specified area's viewers. Since many of these companies have not been able to keep their promise of two-way communications, 130+ channel availability and diverse business oriented channels, they have reduced their rates (MacNeice 2B).

Cable systems do have their short term expenses, also. Since cable service is rented, the monthly bill can be considered a short-term expense, averaging between $17 and $22 a month nationwide (Kaatz 18 & MacNeice B2). This monthly rate can also be reduced.

2. Write on one side of the paper only, and write on every other line or every third line. Give yourself wide margins. Then you will have plenty of room to add details you may have omitted and to revise your sentence structure.

3. When researchers document with footnotes or endnotes, some prefer to prepare each note as they go. Others prefer to enter the note numeral on the rough draft and then prepare the notes later by referring back to the note and the complete source information on the bibliography card. However, researchers who use the internal citation method find documentation easier because the source for the information is written along with the text. Always refer to a handbook or guide for the proper documentation form.

4. Check direct quotes very carefully to make sure that you are quoting the original exactly. If a quotation does not appear to be accurate on your note card or if you are uncertain whether you have paraphrased or directly quoted in a particular instance, then check your notes against the source.

    Use appropriate words to introduce your direct quotes. You can find words more vigorous and explicit than "says" and "states." Try "predicts," "warns," " estimates, " "argues," "thinks," "discovered," "hopes," and other words appropriate to the sense of your quotation.

When you introduce a quotation, mention the name and the title or function of the person responsible for it if possible.

Check the Mechanics Guide, pages 442–443, for the proper punctuation for introducing quotations.

5. After you finish the body of the paper with all of the major sections developed, then add the introductory paragraph to the beginning.

6. Now write the conclusion of the paper. This will be one or several paragraphs in which you discuss what steps are currently being taken to correct the social problem you have investigated, what solutions have been proposed by experts on the subject, and what your own conclusions and ideas are about the topic.

STEP 2   Checking the Rough Draft

Look at the checklist on pages 380–383 of this book. It is a review of the format for your paper and the conventions of documentation, and it can help you in two ways. First, if you check this list against your rough draft, you will prevent unnecessary changes in your final copy. Second, a paper which is accurate in these respects stands a better chance of getting a good grade than one which is not. Obviously, these criteria are not the only ones which will be used in the evaluation of your paper, but correct form and documentation are primary basic requirements for this research paper.

After you have checked the format and documentation of your paper, go over it for corrections in grammar, sentence structure, spelling, and punctuation. It is often helpful to read through the paper once for general sense and continuity and again for the mechanics. Some students find it helpful to read the paper aloud or to have a friend read it over in order to catch sentence structure problems.

Checklist for Research Papers

1. **Title page**
   Does the title page carry, properly spaced, the title, your name,
   the name, number, and section of the course, the professor's name,
   the date of presentation?   _____

2. **Outline**
   a. Is the outline written in standard topic form?   _____

   b. Is it paged with lower case Roman numerals?   _____

   c. Is the outline correctly punctuated and capitalized?   _____

   d. Have you double spaced between Roman numerals?   _____

   e. Are parallel topics grammatically constructed?   _____

3. **First page of text**
   a. Is the title repeated? _____

   b. Are your margins set according to manuscript form? _____

   c. Are the note cards numbered sequentially as you have used them corresponding with the in-text citations in your paper? _____

   d. Have you bound or attached the note cards in the manner requested by your professor? _____

8. **Bibliography/Works Cited**
   a. Does the bibliography or works cited page conclude your paper?

   b. Are the references alphabetized by author's last name, or in the absence of a name, by the first important word of the title of the article? _____

   c. Is the first line of every bibliography entry flush with the left margin? _____

   d. Are second and following lines of each entry indented five spaces? _____

   e. Is a spaced line used in place of an author's name for the second and successive items by that author? _____

   f. Have you given all the necessary bibliographical data in the order and with the punctuation and spacing shown in the bibliography examples on pages 293–305? _____

   g. Have you titled the page WORKS CITED or SELECTED BIBLIOGRAPHY? _____

   h. Have you included in the bibliography only those works which you cited in your paper? _____

9. **Minimum sources**
   a. Have you satisfied the minimum source requirements for this paper? _____

   b. Have you drawn from the variety of sources recommended by your instructor? _____

10. Binding the paper Have you assembled all the pages in their proper order and bound or fastened them together in the manner requested by the instructor?
    Order:
    a. Title page

b. Outline
c. Text of paper
d. Bibliography

Note: If an Endnote page is used for explanatory notes, the Endnote page is placed just before the bibliography.

4. Succeeding pages
a. Are all of the following pages numbered? _____

b. Is your bibliography/works cited sheet paginated? _____

5. Quotations
a. Has each direct quotation of four lines or fewer been put in quotation marks? _____

b. Has each quotation longer than four lines been indented and set off by appropriate spacing, without quotation marks? _____

c. Have double and single quotation marks, italics, ellipses, and brackets been used consistently, according to accepted practice? (See "Mechanics Guide," pages 436–442. _____

d. Has each quotation been smoothly introduced with an appropriate verb and proper punctuation? (See "Mechanics Guide," pages 442–443.) _____

e. Has each quotation been properly acknowledged? _____

6. Documentation
Internal Citation
a. Have you acknowledged all material that was quoted directly or paraphrased or was not original with you? _____

b. Have you followed the correct form? (Check a style manual for the appropriate documentation form.) _____

Endnotes or Footnotes for Explanatory Material
a. Does the raised number in the text correspond in each case with the number of the note that acknowledges the source reference? _____

b. Is the footnote clearly separated from the text? _____

c. Are the footnotes/endnotes indented five spaces from the left margin and raised one half space? _____

    d. Are the notes numbered consecutively? _____

    e. Are the authors' names given first? _____

    f. Are the notes punctuated according to correct usage?
       (Check a style manual.) _____

7. **Note cards**
    a. In addition to the information on the card, does each note card
       carry a subject heading, the source identification, and a specific
       page reference? _____

    b. Have you attached or included a note card for every footnote
       in your paper if required? _____

Stage

8

Writing and Submitting the Final Paper

1. Preparing the Final Revision
2. Proofreading
3. Assembling the Research Packet

Before beginning the final version of your paper, study again the student model of the research paper, "The Formative Years: Effects of Television," which begins on page 389. Observe the form of the title sheet, the outline, the first page of the text, the handling of sources, and the bibliography. Read the annotations.

STEP 1   Preparing the Final Revision

First assemble the materials you will need. This seems obvious, but many students attempt to produce the paper without the tools, and the result is an unprofessional looking paper. Use a good grade of standard bond paper or the heavier grade of erasable bond.

Get out your detailed outline, your notecards assembled in order, and your polished rough draft. Set your margins so that you will have one and a half inch margins at the top and on the left, and about one inch at the bottom and on the right. Begin the first page with the title in all capital letters, about one-fourth of the way down the page.

When the paper itself has been typed, prepare the title page, giving the title of your paper, your name, the name, number, and section of your course, the instructor's name, and the date.

Retype the outline neatly. It is wise to leave the final typing of the outline until last because even in the typing of the final version you may decide to change the order or an item or two in your paper.

Last, prepare the bibliography page. If it is a list only of the sources actually used in your paper (those which you documented) then the bibliography will be titled "Works Cited" or "List of Works Cited." If it includes one or several works which you used as background material but did not actually cite in your paper, then the bibliography will be titled "Selected Bibliography" or "Selected References."

STEP 2 Proofreading

Proofreading is a vital step in submitting an acceptable paper, and it is a step that many students either ignore or fail to devote sufficient time to. It is best to leave some time gaps in the preparation of your paper—at least a day between the writing of the rough draft and the final revision and another day between the writing of the final paper and the proofreading. Start your proofreading when you are fresh; go over every word in every sentence. This is the time to get out the checklist again and check the final paper, correct errors neatly in ink. It is much better to have neatly made corrections than to submit a paper with obvious errors. If the corrections make an untidy appearing paper, it is best to type that page over again or revise it on the computer.

STEP 3 Assembling the Research Packet

When your research packet is ready to submit, use a plain two pocket folder. Write the title of your paper and your name on the front. Then assemble it in the following order (from top to bottom): on the left side put the note cards and bibliography cards; unused note and bibliography cards; clippings; pamphlets, and copies of sources. On the right put the complete paper; the extended introduction; the cause and effect paper; your data enumeration paragraph; the extended definition; and a rough draft if one is requested.

These, then, are the stages and steps to successful expository communication, and by working through them you have discovered that you *can* write.

Title Page

If your instructor requires a title page. you may use one of two formats. Both samples are included. One is a separate title page that comes before the outline. The other is a heading on the first page of the text. Both samples are shown below.

THE FORMATIVE YEARS: EFFECTS OF TELEVISION

Rebecca Rasanen
ENG 1101

Dr. McLaine
12 December 1995

Rebecca Rasanen
ENG 1101
Dr. McLaine
12 December 1995

THE FORMATIVE YEARS: EFFECTS OF TELEVISION

Nowhere is there a greater potential for love, support, caring, and commitment than in the family. Yet, it takes time to love a child. In addition to providing a home and material security, a parent must, as Marian Wright Edelman observes, "Wrap children in a cocoon of caring and activity . . . . the care of the mind and body needs to be grounded in the care of the spirit, which is the glue that holds families and communities together" (XIV). Thus, our obligation as parents is to guide our children to become self reliant adults This, too, involves time. It is a mistake to conclude that baby-sitters, day-care centers, or latch-key arrangements can be a substitute for the consistent discipline and example parents provide. Sadly, this fact escapes many parents, and it is evident particularly in the way children are being raised today. Too many children are forced to grow up in a hurry. As Neal Lawrence asserts, "Family structures are crumbling under the weight of divorce or of parents both who work

THE FORMATIVE YEARS: EFFECTS OF TELEVISION

Rebecca Rasanen

ENG 1101

Dr. McLaine

12 December 1995

THE TITLE

The title is repeated on the outline page.

THE FORMAT

The format of the outline follows the general principles of the standard outline form (See Part 1, Stage 8, page 157–159).

THE THESIS

The student begins with the thesis statement, which is labeled. The student lists four effects of television viewing on children.

THE STAGES OF THE OUTLINE

The outline is very complete, carrying four stages of classified information.

Your outline may not be in four stages, but to be adequate, it should be at least a three-stage outline.

THE FORMATIVE YEARS: EFFECTS OF TELEVISION

Thesis Statement: This steady stream of uncontrolled television viewing seduces and numbs children, causing major problems: loss of inherent creativity, an increase in emotional disorders, poor intellectual development, and diminished social skills.

I. Effect: Loss of inherent creativity

    A. Through desire to conform

        1. Creative play discouraged

           a. With Playdoh

           b. With Ant Farm

           c. In the outdoors

        2. Electronic games and devices encouraged

    B. Through consumerism

        1. Through marketing of video characters

           a. The Mighty Morphin Power Rangers

           b. Walt Disney's *Pocahontas*

        2. Through exploitation

           a. Availability of videos

           b. Manufacturing of merchandise

           c. Promotions by McDonald's

    C. Through seduction by television

        1. Loss of interest in self awareness

        2. Diminishing of natural curiosity

        3. Bypassing of childhood activities

           a. Viewing adult material

           b. Burning out early

Numbering the Pages of the Outline

Since the outline is considered to be a preface to the research paper, it is numbered with lower case Roman numerals. You need not paginate the first page, but all succeeding pages are numbered as follows: i, ii, iii, iv, etc.

II. Effect: Increased emotional disorders

    A. Major effects

        1. Insensitivity to pain

        2. Fear of surroundings

        3. Increase of aggressive behavior

           a. Hit playmates

           b. Become impatient

           c. Disobey those in charge

    B. Other effects

        1. Chance of being arrested

        2. Chance of being sent to jail at a young age

III. Effect: Poor intellectual development

    A. Creates classroom problems

    B. Replaces intellectual activities

        1. Perform poorly on tests

        2. Score below those of other countries

    C. Contributes to poor learning environment

        1. Passive learners

        2. Poor readers

        3. Weak skills in time management

           a. Little lime spent on studying

           b. Excessive television viewing

    D. Effects classroom procedures

        1. Elimination of intellectual activities

        2. Atmosphere of boredom

        3. Loss of teaching innovations

E. Effects desire to learn

    1. Promotes learning as fun and easy

    2. Dominates spare time of student

IV. Effect: Low social skills

  A. Trend toward isolation in the family

    1. Destroys family bonding and unify

    2. Inhibits learning of values and attitudes

  B. Inability to interact with others in society

    1. Distorts reality

    2. Promotes alienation

V. Solutions to the problem

  A. Instilling of family values

  B. Replacing television viewing with human interaction

  C. Promoting active learning

    1. Trip to zoo

    2. Trip to museum

    3. Trip to athletic event

  D. Requiring legislative action

    1. Installation of a computer chip

    2. Blocking of objectionable programs

  E. Relying on parents to become gatekeepers

    1. To control television viewing habits of children

    2. To impart goals and values to children

Rasanen iv

F. Urging parents to interact with children

1. Spend time listening to them

2. Spend time playing with them

3. Share activities with them

The Concluding Statement

The outline ends with the concluding statement—the one sentence that summarizes the paper. It does not introduce new material, nor is it an editorialized statement, such as a warning or a moral.

The concluding statement, like the thesis, is labeled.

Concluding statement: If parents take the time to give their children love, they will not only counteract many of society's ills, but they will also provide their children with a road map for tomorrow.

The Introductory Paragraph

The introductory paragraph includes background information for the subject as well as specific reasons for society's concern about the way children are being reared. The paragraph ends with the thesis statement for a cause/effect paper.

Because research papers are longer than most multi-paragraph essays, the introductory paragraph is extended. It is not just a few sentences. In this case the introduction is written in two paragraphs since the writer did not want the body paragraphs to be shorter than the introductory paragraph.

THE FORMATIVE YEARS: EFFECTS OF TELEVISION

Nowhere is there a greater potential for love, support, caring, and commitment than in the family. Yet, it takes time to love a child. In addition to providing a home and material security, a parent must, as Marian Wright Edelman observes, "Wrap children in a cocoon of caring and activity...the care of the mind and body needs to be grounded in the care of the spirit, which is the glue that holds families and communities together" (XIV). Thus, our obligation as parents is to guide our children to become self reliant adults. This, too, involves time. It is a mistake to conclude that baby-sitters, day-care centers, or latch-key arrangements can be a substitute for the consistent discipline and example parents provide.

Sadly, this fact escapes many parents, and it is evident particularly in the way children are being raised today. Too many children are forced to grow up in a hurry. As Neal Lawrence asserts, "Family structures are crumbling under the weight of divorce or of parents both who work and who have little time to spend nurturing their offspring" (6). For some families, two full-time workers are vital for economic survival. But far too many Americans suffer from

Numbering the Pages of the Text

It is not necessary to number the first page, but you may begin with the second page and continue numbering through the Works Cited page. You may choose to use just the page number (2,3,4, etc.), or you may type your name before the page number. The model theme uses the second form.

Developmental Paragraphs

The first developmental paragraph discusses the loss of inherent creativity. It begins with a topic sentence and gives specific support statements. Notice that the topic sentence is the student's own generalization about the topic.

affluence, trading off time at home with the children for time
spent acquiring material goods. Consequently, children spend a
considerable number of their formative years in out-of-home
settings or simply at home alone, which in either case means
gazing at the television for hours on end. The effect of this
steady stream of uncontrolled television viewing on children
has been attributed by some to be a major cause of many
developmental problems in children. However, the problem is
more accurately described as not what television is doing to
children, but what children are not accomplishing because of the
impact television has had on them. This steady stream of
uncontrolled television viewing seduces and numbs children,
causing major problems: a loss of inherent creativity, an
increase of emotional disorders, poor intellectual development,
and diminished social skills.

   First, children are not exploring their inherent creativity.
As they grow up, society encourages them to put down the
Playdoh and the finger-paints and learn to watch television like
everyone else. Television encourages conformity. The natural
desire to belong is manipulated by the entertainment industry to
turn children into miniature consumers. One season it is Batman
and Superman; the next, it is the Mighty Morphin Power Rangers.
Often children's entertainment is carefully calculated. Less
attention is paid to the quality of the script while primary

Since the research paper is longer than 500 or 600 words, a major point of the paper may be divided into more than one paragraph. But the rule remains. Every developmental paragraph must have a topic sentence. The paragraph will discuss the "many choices" that designers offer.

The information about the products available and sold comes from the student's own experience and observations. Therefore, no internal documentation is needed. Also, since McDonald's advertised their promotions, that information becomes general knowledge.

If there are no pages listed for the electronic generated references, cite only the author's last name.

focus becomes the number of products generated for merchandising (Spratling). Not only are videos of the Power Rangers available in every store, including supermarkets, but McDonald's sold the action figures with their vehicles, called Zords, for each character as well. However, to do so, parents needed to buy a Happy Meal before being able to purchase the figurine set for $1.69. Even the movie industry may be part of this movement to generate more revenue through television by urging children to buy videos of films, such as Toy Story or 101 Dalmations, or to buy any number of products from coloring books to clothing.

One reason may be that product designers offer many choices. There are Power Ranger Halloween costumes, complete with battery operated gloves and boots that simulate sounds of karate. There are masks and decoders that have magical powers, and there are swords that zap the enemy. As a result of the merchandising, parents are hoping to rear a generation that is "Hooked on Phonics," but product manufacturers are ensuring that children are hooked on technology. Children are growing up with Sega Genesis, Nintendo, sneakers with flashing lights, Compact Disk Players, cellular phones, and computers with programs such as "Mortal Kombat." Laurie Farrar of Madison Heights, Michigan, says of her four-year-old daughter, Whitney Hunt, that even before she saw the movie Pocahontas, she had a complete outfit of the character:

In the next paragraph the writer mentioned that the "seduction by television has not gone unnoticed." In discussing this point a long quotation by Gary Trudeau is given. Notice that the quotation is indented. It has no quotation marks surrounding it because the indentation indicates that the passage is a quote. However, single quotes are used within the passage.

Notice the use of the ellipses—the three spaced periods, indicating that the writer chose to eliminate some of the original quotation.

Rasanen 4

hat, blouse, skirt, panties and shoes; she has the doll the
necklace, the bracelet, the earrings, the tape, a coloring
book, talking book and three reading books. And after
several trips to Burger King she's well on her way to collecting all eight figurines associated with the movie. (qtd.
in Spratling)

What is interesting is that Whitney's mother claims that despite
her frequent trips to Burger King, her daughter does not even
like the food there. She goes only to get the figurines
(Spratling).

However, this seduction by television has not gone unnoticed. As children fail to develop intellectually Garry Trudeau,
creator of the comic strip Doonesbury, observes that a child's
creativity, a unique gift is lost with little or no delibera-
tion, children are capable of producing art that is "vibrant,
rhythmic, and balanced. . . ," whose "hallmark is its very lack
of self-awareness" (34). However, as cultural influences bombard
children, they lose interest in this kind of exploration.
Trudeau continues:

One weekend, I sat my son down and pulled out one of his
pieces... 'What would happen,' I asked him, 'if you were to
fill in your drawing with color? Would it make the scene more
alive?' 'Who cares?' he responded, glancing longingly at the
television. (34)

Notice that all quotations are properly introduced. Not only is Neal Lawrence identified as an author, but the title of his article is also given. It is very important to introduce all quotations so that the reader will be able to accept the support statements because they have come from an authority on the subject.

Once again the writer has an indented quotation. Usually a paragraph does not end with an indented quotation, but the writer needs to tie the quotation into the text.

While Trudeau links creativity and curiosity as important parts of the learning process, his own child, like many other children, prefers watching television.

The irony is that children do start out with great creativity and curiosity — eager to explore and hungry to learn. Most children before the age of six draw anything from "scribbled writings" to various "geometric shapes" and "torsoless human figures" (Trudeau 34). In past years, children were fascinated by watching ants working in their "Ant Farm," by catching fireflies in a jar, or just by making mud pies. Neal Lawrence, author of "What's Happening to Our Children?," feels instead that children are being forced to grow up too soon and are "bypassing childhood as we knew it" (6). Lawrence, like others, discovered that children of the 1990's have difficulty maintaining an "untroubled innocence" (6). Televisions impose "adult material on grade schoolers before they are emotionally equipped to assimilate it" (7). He observes that:

> the child of yesterday, who wandered in meadows of fantasy, whose tears were reserved for skinned knees and broken toys, has been replaced by kids who are burned out before they are old enough to vote. (7)

As a result, children are faced with another problem. Television replaces a child's natural curiosity with pseudo- life experiences that produce a high anxiety level in children, causing

Here the writer uses quotations with a paraphrase for variety of sentence structure. The writer is careful to document Hoffman's information with the qtd. entry.

Notice the transition, "Just as a steady diet of television can adversely affect children's emotional development," linking the paragraph before with the developmental paragraph to come.

serious emotional disorders. Psychological research indicates that there are three major effects. First, children become insensitive to pain; second, they are fearful of their immediate surroundings; and third, they become more aggressive (Microsoft Internet 1). George Gerdner, Ph.D., at the University of Pennsylvania, found that children's TV shows contain about twenty violent acts each hour (1). As a result, given a steady diet of these programs, children hit their playmates, disobey those in charge, become impatient, and refuse to complete assignments (1). Kay J. Hoffman, an educator at a progressive school, believes that children reared today are "being hardened too early, jarred into an awake adult consciousness" (qtd. in Lawrence 2). Leonard Eron, Ph.D, and two associates at the University of Illinois, discovered that children who began a steady diet of television when they were eight years old had a greater chance of being arrested and sent to jail as young adults (Microsoft Internet 2). Scientists studying the issue maintain that there is a link between the violence shown on television and the aggressive behavior of children.

Just as a steady diet of television can adversely affect children's emotional development, it can also interfere with their intellectual development. Television viewing replaces activities such as reading and writing, which are vital to a good education. This issue is magnified by the fact that never before has education mattered more in terms of future economic health as it does today. As society moves from the Industrial Age to the Electronic Age, knowledge and skills necessary to an "information economy" must be developed (Resnick 55). Yet, as early as 1983, the Reagan Administration report <u>A Nation at Risk</u> revealed that American students performed poorly on academic achievement tests in comparison to foreign students (Hornblower et al. 56). Another 1992 study, conducted by the Educational Testing Service, showed that while funding in the United States was greater than in any other country (except Israel), American students still scored lower in mathematics and science than did students in ten other nations (56). Studies that analyze American classrooms also found that, coupled with the excessive amount of time students watch television, the enormous class sizes of forty or more and increased teaching loads make schools a frustrating experience for both teachers and students (Howe II 70). Teachers must now devote a great portion of their time keeping order among overstimulated and unruly students in the classroom. School administrators' attitudes stress classroom order over teaching innovation. Beginning teachers soon learn that controlling the class means eliminating intellectual activities that are interesting or exciting because maintaining an atmosphere of boredom helps control the class (Horton and Goroff 32). Thus, teachers find themselves showing videos to keep the students quiet although this practice may be academically unsound because it reinforces television viewing.

Due to these complex classroom problems, educating a child has become an even greater challenge than ever before: children need to spend more time reading and studying to succeed in school. However, television's effect on children creates an expectation that learning is easy, passive, and entertaining. The television addict may find studying an ordeal because of poor reading habits. The 1994 <u>Information Please Almanac</u> shows that daily household television usage is an astounding seven hours a day (748). While not all family members may watch television continually for that length of time, it is evident that television does dominate the spare time of the American family. Patti Doten, in her article "Turning In & Tuning Out," found that 66 percent of Americans regularly watch television as they eat dinner and that parents spend 38.5 minutes a week in "meaningful conversation with their children while children spend 1,680 minutes per week watching TV" (1).

Doten added that because 50 percent of the children have television sets in their room, they are further isolated from the family (1). This trend toward isolation destroys family communication and hinders the development of social skills (1). Like sponges, children readily absorb the values and attitudes they see demonstrated on television (Kiester and Kiester 158). During a child's formative years, he learns values from television. While his parents may try to instill values of kindness, honesty, generosity, and patience, television may introduce negative values (158) such as greed, inhumanity, and dishonesty.

Emphasizing the consequences of excessive television viewing and poor time management, Mihaly Csikszentmihaly, Professor of Human Development in the Departments of Psychology and Education at the University of Chicago, explained:

> Time is not money, but it is life, and so the question of how we use time is crucial. It has been reconfirmed over and over again that those children who spend too much time watching television are not going to learn as well as those who watch less. How much of their free time they spend in active pursuits will have an impact on how much they learn. So, we cannot separate the way in which time is being used from what children learn. (qtd. in Holton and Goroff 31)

Rasanen 10

Children who watch excessive amounts of television are also not learning how to interact with others; nor are they learning how to negotiate, compromise, or resolve conflict. Hours of solitary viewing promotes alienation and distorts reality, for there is no one at home to help explain or interpret what is being shown (Doten 1). Jack Levin, Professor of Sociology and Criminology at Northwestern, says that "TV once was seen as the opiate of the masses, a high tech way of drugging people into submission" (qtd. in Doten 1). Now he believes that not only are the masses "drugged," but they have become "isolated and separated from one another" (qtd. in Doten 1). If he is correct, then perhaps a television set should never be part of a child's
bedroom furniture.

Aside from alienation, perceptions of fantasy and reality can become distorted since most prime time programming depicts an unrealistic view of life. In many sitcoms, the characters never seem to work; they simply "hang out" and discuss their personal problems (Zoglin 74). While the men and women of <u>Cheers</u> spent endless hours talking, viewers were not sure that the characters ever worked. No one ever saw Ward Cleaver of <u>Leave It To Beaver</u> at his place of employment, according to television critic Richard Zoglin. Although Jerry Seinfeld and his friends work, they live in an "in between world; in halls and doorways, in the backseat of taxicabs, in a booth at the local coffee shop" (74). Even most television talk shows revel in entertainment

Rasanen 11

that is voyeuristic and exploitative, rather than on uplifting themes (Winfrey 16).

Since psychological research has confirmed that watching violence on television affects children in major ways, it is important that society begins to find solutions to the problem. While it is important to stimulate children's minds, it is even more important to instill love, empathy, compassion, and sensitivity into their hearts. These values can only be learned through interaction with others. In contrast, television viewing replaces human interaction with a passive, solitary experience; and passive learning is not as effective as active learning. Real-life experiences may be far more inspiring and memorable than any lesson children could extract from a television show. Authors Edwin and Sally Kiester believe that television should be tied to other activities. They urge parents to combine a viewing of National Geographic with a trip to the zoo or to a museum or to participate in a Little League game after watching Major League baseball on television (160).

With multiple television sets in the average household and an abundance of channels to view, most Americans watch television more than four hours a day (Dotin 1). One questions whether or not we have relinquished control of our lives to television producers. A study done by Aletha Huston, Ph.D., observed that children's behavior does become more violent - both verbally and physically - after viewing violent cartoons (1). Studies also confirm the long-range effects of viewing televised violence for children who perceived the world as a "mean and dangerous place" (Microsoft Internet 1). The growing concern over violence on television is reflected in recent legislative efforts that would require television manufacturers to install a special computer chip, enabling parents to block out reception of objectionable programs. Much controversy is expected on this issue as broadcasters argue that these measures would violate the right to free speech (Kaufman B1).

Currently, the debate continues. Broadcasters, Congress, and child psychology experts all propose numerous solutions to a problem that has no easy answers. Unfortunately, by allowing moral values to erode, society has committed a serious mistake. Family life is in decay, and children are the losers. The effect is seen not only on television, but also in newspapers, in magazines, in videos, and on the radio. The current notion is to rely on society's gatekeepers to provide solutions. However, by doing this, we are denying where the primary responsibility for shaping a child's mind and character truly lies with the parents. Parents must recognize that they "have tremendous power to moderate this influence" (Microsoft Internet 2). It is up to parents to draw the boundary lines needed in controlling television viewing habits and to hold to those limits. It is up to parents to impart the goals and values that will vaccinate their children against the moral maladies infecting society today. Children learn through experiences; thus, it is up to parents to spend time with their children-playing with

The Concluding Paragraph

Notice that the concluding paragraph is an extended one. Just like an extended introduction for research papers, there are also extended conclusions. Since the writer introduced the problem, discussed effects on children, it is important that a cause/effect paper offer solutions. The solutions are usually generalizations arrived at by the writer as a result of thinking critically about the subject.

them, listening to them, learning what is on their minds, and sharing activities with them. Compared to material advantages, these activities cost nothing, but they are the things that children need most. If parents take the time to give their children love, they will not only counteract many of society's ills, but they will also be providing their children with a road map for tomorrow.

Works Cited Page

All of the sources that the writer used in the paper are listed on the Works Cited page. All of the entries are listed in alphabetical order. Each entry follows the correct format for the writing of the source information.

The page is numbered because it is considered to be part of the research paper. It is not an appendix.

WORKS CITED

Doten, Patti. "Tuning In and Tuning Out—Family Members Spend More Time Watching Television. . . Alone. " <u>Boston Globe</u> 6 Apr. 1995:1.

Edelman, Marian Wright. Preface. <u>Guide My Feet</u>. Boston: Beacon, 1995: xiv.

Holton. Gerald and Daniel Goroff. "Where Is American Education Going? Report on a Convocation." <u>Daedalus: Journal of American Arts and Sciences</u> 124.4(Fall 1995): 32+.

Hornblower, Margot, et. al. "A Class of Their Own." <u>Time</u> 31 Oct. 1994: 56.

Howe II, Harold. "Priority Strategies for Improved Learning." <u>Daedalus: Journal of the American Arts and Sciences</u> 124.4(Fall 1995): 70-71.

<u>Information Please Almanac.</u> 47th ed. New York: Houghton, 1978: 748.

Kauffman, Susan. "Duke Study Makes Case for TV Warnings." <u>The News and Observer</u> 12 July 1995: B1.

Kiester, Edwin Jr., and Sally Valente Kiester. "Make TV Help Your Kids." <u>Reader's Digest</u> Oct. 1991: 157-162.

Lawrence, Neal. "What's Happening to Our Children?" <u>Midwest Today</u> Dec 1993/Jan. 1994: 2-14.

Microsoft Internet Explorer. "Violence on Television." Online. Internet. 14 Nov. 1995.

Resnick, Lauren B. "From Aptitude to Effort: A New Foundation for Our Schools." <u>Daedalus: Journal of the American Arts and Sciences</u> 124.4(Fall 1995): 55.

Spratling, Cassandra. "Movie-related merchandise has kids begging parents for more." <u>Detroit Free Press.</u> 19 July 1995. n. pag. Newsbank: Box Office Blitz CD Rom Newsbank Comprehansive. 1995.

Trudeau, Gary. "Out of the Crayons of Babes." <u>The New York Times</u> 22 Jan. 1995, final ed. sec 6:34.

Winfrey, Oprah. "What Can We Do to Change TV?" <u>TV Guide</u> 11-17 Nov. 1995: 12-18.

Zoglin, Richard. "Friends and Layabouts." <u>Time</u> 20 Mar. 1995: 74.

A Brief Guide to Mechanics and Style

Manuscript Form

1. **PAPER**
   Ink: Use standard size 8 1/2 x 11 inches composition paper. Do not tear out the paper from a spiral notebook; the edges should not be ragged. The paper must be white.
   Printing: Use standard, unlined typing paper 8 1/2 x 11 inches.

2. **FORM**
   Ink: Write legibly, using a pen with black or blue ink. Write on only one side of the paper.
   Printing: Make sure the type is clean. Use black ink. Double space. Print on only one side of each sheet of paper.

3. **MARGINS**
   Ink and Printing: Leave about an inch and one-half at the left and top, an inch at the bottom. Although the right-hand margin need not be exact, leave about an inch.

4. **INDENTATION**
   Ink: Indent paragraphs about one inch or five spaces in printed copy.

5. **PAGINATION**
   Use Arabic numerals (1, 2, 3, etc.). Place the numeral in the upper right-hand corner to mark all pages after the first. The first page need not be numbered. Do not place a period after the number or enclose the number in parentheses. An alternate form is the last name of the writer and the page number.

6. **TITLE**
   Ink: Center the title on the page on the first ruled line. Leave the next line blank, and begin the first paragraph on the third line. Capitalize the first word of the title and all succeeding words except articles, short conjunctions, and prepositions. Do not put quotation marks around the title or underline it. Place no period after the title.
   Printing: Center the title about three inches from the top. Double-space between the title and the first paragraph. Capitalize the first word of the title and all succeeding words except articles, short conjunctions and prepositions. Do not put quotation marks around the title or underline it. Place no period after the title.

7. **SPACING**
   Leave a space between the title and the body.

8. **ENDORSEMENT**
   Ink and Printing: Endorse the paper with the following information: Name, Class, Date, Title of Paper, the Instructor's name.

Abbreviations

1. Avoid the use of abbreviations in formal writing.
2. Use only acceptable abbreviations such as Mr., Dr., B.C., A.D., etc.
3. The titles *reverend* and *honorable* must not be used with surnames only; those words should be followed by the first name or the initials.
4. In ordinary writing, except in footnotes, bibliographies, addresses, tabulations, spell out:
   a. Names of countries, states, and cities
   b. Names of days and months

c. Words such as chapter, page, avenue, street, manufacturing company, mountain,Christmas, volume, number

d. personal names

Numbers

1. Spell out numbers that can be expressed in two words.
2. Use figures
   a. For numbers not easily written out
   b. For several numbers occurring in the same passage
   c. For street numbers
   d. For room numbers
   e. For page numbers
   f. For chapter numbers
   g. Decimals and percentages
   h. Statistics or tabulations
   i. Hours of the day with A.M. or P.M.
3. Use figures for dates, but do not use *st, nd, rd, or th* with the day of the month.
4. Do not begin a sentence with a number.
5. In expository writing, do not express a sum in both words and figures.
6. Use o'clock following the hour written in words.

Syllabication

1. Do not divide proper nouns.
2. Do not divide words of one syllable.
3. Do not separate a name and the initials, titles, or abbreviations of degrees that go with the name.
4. In typescript and manuscript do not divide short words of two syllables. Only divide words that are more than six letters.
5. Do not divide words that are more than six letters.
6. Divide between syllables (consult a dictionary if necessary).
7. Divide double consonant words between the two consonants.
8. Divide compound words on the hyphen.
9. In words with prefixes, divide, if possible, on the prefix if it has three or more letters.
10. In words with suffixes, divide on the suffix if it has three or more letters.
11. When dividing, carry over three or more letters if possible.

Capitalization

Capitalized (cap)   *Not Capitalized (lc)*

General Rules

1. The first word of a sentence

2. The first word of each item in an
    outline
    I.   Colonial tokens
         A   Authorized by British
             1.   Rosa Americana
             2.   Hibernia coppers
         B. Designed by colonists
3. The first word in each item of a list
    Our investigation showed the fol-
    lowing:
             1. Inadequate lighting
             2. Unpaved streets
             3. Broken walkways

Addresses

1. Specific street names
    4230 Fig Tree Lane

1. Not specific
    The second avenue after the first
    traffic light
2. The second word in a compound number
    5620 Fifty-third Street

Abbreviations

1. For degrees:
    B.A., M.S., Ph.D.
2. For B.C., A.D., A M., P.M.
    in 24 B.C.
    1604 A D.
    at 7:42 A.M.
    at 9:30 P.M.

Brand Names

1. Only the brand name, not the product
    Venus pens
    Ford trucks
    Gala paper napkins

Courses of Study

1. Names of specific courses: English 101
    Chemistry 202
    American History 311

1. Studies other than languages:
    chemistry
    typing
    American history
    biology

Calendar Events

1. All days of the week
2. All months of the year
3. All holidays:
   Fourth of July
   Christmas Eve
   Veterans' Day

1. Seasons of the year:
   spring
   fall
   winter

Degrees and Titles After a Name

1. John Lawton, Ph.D.
2. Titles of Distinction:
   Harvey Cohen, Mayor
   Thomas R. Henry, Jr.
   Stephen P. Warfield, Sr.

1. Ordinary titles used in a general sense
   Tom is a junior officer on board his ship.
   Harvey Cohen was elected mayor last week.

Dialog

1. The first word of the sentence following expressions such as *continued, said, explained, replied:*
   The professor continued, "We must show that we have grown intellectually and that we can tolerate others."

1. Expressions like *he said, replied, continued,* and others introducing the second part of a sentence:
   "We must show," continued the professor, "that we have grown intellectually and that we can tolerate others."

Direct Quotation

1. All words capitalized by an author:
   Miss Anderson wrote, "Captain Wharton was a Saint among the members of his crew."

Institutions

1. Specific names:
   Northwest Medical Center
   The Senior Class of
   Bucknell University
   Leigh Valley High School

1. Used in a general sense
   A medical center usually has visiting hours from 4 P.M. to 8 P.M.

Letters

2. The word *dear* when it follows Mr. in a salutation:
    My dear Dean Harding:

1. Adjectives following the first noun in a complimentary closing
    Very truly yours,
    Your loving niece,

Movements, Events, Periods in History

1. The Anglo-Saxon Period
    The Romantic Movement
    The War Between the States
    World War II
    Declaration of Independence

1. Name of a century not thought of as a movement:
    We live in the twentieth century.

Organizations

1. Special interest groups:
    Democratic party
    Republican party
    American Historical Society
    Lions Club
2. Names of companies:
    Mutual Insurance Company
    Lifelite Corporation

Points of a Compass

1. Sections of the country:
    We moved to the Midwest eight years ago, but he remained in the East.

1. Directions:
    The mountains are six miles south of Bryson City, North Carolina.

Proper Names

1. Political divisions:
    Arlington Heights, Illinois
    Switzerland
    Westmoreland County
    Lake Placid
2. Constellations:
    Orion
    Big Dipper

1. earth, sun, moon:
    The best place on earth to watch the sun rising is here on this mountain top.

3. Planets:
      Mars
      Jupiter
      Earth (if listed as a planet)
4. Streets, parks, buildings, hotels:
      Main Street
      Wrigley Building
      Yellowstone Park
5. Adjectives derived from proper nouns:
      Southern
      Canadian
      Indian
6. Names of ships, planes and trains (also italics):
      the *Seaward*
      the *Caroline*
      the *Hiawatha*
7. All names of races and nationalities:
      Greeks
      Indians
      French

1. Proper nouns which have become common:
      a china cup
      a moroccan leather wallet

Religion

1. Words designating the deity:
      Lord
      Savior
      Allah
      Buddha
      Yahweh
2. Pronouns referring to the deity:
      We are sure He loves us.
3. Sacred books:
      Old Testament
      Bible
      Koran
4. Names of religious groups:
      Baptists
      Catholics
      Jews
      Buddhists

1. Not the word *god* or *goddess* referring to a pagan god unless it is a title:
      the Greek gods
      the Goddess of Liberty

2. The pronoun *whom* may or may not be capitalized in reference to the deity:
      Praise God from whom all blessings flow.

Titles of Essays, Books, Poems

1. First, last, and important words:
   "The Shape of Peace"
   From Here to Eternity
2. Prepositions of five letters or more:
   "The Stage Without a Curtain'

1. Prepositions, conjunctions, and articles:
   "The Death of the Hired Man"

Titles with a Name

1. Preceding a name:
   President Johnson
   the late President Truman
   Captain Ellington
   Aunt Ruth
   Professor Wolff
2. Substituted for a name:
   The President of the United States
   The President will arrive with the Secretary of State.
3. Used in place of a name
   Tell me, Doctor, when will he be released from the hospital?
4. Family relationships not preceded by a possessive or used as a substitute for a name:
   The family held a reunion for Grandmother's eighty-fifth birthday.

1. The name of a worker in a particular field:
   Barron is a television technician for the Rayo Corporation.
2. Officers of organizations:
   The president of the Elks Club called the meeting to order.

3. Family relationships preceded by a possessive:
   My father is a football fan.
4. Titles used in a general sense:
   The old dean looked at this students without saying a word.

Grammar Problems

Rule

Example

A. Pronoun-Antecedent

1. Pronouns agree with their antecedent in person, gender, and number.
2. Use *who, whom,* when referring to persons.
3. Use *that* or *which* when referring to things.
4. Use *that* or *which* when referring to both persons or things.

1. *Each* of us must do *his* or *her* share.
   All of the people in the room raised *their* hands.
2. The *girl who* is standing near the door is my cousin.
3. May I have my *pen which* you have in your hand?
4. Let us not forget the *men* and their *machines* upon *which* we are dependent.

5. In formal writing, do not use *you, they,* or *it* in the indefinite sense.

5. *Incorrect:* They do not want you to talk in the library.
    Correct: The librarians do not like to have students talk in the library.

B. Subject-Verb

1. Verbs agree in number and person with the subject.
2. Intervening phrases between the subject and the verb do not affect the verb.
3   Use a singular verb with nouns that are plural in form but singular in number.
4. In *there is* or *there are* sentences, the verb will agree with the subject that follows it.
5. The relative pronoun *who* may be plural or singular, depending on the antecedent, and the verb will be selected accordingly.

1. *Each one* of the candidates *is* worthy of the office.
2. *Jane,* as well as her mother, *has* returned.
3. The *news is reported* each evening at six o'clock.
4. There *are* six *chairs* in the hall.
5. He is one of those modern *writers who* have attempted to make science fiction popular. (*Who* refers to writers.)

Illogical Comparisons (comp)

1. Avoid a misleading comparison

Original:
    His face is like a movie actor.
Correction:
    His face is like that of a movie actor.
Original:
    Joan Baez is more popular than any folk singer.
Correction:
    Joan Baez is more popular than any other folk singer.

2. Complete all comparisons
3. Tandem comparisons: Complete the first comparison before adding on the second.

Original:
    I like him more than my mother.
Correction:
    I like him more than my mother does.
Original:
    He looks as strong, if not stronger than his brother.
Correction:
    He looks as strong as his brother, if not stronger.
Original:
    The salaries earned by construction workers are at times as high or if not

higher, than the salaries earned by college graduates.

Correction:

At times the salaries earned by construction workers are as high as those earned by college graduates, if not higher.

Original:

Every male passenger will have tong hair, male or female.

Correction:

Every male or female passenger will have long hair.

Original:

After we had stopped at the Information Desk with the help of the boys we found our location on the museum's map.

Correction:

With the help of the boys we found our location . . .

or

After we had stopped at the Information Desk with the help of the boys, . . .

Original:

When writing a research paper, certain rules must be followed.

Correction:

When a student writes a research paper, he has to follow certain rules.

Original:

Riding down a country road, a mailbox covered with flower designs can be seen.

Correction:

Riding down a country road, we saw a mailbox covered with flowers.

Reference Problems (ref)

1. **Vague pronoun reference:** (ref)

   Original:
   After the boys made camp, they remembered that they had forgotten their flashlights, but that didn't bother them.

   Correction:
   After the boys made camp they remembered that they hadforgotten their flashlights, but that oversight didn't bother them.

2. **Indefinite use of pronoun.** (ref)

   Original:
   It says in the newspaper that the number of child abuse cases has risen.

   Correction :
   The newspaper reports that the number of child abuse cases has risen.

3. **Ambiguous pronoun reference:** (ambig)

   Original:
   When Terry met John he told him that he had just been selected as Student Government president.

   Correction:
   Terry told John, "You have just been selected Student Government president."

   or

   Terry told John, "I have just been selected as Student Government president."

4. **No antecedent for pronoun** (ant)

   Original:
   We enjoyed our stay in Italy. They are friendly and hospitable people.

   Correction:
   We enjoyed our stay in Italy. The Italians are friendly and hospitable people.

Sentence Structure (ss)

1. Make your sentence complete when you use *so, too, such*:

    Original:
    They were so tired.
    Correction:
    They were so tired that they went to bed immediately.
    Original:
    The boy was too young.
    Correction:
    The boy was too young to join the Boy Scouts.
    Original:
    That is such a rare coin.
    Correction:
    That is such a rare coin that you should place it in a museum.

2. Be sure that a word calls for the same form of a verb and preposition in tandem constructions If not, write the correct form before the second construction.

    Original:
    The ixora bushes were clipped and the lawn mowed on Saturday.
    Correction:
    The ixora bushes were clipped and the lawn was mowed on Saturday.

3. Do not write sentences that are awkward or difficult to understand: (awk or k)

    Original:
    At the moment of King Henry, the Eighth's death, Elizabeth became queen, although many formalities and traditions had to be gone through.
    Correction:
    At the moment of King Henry the Eighth's death, Elizabeth became queen. However, because of tradition, Elizabeth had to go through several formalities before assuming the throne.

4. Do not write sentences that are obscure: (nc)

    Original:
    The wedding announcement was made in the form of a miniature newspaper with stories and pictures of the couple accompanied with a light buffet.
    Correction:
    The wedding announcement was made at a small reception where a light buffet was served to guests. The

announcement was made in the form of a miniature newspaper with stories and pictures of the couple's courtship.

5. Avoid mixed figures of speech: (fig sp)

Original:
The young candidate for Congress is rapidly gaining a foothold in the public's mind

Correction:
The young candidate for Congress is rapidly gaining a place in the public's mind

6. Express parallel thoughts in parallel form: (// or paral)

Original:
Two things I would like to know how to do well are to play the piano and water skiing.

Correction:
Two things I would like to know how to do are to play the piano and to water ski.

7. Use the correlatives (//)
   both . . . and
   not only . . . but also
   neither . . .nor
   either. . . or
   whether. . . or
   only before the sentence elements that are parallel in form:

Original:
He neither likes beets nor spinach

Correction:
He likes neither beets nor spinach

Original:
I don't know whether to call my neighbor or if I should call the service station for help..

Correction:
I don't know whether to call my neighbor or the service station for help.

Original:
You either begin to set the table or start dinner.

Correction:
You begin either to set the table or start dinner.

8. Do not split constructions: (ss)

Original:
I want to quickly finish my term paper.

Correction:
I want to finish my term paper quickly.

Original:
The house has, although none of the tourists would think so, been visited

by ten thousand people.

Correction:

Although none of the tourists would think so, the house has been visited by ten thousand people.

Shifts (shift)

Avoid unnecessary shifts in:

1. **Tense**

   Original:

   He sent his manuscript to the publisher, but it is returned to him.

   Correction:

   He sent his manuscript to the publisher, but it was returned to him.

2. **Person**

   Original:

   For the inexperienced boatman, it is advisable to moor your boat before attempting to raise the sails.

   Correction:

   For the inexperienced boatman, it is advisable to moor the boat before attempting to raise the sails.

3. **Mood**

   Original:

   We all wished the game was over.

   Correction:

   We all wished the game were over.

4. **Relative pronoun**

   Original:

   She refused to buy the machine that had no cover and which had plastic parts.

   Correction:

   She refused to buy the machine that had no cover and that had plastic parts.

5. **Voice**

   Original:

   As a camp counselor I taught the boys how to make tea from pine needles and how to scale a fish; also, they were taught how to make camp.

   Correction:

   As a camp counselor I taught the boys how to make camp, how to scale a fish, and how to make tea from pine needles.

Punctuation Guide (p)

Apostrophe

1. **Used to show possession:**
    Stephen and Susan's bicycle *(joint ownership)*
    Stephen's and Susan's bicycles *(individual ownership)*
    his brother-in-law's car *(compound word)*
    a nickel's worth of candy
    a month's pay
    the girls' apartment
    the children's playground
    Charles Dickens's novels
2. **Used to show plurals of letters, words, and numbers:**
    a. Dot your *i*'s, cross your *t*'s and don't use so many *and*'s.
    b. Your answer should have three 9's in it.
3. **Used for omission of numbers or letters:**
    a. The class of '49 is having a reunion June 14 at one o'clock.
    b. Who's the one to investigate this haunted house.

Brackets

1. **To enclose a parenthesis within a parenthesis:**
    If he attends the college of his choice (Dixon University [the largest one in the state]), his parents refuse to help with expenses.
2. **To enclose material a writer has inserted within a quotation to explain it or correct it:**
    The detective wrote, "The motive [for the betrayal of his producer] had not yet been determined."
3. **To enclose the word *sic* in a quotation to indicate that an error in spelling appeared in the original quote:**
    "The robbed [*sic*] faculty members were the first in the graduation procession," reported the *Daily News*.

Colon

1. **Before formal appositives:**
    On the sign was written one word: *love*
2. **Before quotations introduced formally:**
    These words from the late President J. F. Kennedy's Inaugural Speech will be long remembered: "Ask not what your country can do for you, but what you can do for your country. "
3. **Before statements introduced formally:**
    Our objections to the building of condominiums on the golf club grounds are several: our homes would depreciate in value, our view would be hampered, our roads could not support the burden of a minimum of 1,200 new cars in the area, and our children

would be deprived of the park they now enjoy.

4. **Before a series introduced with words like** *the following as follows, are these:*
Among the suggestions for world peace were these: total disarmament and withdrawal of all troops.

5. **Between independent clauses when the second clause explains or amplifies the first::**
a. Woodrow Wilson said, "Often the fate of a word is fortuitous: it falls on evil or good days by accident."
b. The popular media, too, has been caught up in the occult revival: horror movies are more popular than ever.

6. **In certain formal uses:**
a. Hours:minutes: 7:45 P.M.
b. Salutation of a business letter: Gentlemen:, Dear Sir:
c. City:publisher: St. Louis: Conrad Publishers
d. Act:scene: Act IV: 3
e. Bible chapter:verse: John 2:4
f. Title of book:subtitle: *The Principles of Writing: A Handbook and a Workbook*
g. Newspaper numbered section: sec 14:6

Comma

1. **To separate coordinate clauses joined by** *and, or, for, nor, yet* .*and but* except when clauses are very short and closely related in meaning:
A letter of application may get you an interview, but you may still not be accepted for the job.

2. **To separate words, phrases, and clauses in a series:**
a. The bowl was filled with oranges, grapes, bananas, and apples.
b. The products at the Chicago Home Show were from Japan, from New Zealand, from Portugal, and from Italy.
c. The weather was clear, the sun was shining, and the humidity was low.

3. **To separate coordinate adjectives not joined by a conjunction:**
The Anglo-Saxons spent days in the Mead Hall listening to loud, boastful promises.

4. **To set off a long introductory subordinate phrase or clause:**
a. *Phrase:* With all chapters of the novel completed, Sarah was ready to submit it to the staff for final editing.
b. *Clause:* Although Americans are admired for their industrious spirit, they are criticized by Europeans for this same characteristic.

5. **To set off nonrestrictive elements:**
a. *Nonrestrictive elements:*
(1) John Ellington, in a gray flannel suit, looks like a typical young American executive of the 1950s.
(2) Hair styling for men, which is always expensive, costs less in this town.
b. *Restrictive elements:*
(1) The boy who walked in late is my roommate.
(2) The man in the-gray flannel suit looks like a typical young American executive of the 1950s.

c. *Read either way:*

  (1) The coin which was made of silver was valued at one thousand dollars. (Several coins are on the table.)

  (2) The coin, which was made of silver, was valued at one thousand dollars. (Only one coin was on the table.)

6. **To set off modifiers or elements out of the normal word order:**
Tired and hungry, the hunters returned to their camp without having found any game.

7. **To set off transitional conjunctions (conjunctive adverbs) like** *however, nevertheless:*
a. They agreed, however, not to file suit against the dog's owner.
b. I wish to travel in Europe this summer; on the other hand, my husband prefers to visit Japan.

8. **To set off** *yes, no,* **and mild interjections** (*oh*):
a. Oh, I forgot to lock the patio doors when I left.
b. No, this is not the time to squander money on luxuries.

9. **To prevent misreading**
Beyond, the road suddenly curved to the right without warning, and we had to be careful to avoid driving our car over the cliff.

10. **To set off appositives:**
The final assignment, the Cause and Effect Theme, will need both footnotes and a bibliography.

11. **To set off a direct address:**
We agree, Ronald, that you should jog at least one hour a day.

12. **To separate verbs of saying such as** *says, responded, asked:*
When Kay was asked how old she was, she answered, "Plenty nine."

13. **Between parts of an address, dates. name and degree, name and title of distinction:**
a. Ray Fletcher lives at 4722 Woodmont Avenue, Arnold, Pennsylvania. He was born on June 22,1954.
b. David L. Tillman, B.A., M.A.., Ph.D. . ,
Linda Foster, Director of Community Services
Brian Cohee, Ambassador from Ireland

14. **For contrast and for emphasis:**
The coach was forced to use the smaller practice field for his first game, not the stadium designed especially for league games.

15. **For omission of a word:**
My older sister lives in Milwaukee, Wisconsin; my brother, in Wheaton, Maryland.

16. **To add a short question:**
It is safe to swim in this canal, isn't it?

17. **To set off an absolute phrase which modifies the sentence as a whole:**
Our world trip over, we finally settled in Arlington Heights, Illinois.

18. **Salutation of a friendly letter**
Dear Jane,

Do Not Use Commas

1. **To separate the subject and its verb:**

a. Only the students who pre-registered for the Occult Seminar, were permitted to attend.

b. In the 1970s horror movies such as *Sixth Sense* and *Night Gallery*, captured the evening viewers, and *Dark Shadows*, chilled the watchers of daytime television.

2. **To separate a verb from its complement:**
His favorite sports are, fishing, hunting, and scuba diving.

3. **Between an adjective and the noun it modifies and between adjectives that are not coordinating:**
The pretty, little, mountain, village near Mt. Etna in Sicily caters to tourists who wish to ski on the slopes.

4. **After a coordinating conjunction:**
No one can teach you how to become a financially successful writer but, a good teacher can help you to learn to write well-organized, well-structured papers.

5. **Before coordinating conjunctions joining two words or two phrases:**
The room was decorated with original paintings done by her children, and with those she had purchased from an artist she had met in Europe.

6. **After the verb of *saying* in an indirect quotation:**
Lara McFarland said, that there would be a large voter turn out for the next election.

7. **With an appositive that is felt to be part of a single proper name, such as William the Conqueror:**
Was it Mary, Queen of Scots, who was beheaded?

8,. **Before a parenthesis, only after:**
[1]Hans Holzer, *Ghosts of the Golden West,* (New York: Ace Books, 1973), p. 24.

9. **After a short, essential introductory adverbial clause or phrase:**
Last night, I met a former classmate of mine-who is now listed in *Who's Who in America.*

10. **After a short prepositional phrase which introduces the sentence:**
After today, I will quit smoking.

11. **To separate a restrictive element from the sentence:**
Georgia is a girl, who enjoys reading science fiction novels.

12. **Between the main clause and a dependent adverbial clause which follows it:**
There would be fewer problems for students in foreign language classes, if they knew English grammar better.

Dash

1. **To indicate hesitation or uncertainty in speech or speech that is broken off abruptly.**
You turn three blocks to the right—or is it only two blocks—before coming to City Hall.

2. **To indicate sudden breaks in thought:**
Did you realize that John—well, I won't even discuss his misfortune.

3. **To indicate a break in sentence structure:**
a. To separate a long appositive that is a series with internall punctuation:
The dogs—poodles, shepherds, terriers, and retrievers—will be judged later this week.
b. To separate an explanatory or parenthetical phrase or clause:
Your mother and I were pleased—proud, we should say—when you received the

Bausch and Lomb Science Award.
c. For special or dramatic emphasis:
If you should miss the plane—heaven forbid!— you will not be able to charter another one for three months.
d. Before an author's name when the name appears at the end of a quotation:
"Wisdom denotes the pursuing of the best ends by the best means. "—Francis Hutcheson.
e. To indicate the omission of words or letters:
Are you familiar with the writer Grant Allen (1848-1899)?
Lt. William C—has been a subject of controversy since his arrest.

Ellipses

1. **Use three spaced periods within a sentence to show an omission:**
"Yet despite strict government restrictions . . . older workers are confronted continually with the same bias: they are too old to do an employer any good."
2. **If the omission is at the end of a sentence, use four spaced periods:**
In 1973 "the Department of Labor found 1,836 employers, employment agencies, and unions violating the Age Discrimination in Employment Act of 1967. . . ."
3. **Use a full line of spaced periods if a paragraph of quoted material has been omitted:**
Not everyone is convinced, though, that age discrimination is much of a problem today. Lon D. Barton, President of Cadillac Associates, an employment agency specializing in executive placement, calls such bias, 'almost a thing of the past.'
. . . .
'It used to be that the sure way to fill a position was to send an eager 25-year-old out for an interview. Today companies seem to be looking for a mature 40-year-old.'[1]

End Punctuation

1. **Period**
   a. *After all abbreviations commonly used in writing:*
   Mrs., Ms., Dr., Sr. (You may omit the periods after some organizations and agencies, such as CBS, AFL, NBC, CIA, TWA.)
   b. *Inside all quotation marks:*
   He sang a song from the 1940s, " Blue Moon."
   c. *Outside parentheses when the parenthetical statement, figure, or word is part of the preceding statement:*
   He paid thirty dollars ($30.00).
   d. *Only one period if the sentence ends with an abbreviation:*
2. **Exclamation mark.**
   a. *Use infrequently.*
   b. *To follow an expression of strong feeling that is a complete sentence:*

[1] Houson, Jack. "45-Year-old's Job Prospects Looking Bleak." *Ft. Lauderdale News and Sun Sentinel*, 24 Mar 1974: 16E.

Wrong: Look before you cross the railroad tracks!
Right: Look out! The train is coming.
c. *Never use more than one:*
I'll never date him again!!! Only one exclamation mark is necessary: I'll never date him again!
d. *Use at end of the sentence even when words such as* oh, no, yes, *introduce the sentence:*
Oh no, I didn't win the million dollar lottery!

3. **Question mark:**
a. *Enclosed within parentheses after a doubtful date or figure:*
The Reverend James Brameton (1964?-1744) wrote in *Art of Politics:* What's not destroyed by Time's devouring hands?
Where's Troy, and where's the Maypole in the Strand?
b. *To follow separate questions within a single interrogative sentence:*
The investigator asked several questions: How old are you? What is your home state? How long have you lived in the apartment? How long do you plan to remain here ?
c. *With quotation marks:*
1. Did you answer question 10, "Comment on Hardy's selection of the name Father Time for Jude's son"?
2. Answer only the first question, "How does Clarisse influence Guy Montag in *Fahrenheit 451 ?*"
d. *Incorrect:*
The comedy (?) is to be presented again at the Forest View Theater on Sunday at 8:00 P.M.

Hyphen

1. **With two or more words forming a compound adjective:**
This was a never-to-be-forgotten vacation.
2. **With compound numbers from twenty-one to ninety-nine:**
If you count carefully, you will find that there are twenty-seven boxes in the stock room.
3. **At the end of a line to mark a division in a word when the remainder of the word is carried over to the next line:**
Not since the Civil War have so many men protested the war policies of their government.
4. **Never put a hyphen at the beginning of a line:**
Incorrect:
Behind the Amnesty debate lies the statistics of the United States invol
-vement in the Vietnam War.

Parentheses

1. **To enclose material that is supplementary, explanatory, or interpretive:**

A growing minority is willing to substitute service in such groups as the Peace Corps or VISTA (Volunteers in Service to America) for imprisonment for draft evaders.

2. **General rule to distinguish difference in use of comma, dash, and parentheses:**
   a. *Commas* set off material close to the thought of the sentence.
      There we met Jerry Frey, who directed us to the department for film editing.
   b. *Dashes* set off material that is loosely connected to the thought of the sentence.
      Bruce Davenport—he's very handsome—is campaigning for Student Government president.
   c. *Parentheses* set off material to indicate the most distant relation to the thought of the sentence.
      Amnesty groups argue that the Vietnam War (lasting eleven years and one month) was illegal because the United States government never officially declared war.
   Note: Do not use parentheses to cancel any part of your writing.
   Incorrect:
   The psychological impact of today's movies (effect) affect great numbers of viewers, especially those between the ages of thirteen and thirty.
   Correct:
   The psychological impact of today's movies affect great numbers . . .

Semicolon

1. **Between the clauses of a compound sentence when independent clauses are not joined by one of the coordinating conjunctions:**
   The dog stopped and sniffed; a rabbit was running swiftly through the hollow log nearby.
2. **Before a coordinating conjunction when the independent clauses contain other punctuation:**
   When the university opened its law school, 450 applicants requested admission; but the dean of Law reported that there were only 170 spaces available that year.
3. **Between clauses (occasionally between phrases) to indicate balance or contrast or to give a more definite separation than a comma would:**
   When the crowd became quiet again, he said, "There will be no sermon; no lecture; no condemnations. We wish only to exchange ideas."
4. **Before a conjunctive adverb** (*therefore, however, hence, accordingly, then, thus, still, moreover, subsequently*) **that is used to separate two independent clauses:**
   The psychiatrist considered shock movies such as *The Exorcist* to be full of fear and confusion; nevertheless, fans were willing to stand in line for hours just to view the movie.
5. **To separate a series that has internal punctuation:**
   The following officers were elected at the last meeting: Tom Harvey, president; Judy Shank, vice-president; Mitchell Turner, secretary; and Barbara Heinz, treasurer.

Quotation Marks

1. **Double quotation marks ("):**
   a. *For a single sentence, to enclose a direct quotation:*

When asked what he would buy if he could have anything in the department store, three-year-old Billy answered, "The toy department."

b. *For several sentences, only at the beginning and end of the entire quotation*
c. *For several paragraphs:*
 1. Begin each paragraph with quotation marks, but place them at the end of the last paragraph only.
 2. In a typed manuscript, indent and single space quotations which are more than five lines long.
 Do not use quotation marks with material indented in this manner (see pages 404–7).
d. *For dialogue:*
 1. Use a separate paragraph for every change of speaker.
 2. Enclose short descriptive, explanatory, or narrative passages with dialogue if they are placed between sentences of dialogue spoken by the same person:
 "No," he said, "I have not hurt myself." However, he leaned against the wall, closed his eyes, sucked in his breath, and bit his bottom lip.
 "Mr. Nye," the boy shouted, "stay where you are, and I will go for help." He had noticed that while Mr. Nye was leaning there, drops of blood began trickling down the side of his face.
c. *For titles:*
 1. Essays, articles, short stories, short poems, or any subdivision of a periodical or book:
 The title of the essay is "Clearcutting: A Devastation of Our Forests."
 Perhaps the article "Fungus Enzyme Changes Wastes Into Sugar" can be used for your research paper.
 Read "That Only a Mother" from the science fiction anthology *Speculations*.
 Before beginning your research, read the chapter "The Use of the Library" from the assigned textbook.
 2. Short muscial compositions:
 "The Way We Were" won the 1973 Academy Award for the best song written for a movie.

2. **Single Quotation Marks ('):**
To enclose a quotation within a quotation:
"Was it you," he asked, "who said, 'Two can live as cheaply as one if one person doesn't eat'?"

Underlining (Italics)

1. **Titles of books, plays, newspapers, magazines, long musical compositions, works of art (exception: the Bible and its divisions):**

titles of books:	*Jude the Obscure*
plays:	*Arsenic and Old Lace*
newspapers:	the *New York Times*
magazines:	*Psychology Today*
long musical compositions:	Beethoven's *Fifth Symphony*

bulletins and pamphlets:	*Your Heart*
works of art	*Pieta*

2. **Names of ships, trains, or aircraft:**

names of ships:	the *Sunward*
names of trains:	*Hiawatha*
names of aircraft:	*Air Force I*

3. **Words, letters, or figures when they are referred to as such:**

   a. He got *stationery* and *stationary* confused.

   b. If the combination of letters *th, sch,* and *pro* are substituted for the figures *17, 34,* and *56,* we may understand the coded message.

4. **Foreign words or phrases that are used in English context:**

   News of the *coup d'etat* reached us shortly after midnight.

Index